My Redeemer Lives

Evidence
For The Resurrection Of Jesus

Evan Minton

My Redeemer Lives: Evidence For The Resurrection Of Jesus,

1st Edition

Cerebral Faith logo created by Evan Minton

Some material has been adapted from "The Evidence For Jesus' Resurrection" a ten part blog post series on CerebralFaith.blogspot.com.

Table Of Contents

Introduction

The oxford theologian and British author C.S Lewis once said *"Christianity, if false, is of no importance, and if true, it is of infinite importance. The only thing it cannot be is moderately important."*[1] Lewis' pithy statement couldn't be more true. Think about it: Christianity teaches that all people have sinned and fallen short of the moral standard of the God who made them (see Romans 3:23, Psalms 14:2-4, Genesis 1:1), and that moved by love, God sent His Son Jesus to die on the cross to pay the penalty on our behalf (Isaiah 53, John 3:16, 1 Peter 3:18), and that if we place our faith in Him, His blood will wash away our moral misdeeds and make us right before God (John 3:16, 1 John 1:9), but that if we don't place our faith in Him, we will remain condemned (John 3:18, John 3:36). What does condemnation mean? Hell. Hell is a place described as a realm of *"eternal fire"* (Matthew 25:41), *"unquenchable fire"* (Matthew 3:12), *"shame and everlasting contempt"* (Daniel 12:2), The Bible describes it as a place where *"the fire is not quenched"* (Mark 9:44-49), a *"lake of burning sulfur"* where the wicked are *"tormented day and night forever and ever"* (Revelation 20:10).[2]

Obviously, this place is not Disneyland. You don't want to end up here. Now, of course, if Christianity is false, then the place described in The Bible should strike fear in the heart of no one. If God does not exist or if The Bible is not His word, then when you die, it's light's out for everyone, no matter how good or how evil you were in this life. If Christianity is false, don't pay it a second thought. On the other hand, if Christianity is true, we ought to give our lives to Christ so that we can receive absolution for our sins and so that we can spend eternity in Heaven, not Hell. If it's true, then it's infinitely important that we come to know it is!

But is Christianity true? How can we know? Should we just put blind faith in the system and hope we got it right? Pascal's Wager, named after the inventor of the calculator, Blaise Pascal[3], says that if the evidence (or lack thereof) for God's existence and the evidence (or lack thereof) for His non-existence are equal, then we should bet on God's existence. Why? Because if we believe that God exists and it turns out that atheism is true, we don't lose anything. It's lights out after death. On the other hand, if we bet on atheism, and it turns out that God **does** exist, then we're in for one Hell of an afterlife (pun intended). If we bet on God, we lose nothing regardless of whether He does or does not exist. If we bet against God, then we better hope He's not there, or it's off to the lake of fire for us! Clearly, the most rational option is to vote on God.

I do not like Pascal's Wager and have never used it in my discussions with non-Christians. Pascal's Wager is flawed because the gambler is only considering Christianity and Atheism. Obviously, if these were the only two options, then of course, you should bet on Christianity against Atheism. But, atheism is not the only competitor against Christianity in the marketplace of ideas. Islam teaches that all Muslims (and only Muslims) will go to Heaven.[4] This means that **if** Islam is true, I am in just as much eternal jeopardy as my atheist friends. When betting Christianity against Islam or vice versa, the stakes are equally high. Likewise, if the Jehovah's Witnesses are right, then I need to (A) become a Jehovah's Witness, and (B) make sure I do enough good works so that God will allow me to become one of the 144,000 of Heaven's population.[5]

So, it is a terrible idea to approach religion as a gambler. We can't just hedge our bets and hope we get it right. Eternity is at stake! Eternity is a very long time to be wrong! We need to be absolutely sure that the religion we hold is true. But how can we do that? The answer: We should weigh arguments and evidence for and against every worldview.

But is there any evidence for any religion? Aren't religions a matter of blind faith or religious experience? Moreover, even if there was evidence for a particular religion, wouldn't that prevent us from having faith in it? After all, isn't the definition of "faith" believing in something without any evidence, or even belief **in spite of** the evidence? If we could prove that one of the world's "faiths" were true, it would cease to be a "faith", wouldn't it?

These are all very good questions. In fact, the author of this work asked these very same questions as a teenager, and during an intense investigation he found surprising answers to them. I will answer each of these questions individually in the sections below.

The Biblical Definition Of Faith

First off, if you've read the cover of this book, it should be obvious to you that I am a Christian theist. I think that Christianity is true and that all religions that oppose Christian beliefs are false. Secondly, I would argue that not only is the popular cultural definition of the word "faith" flawed, it's unbiblical. The Bible depicts faith in a far different way than non-Christians and average church-goers do. Thirdly, I think there is evidence that Christianity is true. In fact, I would say that the evidence is overwhelming and that Christianity can be demonstrated to be true "beyond a reasonable doubt".

Faith is **not** believing something for no reason nor is it believing something **against** reason. According to The Bible, faith is a synonym for trust. I can have evidence for someone's existence and still be able to trust them. By contrast, I can have evidence for their existence and not trust them at all. The following is an illustration I frequently like to employ to get this point across. If you were a kid walking home from school and a man pulled up next to you and said "Come here little boy. I'll take you back to your house." Would you trust him? Certainly not! You'd probably run away as fast as you can! You'd think that this guy is most likely a perv and that if you got in the car with him, you could very well get raped and murdered! You have evidence for this man's existence, but you do not trust him. Let's turn the illustration around. Instead of a complete stranger, it's your mother. Your mother pulls up in her car and says "Sweetie, you don't have to walk all the way home. I'll drive you myself." Would you trust her? Yes. Your experience with your mother shows you that she is a trustworthy individual. Unlike the stranger, you have no qualms getting into the vehicle with her.

You have evidence for the existence of both the stranger and your mother, but you only placed your faith in one of them. If faith is a synonym for trust, then we can certainly have evidence for God's existence and still have faith in Him. The two illustrations above raise another question. **Why** did you have faith in your mother, but not the complete stranger? You put your faith in your mother because she proved to you that she was a trustworthy person. She gave evidence that she is someone you could safely get into a vehicle with. The complete stranger didn't give you any reasons to believe that he was a trustworthy individual. His offer to take you home might possibly have been sincere (after all, not every stranger is dangerous), but he just as well could have been a murdering pedophile! You had no way of knowing either way.

If you stepped into the vehicle with that man, you would be exercising **blind** faith. I would agree with every atheist in the world that **blind** faith is indeed irrational. If you have no reason to believe something, don't. Moreover, in some cases, blind faith could be dangerous. Blind faith in the stranger could make you the victim of rape and murder. Evidence based faith is the opposite of blind faith. It is both rational and safe. Your faith in your mother was rational and safe because you had evidence that she would do you no harm. She never hurt you in the past, why would she start now? Your odds of actually getting home are much higher with your mom than with the complete stranger.

Rational faith is based on evidence. **Blind** Faith is based on nothing. In John 10:37-38, Jesus said *"**Do not believe me unless I do the works of my Father.** But if I do them, even though you do not believe me, **believe the works**, that you may **know and understand** that the Father is in me, and I in the Father."* (emphasis mine). Jesus told his listeners that they should not believe in Him unless He provides evidence to back up his claims. He then says that if they don't believe in Him, they should *"believe the works"*. In other words, the miracles served as powerful evidence to those who witnessed them that Jesus really was from God. Acts 1:3 says *"After his suffering, he presented himself to them and **gave many convincing proofs** that he was alive. He appeared to them over a period of forty days and spoke about the kingdom of God."* (emphasis mine) If the real definition of faith was "belief without evidence", then why would Jesus "give many convincing proofs" to His disciples that He was alive and really was Israel's promised Messiah after all? Wouldn't Jesus be preventing His disciples from exercising faith?

Moreover, The Bible commands Christians to give reasons for what they believe.

1 Peter 3:15 says *"Always be ready to give a defense to anyone who asks you for the reason for the hope that you have, yet do so with gentleness and respect."*

In other words, if an unbeliever asks me why I believe Christianity is true, I am not to say "I have faith". 1 Peter 3:15 commands me to give reasons. 1 Peter 3:15 is a command to do apologetics; to provide the unbeliever with good solid reasons for why Christianity is true. We are to *"demolish arguments and every pretension that sets itself up against the knowledge of God, and we take captive every thought to make it obedient to Christ."* (2 Corinthians 10:5).

I think the most explicit evidence in The Bible that having evidence for God's existence and having faith in Him are not mutually exclusive is found in the Exodus event. Check out The Bible verses below:

*"**By faith** the people passed through the Red Sea as on dry land; but when the Egyptians tried to do so, they were drowned."* -- Hebrews 11:29 (emphasis mine)

*"And when the Israelites **saw the mighty hand of the Lord** displayed against the*

*Egyptians, the people feared the Lord and **put their trust in him** and in Moses his servant."* - Exodus 14:31 (emphasis mine)

The NIV of Exodus 14:31 says *"they put their **trust** in him and in Moses his servant."*, the NLT says *"They put their **faith** in the LORD…."*, The KJV says *"the people feared the Lord, and **believed** the Lord, and his servant Moses."*

Clearly, the Israelites had reasons to believe that God existed and was helping them escape Egypt (i.e all of those plagues and miracles) and yet the text says they put their faith in Him anyway (for a little while at least. We all know they lost faith a bunch of times after this). They especially had evidence that **Moses** existed and the text says they placed their faith in him as well! So, given this piece of scriptural evidence we know that a Christian can still base his belief **that** Christianity is true on the basis of evidence and still be able to have faith **in** God.

Faith is not blind. Despite what many non-Christians and even many Christians want you to believe, biblical faith is not blind faith. Biblical faith is a cerebral faith.

Can Christianity Be Proven?

Well, that depends on what you mean by "proven"? There are different standards of what amounts to "proof". In a court of law, there are different standards of proof (the "SOP"). The SOP varies depending on the kind of case juries are doing. The highest standard of proof is the "beyond a reasonable doubt" standard that is required at criminal trials. *"Reasonable doubt is defined as follows: It is not a mere possible doubt; because everything relating to human affairs is open to some possible or imaginary doubt. It is that state of the case which, after the entire comparison and consideration of all the evidence, leaves the minds of the jurors in that condition that they cannot say they feel an abiding conviction of the truth of the charge."* [5] Homicide Detective J. Warner Wallace explains that *"This definition is important because it recognizes the difference between reasonable and possible. There are, according to the ruling of the court, 'reasonable doubts,' 'possible doubts,' and 'imaginary doubts.' The definition acknowledges something important: every case has unanswered questions that will cause jurors to wonder. All the jurors will have doubts as they come to a decision. We will never remove every possible uncertainty; that's why the standard is not 'beyond any doubt.' Being 'beyond a reasonable doubt' simply requires us to separate our possible and imaginary doubts from those that are reasonable."* [6]

Next to nothing can be proven beyond a **possible** doubt. Can it be proven that you are actually sitting there reading this book? That the ink and paper in front of your eyes are actually there and that your room is actually real? Maybe you're a brain in a vat of chemicals hooked up to electrodes, and a mad scientist is causing you to experience what you think is the external world? Can you prove that beyond any possible doubt that this "brain in a vat" scenario is not true? No. But should that cause you to doubt that your body, this book, and the room and objects around you are actually there? Of course not. If you did, that would most certainly not be a **reasonable** doubt.

I think that Christianity can be proven "beyond a reasonable doubt". However, maybe **you personally** don't think the evidence I will present in this book matches that standard. Maybe you think the evidence simply meets lower SOPs like "the preponderance of the evidence" (i.e it's more likely than not that Christianity is true). I will leave that up to you. Some people consider some arguments more convincing than others. You may not agree with every point I make in this book. Nevertheless, I want you to consider the **overall** case for Christ. For example, several chapters from now, I will be making 9 independent arguments that Jesus' death by crucifixion is a historical fact. Let's say you find 2 or 3 arguments unpersuasive. Still, should that dissuade you from thinking that Jesus' death on a Roman cross is a historical fact? Not if you think 3 or 4 of them are good! You can say "You know, I find arguments 1, 3, 5, and 6 overwhelmingly powerful, but the rest are pitiful." That's fine. I just don't want you to throw the baby out with the bathwater. Don't think that because you find 1 or 2 arguments unpersuasive that therefore, Jesus' execution or His empty tomb aren't facts. Only if you find them **all** unpersuasive can you say "I don't think you established the minimal fact".

What This Book Seeks To Prove

The goal of this book is to present a powerful evidential case for the historicity of Jesus' deity, death, and resurrection. If Jesus claimed to be God, then He died and rose from the dead, then the entire Christian worldview follows!

Why do I say that? Aren't I committing the hasty generalization fallacy in making this assertion?[7] I understand why people would raise this question. Before I get into making a case for Jesus' resurrection, I need to first unpack why it would validate the entire Christian worldview.

First of all, there is strong historical evidence that Jesus claimed to be God. If Jesus said that he was God but he wasn't, then he was either a lying heretic or else he was crazy. If that were the case, there's no way God The Father would resurrect Jesus from the dead knowing that that would vindicate his blasphemous claims and lead many people astray. God would never raise a heretic and a blasphemer. But if God did raise Jesus from the dead, then God implicitly put his stamp of approval on everything Jesus said and did. If Jesus rose from the dead, then that means God

The Father agreed with Jesus' claims for which his enemies killed him as a blasphemer. If God The Father raised Jesus from the dead then that means He agrees with Jesus' claims to be divine.

If that's the case, then whatever Jesus teaches carries a lot of weight. This includes but is not limited to His teaching that (1) the Old Testament was the divinely inspired Word of God. Jesus believed and taught that every word in The Old Testament was true. (2) Since he handpicked the writers of the New Testament, this means the New Testament is divinely inspired given that Jesus is God, (3) He also seemed to believe that Adam and Eve were historical individuals, that (4) the flood story in Genesis 6-9 actually happened, that (5) angels and demons really do exist, and (6) that if you place your faith in him, you will have eternal life but that if you don't place your faith in Him, you'll end up in Hell (John 3:16-18, John 8:24). Who would be in a better position to know whether these 6 propositions are true if not God incarnate?

So if Jesus rose from the dead after allegedly blaspheming the One who raised him, we can believe all of these things as well simply because Jesus believed them. This is why you'll often hear Christian Apologists[8] say *"I don't believe in Jesus because I believe The Bible. I believe The Bible because I believe in Jesus"*. To put it another way, if you get the resurrection of Jesus, you get the whole Christian worldview thrown in as well!

Be Willing To Follow The Evidence Wherever It Leads

If you understand the importance of knowing whether or not Christianity is true, then you'll take the time to read this book. If you do take the time to listen to my arguments, please follow them to their logical conclusions. My friend Neil Mammen has a saying *"Don't let the consequences of your logic cause you to abandon that logic."* [9] Not everyone who denies the resurrection of Jesus does so purely on intellectual grounds. Some people deny that the resurrection occurred simply because they **want** it not to have occurred. Some people aren't Christians not because there isn't enough evidence to establish that it's true, but because they **don't want** it to be true.

If Jesus rose from the dead, then Christianity is true. If Christianity is true, then several implications follow. It means that if you're living in sin, you'll have to repent. Jesus said that if you even look at a woman with lust, you've committed adultery in your heart (Matthew 5:28), and adultery is one of the things God said not to do (Exodus 20:14). If you like to spend your evenings downloading and looking at pornography, you'll have to get that out of your life or answer to God for it (2

Corinthians 5:10). But porn watchers don't want to do that. Watching porn is fun! It's exciting! Porn watchers don't want to give up porn because they enjoy it too much. Others may want to sleep around, bouncing from woman to woman as Charlie Harper did on the hit sitcom *Two and A Half Men.* According to Hebrews 13:4, this is a no-no. If someone engaged in this behavior doesn't repent, they'll be facing judgment. Romans 1:26-28, 1 Corinthians 6:9-11, and 1 Timothy 1:9-11 prohibit homosexual relationships. Some people don't want Christianity to be true because it means they'll have to stop having sex with their same-sex partner. 2 Corinthians 6:14 prohibits a believer marrying an unbeliever. Some people may not want Christianity to be true because they know that if it is, they need to become Christians or else they face Hell, and if they're Christians themselves, they'll be prohibited from marrying their boyfriend or girlfriend who is an unbeliever.

For many people, it's a purely intellectual issue. Merely being presented with the evidence in this book will be sufficient to persuade them to become Christians. For others, they're resistant to following the evidence where it leads because they're in love with their sin, and don't like the idea of having to exchange their pet sin for a relationship with Jesus. Jesus talked about this when he said *"This is the verdict: that light has come into the world. Yet men loved the darkness rather than the light for their deeds were evil. Everyone who does evil hates the light and will come nowhere near the light for fear that their deeds will be exposed."* (John 3:19-20). Echoing Jesus' words, the mathematician and Christian Apologist John Lennox said: *"If religion is a fairytale for those afraid of the dark, then atheism is a fairytale for those afraid of the light."*[10]

So again, *"Don't let the consequences of your logic force you to abandon that logic."* Don't let the consequences of Christianity being true force you to swim against the current of evidence pointing in its favor. The Christian Apologist Frank Turek of CrossExamined.org often exposes someone as resisting Jesus on emotional or moral grounds by asking them one simple question: "If Christianity were true, would you become a Christian?" That's the question I'm posing to you, dear reader. If you knew beyond a reasonable doubt that Christianity is true, would you be willing to give up whatever lifestyle Christ might not approve of in order to follow Him and serve Him? If you were convinced that God exists, would you bow to Him as your Savior and Lord? If you hesitate or if your answer is "no", then your problem isn't in your head, it's in your heart. In that case, this book will be of no use to you, since your problem isn't intellectual to begin with. So, before you proceed, do some introspection and determine whether you're on a truth quest or whether you're on a happiness quest. If your answer to that question is "Yes", then keep reading! God promises that those who sincerely seek Him find Him when they seek Him with all their hearts (see Jeremiah 29:13).

Moreover, if your answer is "No", let me ask you something. Isn't it better to live in the truth than in a lie? Wouldn't it be wonderful if life didn't end at the grave, but that an eternity of uninterrupted bliss followed? Wouldn't it be infinitely awesome if the death of a loved one wasn't a final goodbye, but an "until we meet again"? Wouldn't it be wonderful if death actually had a cure? If Christianity is true, life doesn't end at the grave, death is the beginning of an eternity of uninterrupted bliss, and we will see our loved ones again someday. If Christianity is true, death is not an "eternal" slumber. Christ will empty every casket and every tomb when He returns. I would think you would prefer that Christianity be true, not false! Yeah, you'd have to give up some worldly pleasures, but isn't eternal life worth more than a night of porn or a marriage to someone of the same sex?

Of course, what we **want** to be true doesn't matter. What matters is where the evidence points. If the evidence points away from Christianity, so be it. If it points to Christianity, awesome! My point in the previous paragraph was just an attempt to change your desire if you fell into the category of people who say "No" to Frank Turek's question. If you would at least like Christianity to be true, you might be more open to following the evidence. If you would lament over it being true, then you'd be prone to talk yourself out of the arguments' conclusion. I wanted to make you want it to be true, or at least find Christianity attractive so you might be less prone to suppressing the truth (Romans 1:18-20).

Addressing The Elephant In The Room

Moreover, when you examine the evidence, make sure you don't go in with a presupposition that miracles cannot occur. What is a presupposition? Josh and Sean McDowell explain that *"A presupposition is something assumed or supposed in advance. ... A presupposition is something that is assumed to be true and is taken for granted. Synonyms include: prejudgment, assumption of something as true, prejudice, forejudgment, preconceived opinion, fixed conclusion, preconceived notion, and premature conclusion."* [11] If you go into this concluding from the outset that miracles cannot occur, that will distort your ability to interpret the evidence. You can't go into this investigation with your mind already made up.

The biochemist Michael Behe gives an amusing illustration of this in his book Darwin's Black Box:

"Imagine a room in which a body lies crushed, flat as a pancake. A dozen detectives crawl around, examining the floor with magnifying glasses for any clue to the identity of the perpetrator. In the middle of the room, next to the body, stands a

large, gray elephant. The detectives carefully avoid bumping into the pachyderm's legs as they crawl, and never even glance at it. Over time the detectives get frustrated with their lack of progress but resolutely press on, looking even more closely at the floor. You see, textbooks say detectives must "get their man," so they never consider elephants."[12]

Behe was writing in the context of Darwinists ruling out Intelligent Design theory from the outset, but the analogy is just as applicable in looking at the evidence for Jesus' resurrection. If you presuppose that a miraculous resurrection cannot occur and then interpret the evidence in light of that presupposition, you're like the detectives who refuse to consider that the corpse on the floor may have been killed by the elephant standing directly adjacent to it. Of course, if a naturalistic explanation can account for the data, that's one thing, but to think, either consciously or subconsciously "No matter what the evidence says, Jesus could not possibly have come back to life" is wrongheaded. If a human culprit could be found, tried, and convicted for the murder of the person in Behe's analogy, that would be one thing, but to say "No matter what the evidence says, an elephant couldn't possibly be the culprit" is wrongheaded.

"You've Written About This Before, Why Write This Book?"

Those who follow my blog Cerebral Faith (www.cerebralfaith.blogspot.com) know that this isn't the first time I've written on this topic. I have written about the evidence for Jesus' resurrection elsewhere. I've written about it in blog posts titled "The Minimal Facts Case For Jesus' Resurrection PART 1" and "The Minimal Facts Case For Jesus' Resurrection PART 2". I've also written an abbreviated version of that first blog post titled "A Quick Case For Jesus' Resurrection". And I've done a 20-page chapter on it in my book *Inference To The One True God: Why I Believe In Jesus Instead Of Other Gods*. Furthermore, there's a 10 part blog post series on the Cerebral Faith website (and this has also been featured on CrossExamined.org). Given this, one may wonder why I'm writing a book like this one. The answer: because the evidence is far more powerful and plenteous than I was able to present in the space allotted to me in those articles and book chapter. For example, I gave 3 reasons to believe Jesus' tomb was empty in *Inference To The One True God* and a few of the aforementioned blog posts. However, there are actually many more reasons to believe that this is true. Other criteria of authenticity establish that Jesus' tomb was empty and that Jesus did die by Roman crucifixion. I just didn't mention these in these above writings (except for the 10 part series) because (1) I didn't know about these arguments when I wrote the aforementioned writings, and (2) I didn't want the above writings to be lengthier than need-be.

As for the 10 part blog post series, I originally intended this very book to be a mere compilation of those articles, but I felt that God was telling me that instead of simply shoving my blog posts as-is into a book compilation, I should expand and adapt upon that blog post series.

The reasons for that are that I can add **even more** reasons for accepting the minimal facts than I even went into in the blog post series. I had to keep each article to a decent length. One of the most important principles for a blogger is; Don't talk too long or else people will lose interest. With books, one is at liberty to talk longer than in a blog post because people have an expectation for book chapters to be substantially longer than blog articles. Moreover, when addressing "The Antecedent Probability" objection to the resurrection, I didn't really lay out some of the most important reasons why Jesus' resurrection isn't improbable in part 9 of the blog post series. I mentioned things like God's existence and the religio-historical background weighing in favor of the miraculous resurrection. I simply mentioned them and directed the reader to other sources in which I defend the existence of God and the historicity of Jesus' divine self-understanding. This is perfectly fine in a blog post series (they just simply need to look at other articles I've written on the website), however, readers of a book would have to go beyond the book itself to get that information. Additionally, I haven't written **anywhere** (until now) on why we should affirm that Jesus' ministry consisted of what appeared to be miracles.

I thought that not talking about these issues would make the case a lot weaker and leave many skeptics unsatisfied. Therefore, although the contents of this book substantially overlap with my 10 part blog post series on Jesus' resurrection, entire chapters have been devoted to Jesus' divine self-understanding, His ministry as a miracle worker, His predictions that He would die and rise from the dead, and the arguments for God's existence. Moreover, even in the chapters that heavily mirror my 10 part blog post series, I have added a substantial amount of new material and expanded on some of the points I made in those articles. For example, I explain what "abductive reasoning" is in more depth than I do in the 10 part series. Again, this is because I am at liberty to talk longer in a book than I am on my blog, due to people's' expectations that blog articles will be relatively short, and book chapters will be much longer. Also, during my research for this book, I have discovered that Matthew and Luke are probably independently reporting Jesus' crucifixion and aren't borrowing from Mark. I also include the Talmud among the reliable sources reporting Jesus' crucifixion. So, I have expanded my list from 7 independent sources for Jesus' crucifixion to 9.

In this book, I'll be covering familiar ground while also talking about evidence I had not talked about in my prior writings on this subject. This book will be a mixture of both old and new. Let's now turn to the historical case for Christianity.

Notes

1: C. S. Lewis Quotes. BrainyQuote.com, Xplore Inc, 2017. https://www.brainyquote.com/quotes/quotes/c/cslewis164517.html, accessed November 6, 2017.

2: Some people think The Bible's teachings on Hell impugn God's goodness. I don't, but it's beyond the scope of this series to get into why. If you're bothered by The Bible's teachings on Hell, I recommend checking out my book *A Hellacious Doctrine: A Defense Of The Biblical Doctrine Of Hell* which addresses this biblical doctrine in depth. Each chapter takes on a different objection to the doctrine of Hell, from the "Eternal torment is overkill" argument to the "What happens to the unevangelized" question.

3: Blaise Pascal's, Pensées ("Thoughts"), 1670, page 233. It is in this work that we find what is known as Pascal's Wager.

4: *"And whoever desires other than Islam as religion - never will it be accepted from him, and he, in the Hereafter, will be among the losers."* - Qur'an 3:85

"They have certainly disbelieved who say, 'Allah is the Messiah, the son of Mary" while the Messiah has said, 'O Children of Israel, worship Allah, my Lord and your Lord.' Indeed, he who associates others with Allah - Allah has forbidden him Paradise, and his refuge is the Fire. And there are not for the wrongdoers any helpers." - Qur'an 5:72

5: Ochoa v. Evans, 2009 U.S. Dist. LEXIS 112693 (C.D. Cal. Oct. 1, 2009).

6: J. Warner Wallace. Cold-Case Christianity: A Homicide Detective Investigates the Claims of the Gospels (Kindle Locations 2040-2044). David C. Cook. Kindle Edition.

7: The Hasty Generalization fallacy occurs when someone takes a small sample of a class and then makes an unjustified conclusion about the totality of that specific class in which the sample was found. For example, someone would be committing the hasty generalization fallacy if they said "All men are pigs" based on their past relationships, or if they said "All white men are racists" just because they knew a couple of white men who were indeed racists.

8: Christian Apologists are people who defend the truth of the Christian Worldview. Famous contemporary Christian Apologists include William Lane Craig, Lee Strobel, Gary Habermas, Michael Licona, and Ravi Zacharias.

9: Neil Mammen, "Who Is Agent X: Proving Science and Logic Show It's More Rational To Believe That God Exists", page 5

10: I could never find a place where Lennox said this in writing, but I know he said this in a debate he had with Stephen Hawking. In fact, it's a rather popular quote of his.

11: McDowell, Josh; McDowell, Sean. Evidence That Demands a Verdict: Life-Changing Truth for a Skeptical World (p. lxi). Thomas Nelson. Kindle Edition.

12: Michael J. Behe, Darwin's Black Box (New York: Free Press, 1996), 192.rf

Part 1: Preliminary Issues

Chapter 1

How To Do History

In the previous chapter, I talked about how important it was that we figure out whether or not Jesus rose from the dead.

However, what kind of historical evidence could there be for the resurrection of Jesus? Where does one find this evidence? How does one come up with it? It's important to understand how historical conclusions are derived. It's important to understand the reasoning behind the case for Jesus' resurrection, that is; the procedure at which we will come to the conclusion: Jesus of Nazareth rose from the dead. If one doesn't understand the methodology of how historians come to this conclusion, then one won't be convinced and might even respond with a straw man argument.

What Is The Minimal Facts Approach?

The approach to evidentially demonstrating Christ's resurrection I will be taking in this book is what's come to be known as "The Minimal Facts Approach". New Testament scholars Gary Habermas and Michael Licona use this method in their book *The Case For The Resurrection Of Jesus*.

The Minimal Facts Approach only employs data that meet two criteria:

1: It has a lot of historical evidence in its favor.
2: It is nearly universally accepted by nearly all scholars and historians who study this subject, even the skeptical non-Christian scholars.

A minimal fact, in order **to be** a minimal fact, must meet those two criteria. It must be very well attested and have near universal acceptance among scholars and historians who study this subject, even the skeptical non-Christian scholars.

The Minimal Facts approach argues for the historicity of the resurrection by a two step process:

1: We give a list of facts and the historical evidence that proves they are facts.
2: We arrive at the resurrection as the best explanation of those facts by means of abductive reasoning. I'll explain what Abductive Reasoning is below.

The Criteria Of Authenticity

With regards to that first step, you'll notice that I appeal to both extra biblical sources as well as The New Testament documents. This is where non-Christians get hung up. They think that just because I cite a book or letter from The New Testament that I'm somehow "begging the question" or "reasoning in a circle" because they say that I'm "Quoting from The Bible to prove that The Bible is true". They think I'm saying that because, for example, The Bible says that the tomb of Jesus was empty, that therefore Jesus' tomb was empty. They think I'm arguing like this: "The tomb of Jesus was empty because The Bible clearly says it was empty, and The Bible's the word of God, so you know that what it says is true!"

However, that's not at all how I'm arguing for the factuality of the minimal facts. Yes, I use The New Testament documents, but I am not citing from them as divinely inspired scripture. Rather, I'm treating the New Testament documents as I would any other document from ancient history: as a set of ancient documents that claim to be telling us about historical events. I do not presuppose the inspiration, inerrancy, or even the general reliability of The New Testament when I appeal to it.

When I use the New Testament documents, I treat them just as a historian would any secular document. When historians are examining documents and are trying to figure out whether what those documents say are true, they will employ certain principles or criteria which will make a recorded incident more likely true than it would be without the use of those principles. By doing this, they can come to a conclusion with some degree of certainty that what they're reading about actually happened.

These principles, known as "the principles of historical authenticity" or the "criteria of authenticity" will be described below. I will be applying these to the gospels and New Testament epistles to see what kind of data we can extract about what happened to Jesus. Now, let me explain these criteria:

The Principle Of Embarrassment -- If a document records an event that is embarrassing to the one writing it, embarrassing to someone the writer cares about, weakens an argument he's trying to make, or hurts his cause in any way, it is more likely to be true than false. This principle is built on the common sense belief that if people are going to make up lies, those lies will make themselves look good, make their loved ones look good, strengthen their arguments, or helps their cause. No one makes up lies to make themselves or a loved one look bad, or to weaken an argument they're trying to make.

Here's a hypothetical example of this principle in play. Let's say we had a letter written by George Washington, the first president of The United States, and in that letter, he records an incident where he was riding a horse along the countryside and he had a bad case of diarrhea, causing him to soil himself. Then he says that he went behind a tree, removed his undergarments, and went commando for the rest of the day. A historian examining that document would conclude that this story is more likely to be true than not because such a story is embarrassing to the one who wrote it (i.e. George Washington). Now, no such letter written by George Washington exists (at least to my knowledge). This is merely an illustration to help you see how a historical investigation is done.

The Principle Of Multiple Attestation -- The more independent sources an event is mentioned in, the more likely it is to be true. The more independent sources you have reporting an event, the smaller the odds it is that the event is made up, since it's highly unlikely for multiple people to concoct the same fiction.

Let's say that not only did Washington write about his embarrassing case, but three of his friends each wrote documents recounting the incident as well. If this were the case, the incident of Washington soiling himself would be **even more** likely to be true. Why? Because of the principle of multiple attestation. When you have two or more independent sources record an incident, it's far more likely to be true than not, because the more and more independent sources an event is mentioned in, the less and less likely it is to be made up. If you had three or four different sources recording the same event, what are the odds that all four sources are making up the same thing? So on top of the principle of embarrassment, we would add multiple attestation to this incident.

The Principle Of Early Attestation -- The earlier a document dates relative to the event the document purports to describe, the more reliable the account. The earlier a document is, the less time there was for legend and embellishment to creep in.

The hypothetical documents of Washington's' friends were written only 2 years after the event. This short timescale makes it less likely that they would embellish things and inaccurately recall the day.

The Principle Of Enemy Attestation -- If Document X is saying something that benefits a person, message, or cause that X is hostile or opposed to, we have an indication of authenticity.

This principle's logic runs mirror to The Principle of Embarrassment's. The logic behind this principle is that people who hate you are not going to make up lies to make you look good. People who are opposed to your cause are not going to make up lies that help it.

The Principle Of Historical Fit -- If details in an account conform to well established historical facts of the period, this makes the event in said account more credible.

For example, if Washington's letters and the writings of his 3 friends described the countryside accurately, described what kind of trees were in bloom in the area that they said they were horse riding in, described the kind of clothes the people back in town wore, etc. these things would heighten the credibility of the accounts.

The Principle Of Dissimilarity -- As far as I know, this principle is solely used in examining The New Testament. This principle says that If an event or saying of Jesus cannot be derived from the Judaism that preceded him or the Christian church that came after him, then it's highly unlikely that the saying of Jesus in question is made up. Some object to the use of this criterion on the basis that we would expect Jesus, as a Jewish Rabbi and the founder of the Christian church, to say things that reflect the Judaism that preceded Him and the Christianity that came after Him. This is a good point, but as I point out below, the criteria of authenticity cannot be used negatively. This criterion simply states that if Jesus says something that sounds unJewish and unChristian, then Jesus most likely said it. This is because it would be implausible to say that the early church retroactively put these words in Jesus' mouth or that it was a logical outworking of the Jewish theology of the day. This is probably the most skeptical of all the criteria, and it is used the least often.

The Principle Of Multiple Literary Forms -- Greco-Roman Biographies, creeds, miracles, didactic (these would be sermon summaries), apocalyptic. These are the genres of writings in the first century Roman-Palestinian world. If an event can be found in writings that fall into more than one literary genre, then it's more likely to be true than not.

<u>The Principle Of Eyewitness Testimony</u> -- If a writer claims to be a direct witness to the event he's describing, this is generally taken to make the event more likely to have occurred.

As you can see, although I'll be appealing to the New Testament documents, I won't be "quoting from The Bible to prove The Bible." Instead, I'll merely be treating The New Testament documents like I would any other set of ancient documents. By the way, even non-Christian historians treat The New Testament this way! People like Bart Ehrman and Gerd Ludemann come to conclusions about the historical Jesus by applying these "criteria of authenticity" to the New Testament documents. Bart Ehrman is probably the loudest and most influential historian arguing against Christianity today. This is what Ehrman has said regarding the Gospels in the New Testament: *"The oldest and best sources we have for knowing about the life of Jesus are the four Gospels of the New Testament, Matthew, Mark, Luke, and John. This is not simply the view of Christian historians who have a high opinion of the New Testament and its historical worth; it is the view of all serious historians of antiquity of every kind, from committed evangelical Christians to hardcore atheists."*[1] As resurrection expert and New Testament scholar Gary Habermas once said: *"If you don't use The New Testament, the skeptics will."*[2] So here's something to ponder; if the skeptics are allowed to use the New Testament, why aren't Christian Apologists? If atheists can say "This aspect of Jesus is historical because of criteria of authenticity X", then why can't I? These non-Christian historians certainly don't presuppose the inspiration or inerrancy of scripture. Indeed, they don't even believe them.

Now, when one applies these criteria, what one comes up with are several facts which undergird the inference to the resurrection. These 5 facts will be talked about in part 2 of this work. They are

1: Jesus died by crucifixion.

2: Jesus' tomb was found empty the following Sunday morning.

3: Jesus' disciples believed that Jesus appeared to them alive after His death.

4: A church persecutor named Paul converted to Christianity on the basis of what he perceived was an appearance of the risen Jesus.

5: A skeptic named James converted to Christianity on the basis of what he perceived was an appearance of the risen Jesus.

According to Doctor Habermas, these 5 facts meet the two criteria required to be a minimal fact. They have both a lot of historical evidence in their favor (as we'll see in the upcoming chapters), and moreover, they are nearly universally accepted by scholars and historians who study ancient Palestinian history, even the skeptical ones.[3]

By the way, let me just get a quick word in about these criteria regarding how they can be **mis**used. Some people have tried to disprove things about Jesus through the **negative** use of these criteria. For example, they'll say that because some event or saying of Jesus is **not** multiply attested or **not** embarrassing, that therefore, it isn't historical. You can't use the criteria in that way. They can only be used positively to show that something **is** true, they can't be used negatively to show something **isn't** true. Just because something isn't embarrassing to an author, that doesn't mean it isn't true. Just because something is found in only one source, that doesn't mean it isn't true. Just because something isn't attested by an enemy source, that doesn't mean it isn't true. The criteria only say that if something **is** multiply attested, embarrassing, enemy attested, etc. then that means it probably happened. Think about it this way; Event X may be mentioned in only one source and therefore is not multiply attested. However, Event X may be embarrassing to the author. So even though event X isn't mentioned by two or three other writers, we'd still be justified in concluding X happened on the basis of the criterion of embarrassment. Or something may not be embarrassing, but it may be mentioned by two or three independent writers and ergo is multiply attested.

Abductive Reasoning

Once the 5 facts are established through the historical methodological approach, we then use abductive reasoning to arrive at the resurrection as the best explanation of those 5 facts. Now, what is abductive reasoning? Abductive Reasoning, also known as inferring to the best explanation, is a form of reasoning that takes a collection of evidence and eliminates the list of possible explanations for that evidence until you arrive at only one remaining possibility. If this remaining possibility has the power to explain all of the evidence in question and if it's truly the only one left, then the most logical conclusion is that this explanation is the true explanation.

In his book *Cold Case Christianity: A Homicide Detective Investigates The Claims Of The Gospels,* J. Warner Wallace gives a helpful illustration to show how abductive reasoning works. He says abductive reasoning involves "two E Lists"; an

"Evidence List" and an "Explanation List".[4] Wallace then invites his readers to join him on a hypothetical crime scene. We go up to the scene and find a dead body lying face down on the floor. On this basis, we conclude that the person is dead. But what exactly did he die from? Well, there are only 4 categories in which a death can fall into: Natural, Accidental, Suicide, or Homicide. Many different kinds of deaths occur, but they all fall into one of those categories. As a homicide detective, Wallace only cares about whether a death falls into that last category.

Based solely on the fact that the man is lying face down on the floor, it would be impossible for you to determine which of the 4 explanations is the best. It could be any one of them. Now, suppose that we add more pieces of evidence to our first "E List". We find (1) a dead body lying face down in a pool of blood with (2) multiple stab wounds in his back, and (3) the knife is sticking out of his back, and (4) bloody footprints lead away from the body. No person in his right mind would conclude that this was an accidental death! What? Did this guy just happen to accidentally back into a knife over and over again? Why didn't he back away from the object after he got hurt the first time? Moreover, how does one explain the footprints? Did he walk outside to get a breath of fresh air before coming back in, lying down, and passing away? A natural death is an irrational explanation as well. What kind of natural event is going to cause stab wounds to appear on someone's body, leave a knife sticking out, and cause footprints leading away from the body? Was this a suicide? No. It's unreasonable to think that this man killed himself. If he were going to commit suicide with a sharp object, he would most likely have run it through his stomach, as dishonored samurais did in feudal times. Additionally, it would have been difficult for him to reach back there to cause damage. I have a hard time scratching an itch on my back. I can only imagine how difficult it would be to impale myself multiple times! This is not a suicide. Given that 3 of the 4 explanations have been ruled out, the best explanation is that this was a homicide.

This was all based on what we **do** know, not on what we **don't** know. You, as a detective, would laugh at anyone who accused you of "Murderer Of The Gaps" reasoning. You examined all of the possible explanations and found that only an outside intruder could explain all of the evidence. Likewise, if we exhaust all of the possible natural explanations that attempt to account for the 5 minimal facts and find that only the miraculous resurrection hypothesis can adequately account for the data, then we should conclude "He is risen! He is risen indeed!"

Don't Worry About Alleged Contradictions In The Gospels

   In conversations with skeptics about the evidence for the resurrection, almost inevitably, someone will bring up the charge that the gospel accounts are contradictory. They'll say "How can we believe what the gospels tell us about Jesus!? They're hopelessly filled with contradictions!" Or they'll quote Bart Ehrman saying:

"Did he [Jesus] die on the day before the Passover meal was eaten, as John explicitly says, or did he die after it was eaten, as Mark explicitly says? Did he die at noon, as in John, or at 9 a.m., as in Mark? Did Jesus carry his cross the entire way himself or did Simon of Cyrene carry his cross? It depends which Gospel you read. Did both robbers mock Jesus on the cross or did only one of them mock him and the other come to his defense? It depends which Gospel you read. Did the curtain in the temple rip in half before Jesus died or after he died? It depends which Gospel you read. Or take the accounts of the resurrection. Who went to the tomb on the third day? Was it Mary alone or was it Mary with other women? If it was Mary with other women, how many other women were there, which ones were they, and what were their names? Was the stone rolled away before they got there or not? What did they see in the tomb? Did they see a man, did they see two men, or did they see an angel? It depends which account you read." [5]

Listening to Ehrman or another unbeliever list these supposed contradictions off can seem a little overwhelming, and some apologists feel tempted to respond to every one of them and provide some sort of plausible harmonization scenario for each. However, in a minimal facts approach, we need not bother with any alleged contradictions in the gospel accounts. For one thing, while I think apologists should provide scenarios to harmonize these differences, since I take biblical inerrancy to be very important (and I think Norman Geisler and Thomas Howe do a great job at this in their book *The Big Book Of Bible Difficulties*), nevertheless, since inerrancy isn't something being presupposed in our case, we can ignore any errors The New Testament may or may not have made.

   Moreover, I want you to notice something: all of these discrepancies are in the secondary details, not the primary details.

   The gospels are completely in harmony when it comes to the primary details. All 4 gospels agree on the following facts:

Jesus was crucified in Jerusalem on Passover Eve under Pontius Pilate at the instigation of the Sanhedrin, and afterwards, he was buried in a tomb owned by Joseph of Arimathea, which was sealed by a huge round stone. The following Sunday morning, at least one woman went to the tomb and found it empty. Jesus then appeared to the women and to the disciples alive.

All four Gospels attest to these facts.

The only places where there seem to be discrepancies are in the peripheral details, which don't really make an impact on the story. For example, who went to the tomb? One woman, or several? How many angels were at the tomb? One angel or two? Do the answers to these questions really matter in the overall scheme of things? No. If the gospels contradict each other, they only do so in the minor, secondary, peripheral details. They're completely harmonious in the core details of the story.

Dr. William Lane Craig said *"Historians expect to find inconsistencies like these even in the most reliable sources. No historian simply throws out a source because it has inconsistencies."* [6] and he's absolutely right. Historians look at whether accounts harmonize in the primary details. If they conflict only in the peripherals, they don't throw the sources out. Let's use a non-biblical example to demonstrate this point.

When the Titanic sank, there were differing accounts as to how it sank. Some said the Titanic went down in one piece, others said it broke in half before it went down. Some said people continued to play music as the ship sank, others said there was no music. Some said there were shootings happening when the Titanic was sinking, but others disagreed. How in the world could eyewitnesses not agree on these things? I don't know! But I don't hear anyone claiming that because of these discrepancies in the eyewitness accounts that therefore the Titanic didn't sink![7] Eyewitnesses may differ as to whether the Titanic broke in half, but they all agreed that it sank! The gospel authors may disagree about how many women went to the tomb, but they all agree that the tomb was empty! The gospel authors may disagree as to how many thieves ridiculed Jesus at His crucifixion, but they all agree that Jesus was indeed crucified!

Moreover, as Detective J. Warner Wallace points out in *Cold Case Christianity*, this is exactly the kind of thing you would expect from true, eyewitness accounts. True eyewitness accounts generally have many differences in the peripheral details, but they all are in harmony in the core of the story. In fact, when judges hear multiple witnesses all give exactly the same story in exactly the same way, they conclude "collusion!" They got together, concocted this story, and made sure that they all were on the same page.

Objection: But The New Testament Writers Were Biased!

Some non-Christians would object to me using The New Testament even if they fully understand that I'm not treating it like divinely inspired scripture. They say we can't trust what The New Testament writers wrote because they were biased. They say that they had an invested interest in writing down the things they wrote down. They say it's propaganda. It's a religious text. It's meant to be a tool for converting people and nothing more. So, therefore, these non-Christians argue, we should only look at extra-biblical sources in trying to figure out the truth about what happened to Jesus.

This argument doesn't work for three reasons. First of all, **everyone** is biased to some degree or other. Jews have an invested interest in writing about the Holocaust (namely to try to prevent such an atrocity from ever happening again), and African Americans have an invested interest in writing about the unfairness of slavery, so rejecting what a document says because they're supposedly biased is just fallacious. Basically, it's just another example of the ad hominem fallacy (i.e rejecting what a person says as true simply because of who they are). If you're going to reject a source on these grounds, you would throw out every history book ever written. In fact, you'd have to reject not only every source from ancient history, but you'd have to reject every blog, every news site, every radio program, every newspaper, you'd basically be forced into a state of hyper-skepticism. You couldn't even believe your mother when she tells you she loves you and are a good person! I'm not joking! Isn't she biased? No one writes about anything unless they're interested in their subject.

Secondly, bias does not automatically mean someone is distorting the facts. Someone can be biased, and someone can be right at the same time. In fact, ironically, bias can actually drive a person to be **more** accurate in their reporting. For example, one might say (and in fact, some have said) that I'm biased in favor of Christianity and that I have an invested interest in winning unbelievers to the faith and equipping believers to defend their faith. True enough. I've said so outright in various places on my blog. However, I would submit to you that my bias drives me to be more accurate, more truthful, and more careful in my writing. The reason is that I don't want to discredit myself. If I even misattribute a quote to someone or take a Bible verse out of context, I'm mortified! I want to ensure that everything I say is true so that my credibility doesn't suffer.

Thirdly, the criteria of authenticity that I mentioned several subsections ago help to establish facts as historically true regardless of whether an author has a bias or not. Multiple attestation, embarrassment, enemy attestation, etc. These can be used to extract historical pieces of information.

As Dr. William Lane Craig said, *"Notice that these "criteria" do not presuppose the general reliability of the Gospels. Rather they focus on a particular saying or event and give evidence for thinking that specific element of Jesus' life to be historical, regardless of the general reliability of the document in which the particular saying or event is reported. These same "criteria" are thus applicable to reports of Jesus found in the apocryphal Gospels, or rabbinical writings, or even the Qur'an. Of course, if the Gospels can be shown to be generally reliable documents, so much the better! But the "criteria" do not depend on any such presupposition. They serve to help spot historical kernels even in the midst of historical chaff. Thus we need not concern ourselves with defending the Gospels' every claim attributed to Jesus in the gospels; the question will be whether we can establish enough about Jesus to make faith in him reasonable."* [8]

The criteria of authenticity do an end-run around the historical reliability of the gospels (which might be affected by a bias). Even in the most unreliable of sources, these criteria can extract nuggets of historical data. For example, one might say "X is an unreliable source, but we can still believe what it says when it reports Y because it's embarrassing to X to mention such a thing." or "X is an unreliable source, but X's mentioning of Y is corroborated by several other sources, so it's multiply attested and therefore, likely to be true." Therefore, this objection to the use of The New Testament documents falls flat.

Summary and Conclusion

Hopefully, you now know how history is done and how the minimal facts are arrived at. Hopefully you'll see that the approach we apologists take when arguing for the historicity of Jesus' resurrection isn't a question begging "The Bible says it! I believe it! That settles it!" kind of approach. Rather, this approach treats The New Testament documents the same way we would treat any set of ancient documents. Moreover, non-Christian historians approach the New Testament in the same way and come to the same conclusions. Using the historical methodological approach, they agree that the minimal facts are indeed facts. They just disagree with Christian scholars on how to explain those 5 facts. That's where abductive reasoning comes in. We need to see whether any of the proposed naturalistic explanations non-Christian scholars propose are any good. I submit to you that they are not, and only the miraculous resurrection can account for all 5 facts. Finally, we need to not get distracted by claims that the gospel accounts are contradictory. For one thing, all alleged contradictions are in the peripheral details that don't make an impact on the story. Moreover, if historians threw sources out because of such differences, little could be known about history.

Now that you know the reasoning process behind the minimal facts approach, it's now time to begin looking at the evidence for the truth of Christianity. First, we'll examine whether Jesus ever claimed divinity for Himself, and then we'll determine if Jesus rose from the dead.

Notes

1: Bart D. Ehrman, Truth and Fiction in The Da Vinci Code (Oxford: OUP, 2004), 102.

2: Gary Habermas said this in a lecture at the "To Everyone an Answer: 10th Annual EPS Apologetics Conference". The lecture was titled "The Resurrection Evidence that Changed Current Scholarship" and can be viewed on YouTube here, uploaded by Biola University's YouTube account à
https://www.youtube.com/watch?v=5znVUFHqO4Q

3: Doctor Habermas came up with the number that around 95-99% of non-Christian scholars accept the 5 minimal facts presented above. The empty tomb, while not having such near unanimity as the other 4 facts, does have support from an impressive majority of 75% of scholars. He came up with this number by surveying the literature.

4: See J. Warner Wallace, "Cold Case Christianity: A Homicide Detective Investigates The Claims Of The Gospels", David C Cook, pages 34-39

5: (Bart Ehrman vs. William Lane Craig Debate, Is there Historical Evidence for the Resurrection of Jesus?, debate transcript
http://www.reasonablefaith.org/is-there-historical-evidence-for-the-resurrection-of-jesus-the-craig-ehrman).

6: William Lane Craig, "Q&A: Inerrancy and The Resurrection",
https://www.reasonablefaith.org/writings/question-answer/inerrancy-and-the-resurrection

7: See "Titanic: First Accounts", by Tim Maltin (Editor, Introduction), Nicholas Wade (Afterword), Max Ellis (Illustrator), Penguin Classics

8: William Lane Craig, "Q&A: Establishing The Gospels' Reliability",
http://www.reasonablefaith.org/establishing-the-gospels-reliability

Chapter 2

Did Jesus Claim To Be God?

Who did Jesus think he was? Did He think He was God? I'm not asking whether The Bible teaches whether Jesus is God. I think it's undeniable that it does. Few can read John 1, Colossians 1, or Hebrews 1 and walk away thinking that The Bible doesn't boldly assert that Jesus is God Almighty. These texts so powerfully support the deity of Christ, that the exclusive translation of the Jehovah's Witnesses (called The New World Translation) has to render the wordings in these passages differently so as to downplay their significance.

What I'm asking is whether the historical Jesus believed that He was God. Obviously The New Testament calls Him that, but is that what the historical Jesus believed about Himself? Would he, if he read John 1:1-3 think "Yep, I'm all that and more" or would He say "Whoa! John! Delet dis! You are doing God a blaspheme!"? In this chapter, I will examine Jesus' claims in the gospels to see whether he believed that He was divine. Remember, I won't be treating this issue from the perspective of a theologian, citing Bible verses and saying "The Bible says Jesus said this, therefore, Jesus must have said it. And this proves that Jesus had a divine self-understanding". No. I will be employing the historical "criteria of authenticity" that we talked about in the previous chapter. In other words, I'll be combing through the gospel data from the perspective of a historian.

First, we'll look at what Jesus said, then we'll employ the criteria of authenticity to conclude that Jesus actually said it, and finally, we'll unpack the theological significance of what Jesus said.

Although I already explained this in the introduction, let me refresh your memory on why it's important to establish whether or not Jesus thought of Himself as God. If Jesus claimed to be God, then there's only two possibilities: He was making true claims or false claims. If the latter is the case, then Jesus is a devious cult leader in the same boat as Jim Jones or David Koresh. He was either intentionally deceiving the masses or he was insane.

C.S Lewis spelled this out quite nicely in his book *Mere Christianity*. Lewis wrote: *"I am trying here to prevent anyone saying the really foolish thing that people often say about Him: I'm ready to accept Jesus as a great moral teacher, but I don't accept his claim to be God. That is the one thing we must not say. A man who was merely a man and said the sort of things Jesus said would not be a great moral teacher. He would either be a lunatic — on the level with the man who says he is a poached egg — or else he would be the Devil of Hell. You must make your choice. Either this man was, and is, the Son of God, or else a madman or something worse. You can shut him up for a fool, you can spit at him and kill him as a demon or you can fall at his feet and call him Lord and God, but let us not come with any patronizing nonsense about his being a great human teacher. He has not left that open to us. He did not intend to."* [1]

Lewis' statement here has become known as the "Liar, Lunatic, Lord Trilemma". The reasoning is abductive reasoning (recall the previous chapter).

1: Jesus is either a liar, a lunatic, or The Lord.
2: Jesus is not a liar or a lunatic.
3: Therefore, Jesus is The Lord.

This is a logically valid syllogism (it's a disjunctive syllogism). It's pure abductive reasoning. If liar and lunatic can be ruled out, then the only remaining option is that Jesus is The Lord. If Jesus rose from the dead, then I think both liar and lunatic can be ruled out. If Jesus were a liar or a lunatic, why would the God of Israel resurrect a man who committed identity theft against Him? To claim to be God when you are not is clear-cut blasphemy. If Jesus rose from the dead, then this means God must not be all that upset with Jesus claiming His identity for Himself. In fact, to raise Him from the dead would be a clear indication that God approved of Jesus' ministry.

The divine self-understanding, therefore, is an important pre-requisite to the case for the resurrection, for the resurrection would serve as a vindication of Jesus' entire ministry.

C.S Lewis' Trilemma all hinges on whether or not Jesus did indeed claim to be God. In this chapter, I will examine 3 titles Jesus attributed to Himself which, at face value, don't seem to be particularly lofty. However, when those titles are closely examined, they are loaded with divine implications. Those titles are: (1) Son Of Man, (2) Son Of God, and (3) The Messiah. Additionally, I will verify that Jesus **did** make these claims using the "criteria of authenticity" that we looked at in the previous chapter. Then I'll look at some objections non-Christians have made to show either that Jesus couldn't be God or at least that He didn't believe that He was.

Title #1: Son Of Man

Over and over and over again, Jesus refers to Himself as the "Son Of Man" in the gospels. He calls Himself the Son Of Man so often that scholars and theologians have dubbed it "Jesus' Favorite Self-Designation".[2] If you do a study of the term "Son of Man" in the Gospels you'll see that he refers to himself as the Son Of Man far more often than He calls Himself the Son Of God. For example, He said things like, in Mark 10:45, *"For even the Son of Man did not come to be served, but to serve, and to give his life as a ransom for many."* And *"Foxes have dens and birds have nests, but the Son of Man has no place to lay his head."* (Matthew 8:20). In fact, according to GotQuestions.org, Jesus refers to Himself as The Son Of Man 88 times in The New Testament![3]

How Do We Know Jesus Actually Called Himself This?

Reason 1: The Principle Of Dissimilarity.
While Jesus calls Himself the Son Of Man over and over again in the gospel accounts, Jesus is **never** called by the title in **any New Testament epistle!** The early church fathers do refer to Jesus as The Son Of Man in a few places, but **hardly ever**. Most of the church fathers (e.g Irenaeus, Polycarp, Ignatius, Tertullian) were prone to call Jesus "God", "Son Of God", "Jesus", or "Jesus The Messiah", but hardly ever "The Son Of Man". Given that this title is sparse outside of the gospel records, it's very unlikely that the early church made up this title and retroactively inserted it into Jesus' biographies. If that were the case, we would expect them to refer to Jesus by this title far more often than they do. Therefore, by the principle of dissimilarity, it's highly probable that Jesus actually referred to Himself by this title.

Reason 2: Principle Of Embarrassment - Jesus The Homeless Dude
Another reason to believe the "Son Of Man" title is historical is because of its use in Matthew 8:20. In Matthew 8:20, Jesus says *"'Foxes have holes and birds of the air have nests, but the Son of Man has nowhere to lay His head.'"* - (NKJV)
It is unlikely that Matthew made this sentence up. Why? Because it depicts Jesus as homeless. It's unlikely the early church would make up a saying of Jesus that emphasizes his homelessness. Therefore, by the principle of embarrassment, this saying by Jesus is very likely to be historical. Remember, the principle of embarrassment is when a writer mentions something in his writing that is

embarrassing to himself, embarrassing to someone he cares about or admires, or has the potential to hurt an argument he's trying to make. I gave an illustration of this in the previous chapter which involved George Washington soiling his britches.

Reason 3: Principle Of Embarrassment - Bad, Bad Company Until The Day I Die.

"The Son of Man came eating and drinking, and they say, 'Look, a glutton and a winebibber, a friend of tax collectors and sinners!' But wisdom is justified by her children." - Matthew 11:19 (NKJV) Once again, this instance seems likely on the basis of the principle of embarrassment. Why would the church make up a reputation of Jesus being a glutton, or a drunkard, or a friend of sinners? This wasn't actually true of Jesus, but people who hated him called him that.

Reason 4: Multiple Attestation

Jesus calls Himself the Son Of Man not only in the Gospel of Mark, but in the gospel of John as well. *"For as the Father has life in himself, so he has granted the Son to have life in himself. And he has given him authority to judge because he is the Son of Man."* (John 5:27). Mark and John are independent sources, therefore, it is multiply attested that Jesus called Himself the Son Of Man. It is unlikely that both Mark and John would have made this saying up independently of one another.

While many scholars think Matthew and Luke borrowed material from Mark on many of the paralalle narratives they report,[4] absolutely no one thinks John borrowed from any of the synoptics. So, since the synoptic gospels and the gospel of John report Jesus as calling Himself "The Son Of Man", we therefore have 2 independent sources.

Reason 5: Principle Of Embarrassment, Son Of Man -- Inept Disciples

There are places in the gospels in which Jesus calls Himself the Son Of Man, and in the context of that self-designation, the disciples appear inept. If the early church or the disciples (whoever you think authored the gospels) were merely making these accounts up, why would they depict the disciples as dimwitted? For example, In Mark 8:31-33, we read *"He then began to teach them that the Son of Man must suffer many things and be rejected by the elders, the chief priests and the teachers of the law, and that he must be killed and after three days rise again. He spoke plainly about this, and Peter took him aside and began to rebuke him. But when Jesus turned and looked at his disciples, he rebuked Peter. 'Get behind me, Satan!' he said. 'You do not have in mind the concerns of God, but merely human concerns.'"* Okay, so let me get this straight, the apostle Peter, the number 1 apostle is called **Satan** by Jesus! If Mark was Peter's secretary, as the early church fathers held, this is even more jarring, for then, if this account is being made up, Peter would essentially be telling Mark "Hey, put this tidbit in. Jesus predicted his death, but I rebuked him for it. Then he got mad at me and called me Satan." Do you honestly think Peter would have Mark write that down if it weren't true? Even if it **were** true, Peter probably would want to keep this incident quiet! He especially wouldn't have Mark record this if it **weren't** true! By the criterion of embarrassment, we have good reason to believe that this conversation really went down, but in this conversation, Jesus called himself The Son Of Man.

Now, you might question the traditional authorship of the gospels. My argument here doesn't depend on whether this gospel was the result of a collaboration between John Mark and the apostle Peter. Even if you wanted to attribute this work to an early church father (like Polycarp, for example), the criterion would still apply. After all, the early church obviously respected Jesus' disciples. In fact, if Roman Catholics are correct, Peter may have even been the first Pope. So whether Peter and Mark co-authored the gospel that bares Mark's name or whether some unknown person in the early church penned this, we still have good reason to believe that they would not include this unflattering account of the apostle Peter unless it actually occurred. That said, if the case for traditional authorship is sound (and I do indeed think that authors like Craig Blomberg and J. Warner Wallace do make a successful case that Mark wrote Mark[5]), then the criterion of embarrassment has **even more** force, for then we have Peter saying this about **himself**.

Another example of The Son Of Man saying appearing in a context unflattering to the disciples is found in Mark 9:9-10: *"As they were coming down the mountain, Jesus gave them orders not to tell anyone what they had seen until the Son of Man had risen from the dead. They kept the matter to themselves, discussing what 'rising from the dead' meant."* Jesus told His disciples to keep quiet about the transfiguration until after He had risen from the dead, and he calls Himself The Son Of Man in this account. The disciples are confused by what Jesus said. They had no idea what it would mean for Jesus to rise from the dead, and evidently, they were too afraid to ask. This doesn't look like something the early church would make up if it weren't true.

What Did Jesus Mean?

Now that we've established that the historical Jesus referred to Himself as The Son Of Man, we have to ask ourselves what Jesus meant by this phrase. It's popular to hear preachers say that when Jesus referred to himself as The Son Of God, he was expressing his deity, and that when he referred to Himself as The Son

Of Man, he was expressing his humanity. So, Son of God and Son Of Man are thought to be two expressions of Christ's dual nature.

However, the fact of the matter is that Son Of Man is just as much of an expression of divinity as Son Of God. Most scholars agree that Jesus was saying that He was the divine Son Of Man figure mentioned in Daniel's Old Testament prophecy…in Daniel 7.

Daniel 7:13-14 says *"In my vision at night I looked, and there before me was one like a son of man, coming with the clouds of heaven. He approached the Ancient of Days and was led into his presence. He was given authority, glory and sovereign power; all nations and peoples of every language worshiped him. His dominion is an everlasting dominion that will not pass away, and his kingdom is one that will never be destroyed."*

So, Jesus was saying that He was the same person mentioned in Daniel 7. What's striking about this is how Daniel describes this Son Of Man figure. Daniel says that He is given authority and sovereign power over all peoples and nations. Moreover, that people all over the world worship him! Daniel says that the Son Of Man is given an everlasting dominion, a dominion that will not pass away. This is a pretty exalted figure that Daniel is describing!

In this context, Caiaphas' reaction at Jesus' trial makes perfect sense. In Mark 14:61-64, Caiaphas asked Jesus *"Are you the Messiah, the Son of the Blessed One?' and Jesus responded 'I am, and you will see the Son of Man sitting at the right hand of the Mighty One and coming on the clouds of heaven.' Caiaphas then tore his clothes and said 'Why do we need any more witnesses? You have heard the blasphemy. What do you think?'"* and they all condemned Him worthy of death.

Jesus' response was considered blasphemous because Jesus was claiming to be God. He was claiming to be this divine Son Of Man figure in Daniel 7:13-14 who would (A) be sovereign over all creation, and who (B) would be worshipped by every nation, and who (C) would be given an everlasting dominion. Moreover, by saying that He would *"be seated at the right hand of the Mighty One"* (referencing Psalm 110:1), He was putting Himself on the same level of authority with God The Father. In other words, Jesus was saying "I'll be sitting on God's throne." To sit at God's right hand is to sit on God's throne. To sit on God's throne is to imply equality with God. Additionally, we must pay attention to Jesus' *"coming on the clouds of Heaven"*. Not only does this indicate that Jesus believed Himself to be Daniel 7's "Son Of Man", but according to Old Testament scholars, Yahweh alone was considered "the cloud rider". Bible Scholar Michael S Heiser explains that *"Throughout the Ugaritic texts, Baal is repeatedly called "the one who rides the clouds," or "the one who mounts the clouds." The description is recognized as an official title of Baal. No angel or lesser being bore the title. As such, everyone in Israel who heard this title associated it with a deity, not a man or an angel. Part of the literary strategy of the Israelite prophets was to take this well-known title and attribute it to Yahweh in some way. Consequently, Yahweh, the God of Israel, bears this descriptive title in several places in the Old Testament (Isaiah 19:1; Deuteronomy 33:26; Psalm 68:33; 104:3). For a faithful Israelite, then, there was only one god who "rode" on the clouds: Yahweh."* [6]

Is it any wonder that the high priest threw a hissy fit when Jesus said He would come on the clouds of Heaven? Jesus (A) is seated at God's right hand, implying equality with God, (B) is "The Son Of Man" whom Daniel 7 says will be given sovereignty over all creation, and will receive worship from people all over the world, and (C) will come on the clouds of Heaven; he's "the cloud rider", a title that belonged to Yahweh alone.

Jesus' claim to be The Son Of Man would indeed be blasphemous if it weren't true. However, If Jesus rose from the dead, then God put His stamp of approval on Jesus' teaching. We'll see later on in this book whether the historical evidence supports the Christian belief that he did in fact rise from the dead.

I think it's safe to say that Jesus, in referring to Himself as The Son Of Man, was claiming to be God.

If you're still not convinced that Son Of Man carries divine connotations, consider that Jesus, as The Son Of Man, claimed to be able to forgive sins.

In Luke 5:17-26, a paralyzed man is lowered down to Jesus from above the roof. The paralyzed man's friends did this because the house Jesus was in was so crowded that they couldn't get through the door. Since they couldn't get in through the door, they climbed on top of the roof, punched a hole in the roof, and lowered the paralyzed man down to Jesus. Jesus saw how much faith they had in Him, so He said to the paralytic *"Your sins are forgiven"* The Pharisees' reaction was quite understandable. They said *"Who is this fellow who speaks blasphemy? Who can forgive sins but God alone?"* So Jesus responded *"Which is easier: to say, 'Your sins are forgiven,' or to say, 'Get up and walk'? But I want you to know that the Son of Man has authority on earth to forgive sins."* So he said to the paralyzed man, *"I tell you, get up, take your mat and go home."*

The Pharisees were correct in pointing out that only God has the authority to forgive sins. If you do something wrong to me, I have the right to forgive you, but if you do something wrong to me, and some third party comes along and says "I forgive you." we would immediately see something off. The only third party who has the right to do that is God Himself. And yet Jesus said that The Son Of Man has the authority to forgive sins.

"But how do we know this story of Jesus healing the paralytic man is even historical in the first place?" you might ask. "How do we know the story of Jesus healing and forgiving the paralyzed man wasn't just made up?" Good question. For one thing, we've already established on the basis of the criterion of dissimilarity that the "Son Of Man" saying is unlikely to have been retroactively inserted into the mouth of Jesus, given that the early church themselves hardly ever call Jesus by that title. If the title isn't made up, why would instances in which Jesus uses the title be? But, this isn't the only place in which Jesus forgave someone's sins. In Luke 7:36-50, we read *"One of the Pharisees asked him to eat with him, and he went into the Pharisee's house and reclined at table. And behold, a woman of the city, who was a sinner, when she learned that he was reclining at table in the Pharisee's house, brought an alabaster flask of ointment, and standing behind him at his feet, weeping, she began to wet his feet with her tears and wiped them with the hair of her head and kissed his feet and anointed them with the ointment. Now when the Pharisee who had invited him saw this, he said to himself, 'If this man were a prophet, he would have known who and what sort of woman this is who is touching him, for she is a sinner.' And Jesus answering said to him, 'Simon, I have something to say to you.' And he answered, 'Say it, Teacher." 'A certain moneylender had two debtors. One owed five hundred denarii, and the other fifty. When they could not pay, he cancelled the debt of both. Now which of them will love him more?' Simon answered, 'The one, I suppose, for whom he cancelled the larger debt.' And he said to him, 'You have judged rightly.' Then turning toward the woman he said to Simon, "Do you see this woman? I entered your house; you gave me no water for my feet, but she has wet my feet with her tears and wiped them with her hair. You gave me no kiss, but from the time I came in she has not ceased to kiss my feet. You did not anoint my head with oil, but she has anointed my feet with ointment. Therefore I tell you, her sins, which are many, are forgiven—for she loved much. But he who is forgiven little, loves little.' And he said to her, 'Your sins are forgiven.' Then those who were at table with him began to say among themselves, Who is this, who even forgives sins?' And he said to the woman, "Your faith has saved you; go in peace."*

The criterion of embarrassment applies here, for as Frank Turek and Norman Geisler point out, the woman wiping Jesus' feet with her hair could easily be perceived as a sexual advance (especially considering that she was a prostitute).[7] Who can forgive sins but God alone? Who indeed!? Jesus must have thought He was God!

Title #2: Son Of God

Jesus also claimed to be the Son Of God. Now, skeptics will argue that there's nothing divine about the title Son Of God since others have been called a son of God. Certain holy men were called sons of God. Even in The Bible, in the Old Testament, angels were called sons of God (see Genesis 6, Job 1:6).

The problem is that when you look at the contexts in which Jesus claimed to be the Son of God, you find that he meant it in a much different way.

First, how do we know that Jesus claimed to be the Son Of God? Also, what did He mean by it?

Reason 1: The Principle Of Embarrassment -- Doesn't Know The Day Or The Hour

Mark 13:32, Jesus says, in regards to His second coming *"But about that day or hour no one knows, not even the angels in heaven, nor the Son, but only the Father."*

The majority of even non-Christian historians consider this to be an authentic statement of the historical Jesus. Why? Because if the gospels are fabricated to make Jesus look divine, they certainly wouldn't have made up a statement that makes Jesus look less than omniscient. This passage is uncomfortable to explain if you're trying to make Jesus look divine. Therefore, these scholars conclude, on the basis of the historian's principle of embarrassment, that Jesus must have made this statement.

Jesus calls himself the Son of God in Mark 13:32. This passage establishes that Jesus believed Himself to be divine. How?

Because this passage employs a figure of speech known as anabasis. Anabasis is an ascending scale with increasing emphasis. An example of anabasis would be if I said "I wouldn't do such and such for a hundred dollars, I wouldn't do it for a thousand dollars, I wouldn't even do it for a million dollars!" Here, you see an ascending scale (i.e. the amount of money) with an increasing emphasis that I would not do such a thing. We see that same figure of speech in Mark 13:32. Jesus says that no one knows the day of His second coming, not even the angels in Heaven (who are higher than humans), not even the Son (who is higher than the angels), but only the Father in Heaven. So, Jesus believed that he was superior to both angels and humans.

Reason 2: The Parable Of The Tenants -- Historical Fit,

Let's take a gander at Jesus' "Parable Of The Wicked Tenants" recorded in Mark 12:1–9. This parable features a vineyard, the owner of the vineyard, wicked tenants, people who try to retrieve the vineyard from the tenants but are either beaten or killed by them, and the vineyard owner's son. Israel is represented by the vineyard (see also Isaiah 5:1–7), God is symbolized by the owner of the vineyard, the Jewish leaders are symbolized by the tenants, the prophets are symbolized by the servants who come to retrieve fruit from the vineyard, and the son of the vineyard owner is Jesus. Let's read this parable together:

"Then he began to speak to them in parables. "A man planted a vineyard, put a fence around it, dug a pit for the wine press, and built a watchtower; then he leased it to tenants and went to another country. When the season came, he sent a slave to the tenants to collect from them his share of the produce of the vineyard. But they seized him, and beat him, and sent him away empty-handed. And again he sent another slave to them; this one they beat over the head and insulted. Then he sent another, and that one they killed. And so it was with many others; some they beat, and others they killed. He had still one other, a beloved son. Finally he sent him to them, saying, 'They will respect my son.' But those tenants said to one another, 'This is the heir; come, let us kill him, and the inheritance will be ours.' So they seized him, killed him, and threw him out of the vineyard. What then will the owner of the vineyard do? He will come and destroy the tenants and give the vineyard to others." (Mark 12:1–9)

The principle of historical fit applies here. How? Because (1) the parable reflects the actual experience of absentee landowners of that time period and (2) also uses images and themes found in Jewish parables (e.g Israel as the vineyard, God as the owner). Moreover, it's unlikely the early church made up this parable since the parable features no resurrection of the slain son, which they would probably want to emphasize.

This parable shows us that Jesus considered himself to be God's final messenger, distinct from all other prophets, God's own son, and heir to Israel itself!

Reason 3: The Principle Of Embarrassment -- No One Knows The Son Except The Father

In Matthew 11:27, Jesus says *"All things have been delivered to me by my Father; and no one knows the Son except the Father; and no one knows the Father except the Son and anyone to whom the Son chooses to reveal Him."* This is very likely to be what Jesus really said. Why do I say that? I say that on the basis of the principle of embarrassment. I find it to be highly unlikely that the early Christian Church inserted this into the mouth of the historical Jesus because it says that the Son is unknowable. —*"no one knows the Son except the Father"*—, but the conviction of the early church is that we can indeed come to know the Father. What does this saying tell us about Jesus' belief about himself? It tells us that Jesus believed that he and only he was the absolute Son of God and the ultimate revelation of God to the human race.

Reason 4: Principle Of Embarrassment - Jesus' Baptism

Matthew 3:13-17 says *"Then Jesus came from Galilee to the Jordan to be baptized by John. But John tried to deter him, saying, 'I need to be baptized by you, and do you come to me?' Jesus replied, 'Let it be so now; it is proper for us to do this to fulfill all righteousness.' Then John consented. As soon as Jesus was baptized, he went up out of the water. At that moment heaven was opened, and he saw the Spirit of God descending like a dove and alighting on him. And a voice from heaven said, 'This is my Son, whom I love; with him I am well pleased.'"*

In this passage, John the Baptist hears a voice from Heaven (obviously God) proclaiming Jesus to be His son. This passage is very likely to be historical on the basis of the principle of embarrassment. Why would Jesus, whom the early church believed to be sinless, need to get baptized? Baptism was seen as a way to wash away sins and show the public that you were serious about getting right with God. This is why Matthew 3:11 calls John's baptism a baptism of repentance. Why in the world would the sinless son of God need to get baptized? If you're sinless, you don't need to undergo a "baptism of repentance" because you have nothing to repent of! I think there are plausible explanations for why Jesus submitted himself to baptism, but given the awkwardness and the questions this event raised, it seems unlikely that the early church would have made this up.

Reason 5: Multiple Attestation

Jesus is recorded as calling Himself The Son Of God in both the synoptic gospels and the gospel of John. Therefore, it is multiply attested in a minimum of 2 independent sources that Jesus applied this title to Himself.

Title #3: The Messiah

Jesus also believed that He was the Messiah that the Old Testament prophesied about. This can be seen through an examination of two different events that occurred during the ministry of Jesus ((there are more, but I cut them down to two to keep this chapter from being overly lengthy)). It should be noted that I won't be examining these events in chronological order.

1: Jesus' Triumphal Entry Into Jerusalem.

In the synoptic gospels (Matthew 21:1-11, Mark 11:1-11, Luke 19:28-44), and in John's gospel (John 12:12-19), Jesus enters Jerusalem riding on the back of a donkey while the people shout *"Hosanna!"* and *"Blessed is he who comes in the name of the Lord!"* and *"Blessed is the coming kingdom of our father David!"* and *"Hosanna in the highest!"* This is very likely a historical incident because it's multiply attested. Jesus' triumphal entry into Jerusalem is multiply attested because not only is it mentioned in the synoptic gospels, but it's also mentioned in John's gospel.

Now, this shows that Jesus believed himself to be the Messiah because there was a prophecy about the Messiah written in the Old Testament; Zechariah 9:9 which says *"Rejoice greatly, Daughter Zion! Shout, Daughter Jerusalem! See, your king comes to you, righteous and victorious, lowly and riding on a donkey, on a colt, the foal of a donkey."* This is also in fulfillment of Zechariah 14:1-5 which says that the Messiah would come to Jerusalem from the Mount of Olives.

2: Jesus quotes Isaiah 61:1 and Isaiah 35:5-6

In Matthew 11, John the Baptist's disciples come to Jesus at John's request. The reason they came to Jesus was that John had heard (while in prison) about all the miraculous works that Jesus had been doing. (Matthew 11:2). John's disciples asked Jesus *"Are You the Coming One, or do we look for another?"* (Matthew 11:3, NKJV). *"Jesus answered and said to them, 'Go and tell John the things which you hear and see: The blind see and the lame walk; the lepers are cleansed and the deaf hear; the dead are raised up and the good news is preached to the poor. And blessed is he who is not offended because of Me.'"* - Matthew 11:4-6 (NKJV)

Continuing on in Matthew 11:7-11, *"As they departed, Jesus began to say to the multitudes concerning John: 'What did you go out into the wilderness to see? A reed shaken by the wind? But what did you go out to see? A man clothed in soft garments? Indeed, those who wear soft clothing are in kings' houses. But what did you go out to see? A prophet? Yes, I say to you, and more than a prophet. For this is he of whom it is written:*
'Behold, I send My messenger before Your face
Who will prepare Your way before You.'
Assuredly, I say to you, among those born of women there has not risen one greater than John the Baptist; but he who is least in the kingdom of heaven is greater than he." (NKJV)

First off, this recorded event is very likely to be historical for a number of reasons. For one thing, this incident records John The Baptist doubting Jesus, and that's why he sent two of his disciples to ask Jesus if he was "the coming one" (i.e the messiah) or if they should keep waiting. Since the early church believed John to be the one who preceded and announced the coming of the messiah (the one prophesied about in Isaiah 40:3 and Malachi 3:1), it's therefore highly unlikely that the church made this incident up. On the basis of the principle of embarrassment, this incident is very likely to be historical. There's just no discernable reason why the church would make the messiah's prophet doubt him.

Secondly, this incident is likely to be historical because right after, he says to a crowd of people "*Assuredly, I say to you, among those born of women there has not risen one greater than John the Baptist;*" But surely this should be properly said about Jesus, right? After all, he's God incarnate, right? He's the sinless God in human flesh! It's unlikely the early Christian church, who believed that Jesus wasn't just a prophet and the Jewish messiah, but that He was Yahweh in bodily form, would have Jesus say that no man born of woman was greater than John The Baptist (or anyone for that matter). Once again, the awkwardness of this statement makes it likely that Jesus really said this and that this recorded incident really happened.

How does this show that Jesus believed he was the messiah? Because in answer to John's disciples' question ""*Are You the Coming One, or do we look for another?*" Jesus answered these disciples by appealing to his miracles.

Moreover, most scholars recognize that Jesus' answer draws from two passages in Isaiah:

"The Spirit of the Lord God is upon Me, Because the Lord has anointed Me To preach good tidings to the poor;" – Isaiah 61:1 (NKJV)

"Then the eyes of the blind shall be opened, And the ears of the deaf shall be unstopped. Then the lame shall leap like a deer, And the tongue of the dumb sing. For waters shall burst forth in the wilderness, And streams in the desert." – Isaiah 35:5-6 (NKJV)

It seems clear that Jesus is combining these two passages to answer the question about his identity; i.e., Jesus is essentially saying "I am doing just what Isaiah said the Messiah would do."

Is The Messiah God?

While there's nothing **explicitly** divine about claiming to be the messiah, when you look at what several pre-Christian Jewish sources say about the messiah, you see that there is **implicit** divinity in the claim.

For example, in the extra-biblical Psalm of Solomon, he is called *"The Lord Messiah"*, who *"will strike the earth with the word of his mouth forever…. And he himself [will be] free from sin…. and he will not weaken in his days."* (17:32-37) In Isaiah 9:6, the prophet Isaiah says *"For unto us a Child is born, Unto us a Son is given; And the government will be upon His shoulder. And His name will be called Wonderful, Counselor, **Mighty God,** Everlasting Father, Prince of Peace."* (NKJV)

Moreover, the following prophecy foretells the messiah's birth in Bethlehem. *"But you, Bethlehem Ephrathah, Though you are little among the thousands of Judah, Yet out of you shall come forth to Me, The One to be Ruler in Israel, Whose goings forth are from of old, From everlasting."* – Micah 5:2 (NKJV)

Micah says that the messiah would be born in Bethlehem. Out of Bethlehem would come forth a ruler. What's striking about this passage is that it says that his goings forth are *"from everlasting"*! In other words, eternity past! Question; who is beginningless in his existence? Whose origins are from everlasting? God!

Finally, let's return to the prophesies about John The Baptist recorded in Isaiah 40:3 and Malachi 3:1.

"A voice of one calling: 'In the wilderness prepare the way for the LORD; make straight in the desert a highway for our God." – Isaiah 40:3

"I will send my messenger, who will prepare the way before me. Then suddenly the Lord you are seeking will come to his temple; the messenger of the covenant, whom you desire, will come,"'says the LORD Almighty." – Malachi 3:1

In Matthew 11:10 and Luke 7:27, Jesus says that John The Baptist was the person Malachi 3:1 was talking about. Who's going to arrive subsequent to this messenger preparing the way for him? These prophecies say that it would be the Lord, God! God says through the prophet Malachi *"I will send **my** messenger, who will prepare the way before **me**. Then suddenly **the Lord** you are seeking will come to his temple; the messenger of the covenant, whom you desire, will come,"'says the LORD Almighty."* Therefore, Jesus' claim to be the messiah is fraught with divine significance!

Other Claims To Be God

There are several other claims by Jesus in which He claims to be God, but these cannot be confirmed by the historical criteria of authenticity. Now, I don't want my Christian readers to get me wrong! I am not at all saying that Jesus didn't utter these. I do think He said these, I'm just saying we cannot confirm these through the historical criteria of authenticity. Remember, we're treating the New Testament documents as just ordinary historical documents and are applying the same tests of authenticity historians apply to secular documents, and none of the tests can be used to confirm that these are historical sayings. Nevertheless, I'll still mention them for those who may be interested in knowing what those claims are.

One of the claims is in John 10:30 where Jesus says *"I and the Father are one"*. The Greek word there translated as "one" means "one in essence" or "one in nature". Jesus said outright that He and His Father share the same essence. In the verses that follow, we read that the Jews pick up stones to kill Him on charges of blasphemy because they said *"You, a mere man, are claiming to be God!"*

In John 8:56-59, Jesus said to some of the Jews *"Your father Abraham rejoiced at the thought of seeing my day; he saw it and was glad."* The Jews responded *"You are not yet fifty years old, and you have seen Abraham!"* and Jesus said *"Very truly, I tell you, before Abraham was born, I Am."* The Jews then tried to stone him, but Jesus evaded them.

Why did the Jews try to stone Jesus when He said *"Before Abraham was born, I Am"*? In the book of Exodus, God appears to Moses in the form of a burning bush. God tells Moses to go to Egypt to order Pharaoh to set the Israelites free. Moses asks God *"Suppose I go to the Israelites and say to them, 'The God of your fathers has sent me to you,' and they ask me, 'What is his name?' Then what shall I tell them?"* and The Lord responds *"I am who I am. This is what you are to say to the Israelites: 'I am has sent me to you."* (See Exodus 3)

Here's the thing; Jesus is either using bad grammar ("I Am" is the wrong tense) or he's taking the name that God claimed for himself in Exodus 3 and is applying it to himself. Jesus is saying in a not so subtle fashion, that he is the One who appeared to Moses in Exodus 3 (i.e. God).

Objections From Skeptics

Before I move on, I want to take a look at objections raised by skeptics. These objections either argue that Jesus didn't believe He was God or they challenge the nature of the incarnation as incoherent and therefore impossible. With regards to the latter, I will switch from historian mode to theologian/philosopher mode, since whether or not God has the ability to acquire a human nature isn't a historical question, but a theological and philosophical one. With regards to the former, I will stay true to the standard procedures of the historian.

Objection 1: Jesus said "The Father Is Greater Than I"

Jesus said, *"The Father is greater than I."* (John 14:28). This verse is raised frequently by Muslims who try to argue that Jesus never believed that He was God.

Obviously, they argue, if Jesus claimed to be God, he would never say that the Father is greater than He is, because if Jesus is God, Jesus would be equally as great as his father.

This is merely a differentiation between God the Father and God the Son. As the human version of the invisible God (Colossians 1:15), Jesus was in a lower place than the Father. Jesus had taken on human nature. As I'll mention later in this chapter, His omniscience was tucked away into His subconscious, so that He didn't know everything in the conscious life. Jesus got tired, He had to eat and drink to keep his body alive. Hebrews 2:9 says He was made to be *"a little lower than the angels."* But after the resurrection, all of these limitations were removed from Jesus. Taking John 14:28 in context, this makes sense why Jesus said *"If you loved me, you would be glad that I am going to the Father, for the Father is greater than I."* Jesus says that his disciples should be glad that He's going away. Why? Jesus gives the answer in the very next sentence *"...for the Father is greater than I."* The reason they should be glad is that Jesus is going to ascend back to the throne He sat on with The Father. Those human limitations he had are going to be removed. He will no longer be hungry, thirsty, tired. He will no longer have to learn anything, His omniscience will be 100% consciousness and 0% sub consciousness.

The Father at that time was greater than The Son because The Father wasn't incarnate, so He didn't have any of the human limitations His son Jesus had. The Father wasn't ontologically greater than the Son, but functionally greater than the Son.

Think of it this way; if I said "The President Of The United States is greater than I...." I would not mean that I am an inferior being to the president. He's a human being and I'm a human being. But the president is greater than I am in some ways. He's got more military capacity than I do, he's got more money than I do, he lives in a nicer house than I do, but he isn't a superior being. I think that when Jesus said "the Father is greater than I" he meant that The Father was greater in a similar sense. This interpretation is all the more plausible given the numerous places in which Jesus claims divinity for Himself. A rule of biblical hermeneutics is to interpret unclear verses in light of the clear ones. In light of everywhere else that Jesus claims to be God, my alternative interpretation should be preferred.

Objection 2: Jesus Said No One Is Good But God Alone

Somebody approached Jesus and said, *"Good teacher,"* to which Jesus replied, *"Why do you call me good? Only God is good."* (Mark 10:17-22). Doesn't this show that Jesus didn't believe he was God?

There are basically two ways to interpret this passage. The objector tries to make the point that when Jesus said *"Why do you call me good? No one is good but God alone."* he was implying "so don't call me that. Call me 'Sinner Jesus' like everyone else". The other way to interpret it is as Jesus trying to get the man to think about the implications of what he was saying. "Why do you call me good? No is good but God alone. If you truly think I'm good, and only God is good, what does that entail?" In other words, Jesus was saying "Why do you call me good? Only God is good *wink* *wink*". Again, given all of the claims of Jesus we've surveyed in this chapter, I think the latter is the more plausible interpretation.

Objection 3: When Jesus Talked About "The Son Of Man", He Was Referring To Someone Else.

This is the view of Dr. Bart Ehrman. He argues that the various sayings in which Jesus uses the term "The Son Of Man", He isn't referring to Himself, but to someone else. He can do this because Jesus frequently spoke in the third person. So when Jesus says *"Whoever denies the Son of Man, the son of Man will deny him in Heaven"*, Ehrman takes that to mean that Jesus is saying that if you deny the son of man before people, whoever this might be, then the son of man (whoever he is) will deny him before Jesus' Father in Heaven.

I find this to be a very implausible interpretation. This is because there are just some texts for which this cannot work. For example, in Luke 9:44, Jesus tells His disciples *"The Son of Man must be delivered over to the hands of sinners, be crucified and on the third day be raised again.'"* Is Jesus referring to Himself or to someone else? Well, Jesus was crucified and was raised from the dead (see the rest of this book), so it would appear that Jesus is referring to Himself here. The only other possibility is that Jesus is saying that this other guy called The Son Of Man would go through exactly the same thing He Himself went through, but that seems implausible, and I think the burden of proof is on Ehrman to prove to us that Luke 9:44 doesn't refer to Jesus. It seems more plausible to conclude that Jesus is talking about Himself than to conclude that some other person called The Son Of Man would go through exactly what He went through. By the way, we have good reason for affirming Luke 9:44's historicity because in context, the disciples fail to understand what Jesus is talking about, so the criterion of embarrassment applies.

At Jesus' trial, one cannot make sense out of Jesus' condemnation by the Sanhedrin on the view that Jesus was referring to someone else. Remember that at the trial, the High Priest asks Jesus, *"Are you the Messiah, the Son of the blessed One?"* And Jesus responds, *"I am. And you will see the Son of Man seated at the right hand of power and coming with the clouds of heaven."* And the High Priest says that Jesus committed blasphemy in saying that. Dr. Ehrman himself admits that this incident doesn't make any sense on his view. He writes *"It is difficult to understand the trial because the charge of blasphemy cannot be rooted in anything Jesus said. It wasn't blasphemous to call oneself the Messiah nor to say that the Son of Man was soon to arrive. Yet the High Priest accused Jesus of blasphemy."* So why exactly did the High Priest get so upset? Dr. Ehrman writes *"One could conceive of his statement as blasphemous only by assuming that Jesus was the*

Son of Man because then Jesus would be saying that he had a standing equal with God.[8] Indeed.

Objection 4: Jesus Is Not Omniscient

"Jesus may have **claimed** to be God", the skeptic might retort, "But he couldn't actually **be** God. You wanna know why? Because God is omniscient. Jesus is not omniscient. Therefore, Jesus can't be God."

This objection appeals to Mark 13:32 where Jesus says that He does not know the day or the hour of His coming. God is omniscient. If Jesus is not omniscient, then Jesus is not God regardless of what He may have claimed elsewhere. The problem with using Mark 13:32 as a proof text for Jesus' non-divinity is, as we saw in earlier in this chapter, that it is ironically good evidence **for** Jesus' deity rather than **against** His deity.

But how could Jesus be God and not know the time of His second coming? After all, The Bible says that God knows the future (see Psalms 139:1-4). William Lane Craig defends a model of the incarnation in a book he co-authored with J.P Moreland called *Philosophical Foundations For A Christian Worldview.* This model has three "branches" to it. The first branch asserts that Jesus is one person with two natures (divine and human), the second branch posits that the divine Logos (John 1:1) was the soul that animated Jesus' body. The third branch posits that most of the divine attributes of Jesus were "subliminal". For example, the reason that Jesus didn't know the time of His second coming is that when Jesus became incarnate, all of his knowledge about everything there is to know about everything was shoved into Jesus' subconscious.

This would explain not only why Jesus didn't know the time of his second coming, but also why we don't have the picture of a baby Jesus speaking full blown Hebrew in the manger scene. It would also explain how Jesus *"grew in wisdom and stature"* (Luke 2:52) while still being the omniscient God of the universe. His knowledge was limited in His conscious life, but His vast knowledge of everything from auto mechanics to quantum mechanics was tucked away into His subconscious. In this sense, Jesus could both know and not know something at the same time.

A while back, I heard a song that I learned at vacation Bible school when I was 3 years old. I hadn't thought of that song in over a decade. Yet when it started playing, I immediately recognized it and was able to sing along. I knew the song, and I knew the words, but the knowledge was tucked away in my subconscious and therefore, I wasn't aware of the fact that I knew the song. I can imagine that much of the human Jesus' divine knowledge was tucked away in a similar fashion. So, even though He was omniscient, He still had to learn the Hebrew equivalent of His ABCs and 123s. By the way, the song I remembered was "Deep and Wide".

I think this is a very plausible explanation for how Jesus could be God (who is omniscient) and yet have need of learning and not exhaustively know the future. I think Jesus' other attributes, like omnipresence and omnipotence, can simply be explained by the fact that the human nature of Jesus and the divine nature have different attributes by their very natures. Some aspects belonging to Jesus' divine nature don't belong to Jesus' human nature. For example, in Jesus' divine nature, He is everywhere present, but the homo-sapien body Jesus inhabited could only be in one place at one time. In Jesus' divine nature, He is beginningless, but His human body had a beginning in the womb of Mary (John 1:14). As for Jesus' omnipotence, Jesus very well may have had access to this attribute even as a man, but simply chose not to use it. After all, if he didn't have access to His omnipotence, Satan's temptation to turn stones into bread would have been devoid of any force. Jesus could have simply responded "Gee Satan, I'd love to, but I can't." (see Matthew 4). Only if Jesus truly had the ability to make stones become an edible substance would Satan's temptation been sincere.

Objection 5: How Could God Die?

I hear this objection against Christ's deity more from Muslims than I do other non-believers. "How could God die?" they ask. The problem with this criticism is that these objectors don't understand the dual nature of Christ. Jesus is God, but he's also a human being. He is The Word who became flesh and made His dwelling among us (John 1:14). When Jesus died, his human nature died, but his divine nature did not (Luke 23:46). This isn't really that tricky to comprehend. The way Jesus died is the same way other humans die. When humans die, their immaterial souls leave the physical body and go to either Heaven or Hell to await the bodily resurrection. When Jesus died on the cross, the divine Logos left the body of Jesus of Nazareth. Three days later, the divine Logos or Word came back into the body of Jesus. The divine Logos who existed prior to the creation of the world (John 1:1) never stopped existing. It's just that the Logos left the body of Jesus of Nazareth until the resurrection three days later.

Conclusion

We've examined the historical case for Jesus' self-understanding. Jesus believed Himself to be God. Now we must face C.S Lewis' trilemma. Was Jesus lying about his identity? Was he crazy? Or was he and is he Who he claimed to be? If Jesus rose from the dead, that's pretty good evidence that he was telling the truth. It is to this topic that we now turn.

Notes

1: C. S. Lewis, Mere Christianity (New York: Macmillan, 1952), p. 56.

2: To give one example, Dr. Michael Licona calls this Jesus' Favorite Self-Designation in his BeThinking article "Jesus - The Son Of Man?" -- https://www.bethinking.org/jesus/jesus-the-son-of-man

3: GotQuestions.org, "What does it mean that Jesus is the Son of Man?" ---- http://www.gotquestions.org/Jesus-Son-of-Man.html

4: New Testament scholars generally think Matthew and Luke used Mark as a source for a lot of the material they cover. For one thing, in the first chapter of Luke, he explicitly tells us he used sources. It isn't unreasonable to think that the gospels of Matthew and Mark could have been sources that he drew upon. But perhaps most powerfully is that when you lay the gospel narratives side by side, often they report the same events using the same words, verbatim, as though copy/pasting was done. Now, this isn't the case for everything the gospels report. There is certainly material unique to Mark, material unique to Matthew, and material unique to Luke. In these latter cases, scholars believe Matthew and Luke were reporting events independently from each other and from Mark. But whenever verbatim reporting occurs, they conclude that they're using Mark. However, John is so drastically different in its content from Matthew, Mark, and Luke, that no one thinks John depended on these earlier gospels for his material.
    This is how scholars generally determine if something found in the gospels is independent.
*Mark + anywhere else = Mark
*John
*Matthew (only) = M
*Luke (only) = L
* Q (Alternate source to which Matthew and Luke refer)

5: See Craig Blomberg's "The Historical Reliability Of The Gospels" (InterVarsity Press) and J. Warner Wallace's book "Cold Case Christianity: A Homicide Detective Investigates The Claims Of The Gospels" (David C Cook), for a case for the Gospels' traditional authorship. It's common for skeptics (both scholars and laymen) to argue that the gospels weren't written by the people who bare their names. I think this is rubbish, to be honest, and I think that conservative scholars like Blomberg make a compelling case that it is. Nevertheless, the minimal facts approach doesn't depend on whether the gospels were really written by Matthew, Mark, Luke, and John. These could be the gospels of Bob, Mary, Billy, and Tony and the criteria of authenticity can still be applied to them.

6: Michael S, Heiser, "What's Ugaritic Got To Do With Anything?"-- https://www.logos.com/ugaritic

7: Frank Turek, Norman Geisler, "I Don't Have Enough Faith To Be An Atheist", Crossway, page 278

8: Bart D. Ehrman, As cited in the transcript of "The Work Of Bart Ehrman: William Lane Craig Speaks At Gracepoint Church" -- http://www.reasonablefaith.org/media/the-work-of-bart-ehrman-gracepoint-church

Part 2: Examining The Resurrection

Chapter 3

Fact 1 - Jesus Died By Crucifixion

Now that we've determined that Jesus believed He was God, it's now time to figure out whether or not we should believe Him. Anyone can claim to be God. You can make that claim. I can make that claim. Who cares? But if Jesus died and then returned from the dead then that is pretty good evidence that he was telling the truth.

I shall defend the resurrection, as I said in chapter 1, by means of a two step process: (1) I'll establish the data, and (2) I'll argue that only a miraculous resurrection can best account for the data. In the case of the former, I will be using facts that meet two criteria. They are very well evidenced and nearly all scholars who study the subject accept them as true (even the skeptical non-Christian scholars).

The data to be explained are

1: Jesus died due to Roman crucifixion.

2: Jesus' tomb was found empty the following Sunday morning.

3: The 12 Disciples sincerely believed they saw Jesus alive shortly after His death.

4: A church persecutor named Saul Of Tarsus converted to Christianity on the basis of what he perceived to be an appearance of the risen Jesus.

5: A skeptic named James converted to Christianity on the basis of what he perceived to be an appearance of the risen Jesus.

These are the facts that need to be explained. In this chapter, I will give the evidence for that first minimal fact: that Jesus died by crucifixion.

Reason 1: Jesus' Death By Crucifixion is Multiply Attested

Jesus' death by Roman crucifixion is overwhelmingly multiply attested. It is mentioned in 4 secular sources, The Jewish Talmud, the synoptic gospels, John's gospel, and Paul's epistles.

Source 1: Josephus

The first-century Jewish historian named Flavius Josephus (37-100 A.D) wrote about Jesus' crucifixion in his book *Antiquities Of The Jews* in book 18. Josephus wrote: *"Now, there was about this time, Jesus, a wise man, if it be lawful to call him a man, for he was a doer of wonderful works,--a teacher of such men as receive the truth with pleasure. He drew over to him both many of the Jews, and many of the Gentiles. He was [the] Christ; and when Pilate, at the suggestion of the principal men amongst us, had condemned him to the cross, those that loved him at the first did not forsake him, for he appeared to them alive again the third day, as the divine prophets had foretold these and ten thousand other wonderful things concerning him; and the tribe of Christians, so named from him, are not extinct at this day."*

Here we have a first century, non-Christian historian saying that a man named Jesus existed, drew a crowd of people who listened to His teachings, but was killed by Roman crucifixion under the governor Pontius Pilate at the request of "some of the principal men among us" which we can infer to be the Jewish Sanhedrin. This is historical evidence for the crucifixion of Jesus coming from a source with no theological axe to grind.

Now, some skeptics will object that this passage, known as "The Testimonium Flavianum", really isn't good historical evidence for the crucifixion because the passage seems to have been interpolated by a Christian scribe. I would agree that it has clearly been interpolated by a Christian scribe as would a large number of historians and scholars who study ancient history. The Church Father Origen informs us that Josephus did not believe Jesus to be the messiah,[1] so it would be highly unlikely that he would say things like "If it be lawful to call him a man" for such a sentence implies that Jesus was more than human, or that Josephus would say "He was the Christ" as this is an explicit declaration that Jesus is the Messiah, a statement only a Christian would make. What's worse is that near the very end of this passage, Josephus says that Jesus rose from the dead! Again, only Christians believe Jesus rose from the dead. Josephus, being a non-Christian, would never make these statements. This passage was obviously altered by a scribe who **did** believe these things; a Christian scribe.

But while I agree with the skeptic that the Testimonium Flavianum was altered by a Christian, I don't believe it follows that we can't use this passage as extra-biblical evidence for the death of Jesus. The majority of scholars today hold the position that The Testimonium Flavianum was only **partially** interpolated. That is to say; most of the passage is legitimate (it's not like a Christian scribe made the entire Testimonium Flavianum up), but only certain phrases were inserted by a Christian scribe. There are two primary arguments that historians give for adopting this "Partial Interpolation" view.

When You Remove The Obvious Christian Additions, The Passage Remains Coherent

Christopher Price wrote *"Perhaps the most important factor leading most scholars to accept the partial-authenticity position is that a substantial part of the TF reflects Josephan language and style. Moreover, when the obvious Christian glosses — which are rich in New Testament terms and language not found in the core — are removed or restored to their original the remaining core passage is coherent and flows well. We can be confident that there was a minimal reference to Jesus . . . because once the clearly Christian sections are removed, the rest makes good grammatical and historical sense. The peculiarly Christian words are parenthetically connected to the narrative; hence they are grammatically free and could easily have been inserted by a Christian. These sections also are disruptive, and when they are removed the flow of thought is improved and smoother."*[2]

I think that Price is right. Compare the clearly interpolated version of the Testimonimum Flavianum which I included above with the version below:
"Now, there was about this time, Jesus, a wise man, for he was a doer of wonderful works,--a teacher of such men as receive the truth with pleasure. He drew over to him both many of the Jews, and many of the Gentiles. And when Pilate, at the suggestion of the principal men amongst us, had condemned him to the cross, those that loved him at the first did not forsake him, and the tribe of Christians, so named from him, are not extinct at this day."

You can see that the flow of thought isn't bothered by the removal of the obvious Christian additions. How often is it that you can erase whole sentences from a paragraph and still have it make complete sense? On this basis, therefore, it's highly probable that there was an original passage about Jesus' crucifixion and it did not include phrases that expressed belief in his messiahship and resurrection.

The Reference to James the Brother of Jesus Suggests an Earlier Reference to Jesus

Later on in Josephus' writings, Josephus makes a reference to Jesus' brother James and records his martyrdom at the hands of the Jewish Sanhedrin. While the Testimonium Flavianum is hotly debated, I know of no scholar who doubts the validity of Josephus' reference to James. The reference to James's Martyrdom increases the likelihood that the Testimonium Flavianum is also valid. In Josephus' reference to James, he refers to Jesus as *"the **so-called** Christ"* without further explanation. That's all he says. All he says about James is that he's the brother of *"Jesus, the so-called Christ"*. In the passage about James, Josephus doesn't go into any explanation of who Jesus was, what He did, no claims of Him dying and rising from the dead, no mention of any miracles, or anything like that. The only thing Josephus says about Jesus in this latter passage is that He's James' brother. What this implies is that Josephus presupposed that his readers already knew who he was referring to. But why would Josephus make such an assumption? If The Testimonium Flavianum is legitimate, then it makes sense why Josephus assumes his readers already knew who he was talking about; i.e because He already briefly explained who Jesus was and what He did earlier.

For these and other reasons, most scholars think that the Testimonium Flavianum is an authentic passage. If it's an authentic passage, then we can certainly use it as evidence for the existence and crucifixion of Jesus. However, even if the Testimonium Flavianum couldn't be used, that wouldn't hurt our case very much as we would still have many other sources that record the event, as you'll see below.

Source 2: Tacitus

Tacitus was a Roman historian writing in the early second century. In the 15th volume of his work *Annals,* Tacitus recounts the terrible burning down of Rome by Emperor Nero and mentions how he tried to get the suspicions off of himself and onto the Christians by unleashing a terrible persecution against them. It is in this passage that he makes a reference to Jesus' crucifixion. The Annals of Tacitus dates to AD 115. Tacitus writes *"Christus, the founder of the name, was put to death by Pontius Pilate, procurator of Judea in the reign Of Tiberius..."* (Cornelius Tacitus, Annals, 15:44)

Source 3: Mara Bar Serapion

Mara Bar-Serapion was a Syriac stoic philosopher in the Roman province of Syria. At some point, he was arrested, and while in prison, he wrote a letter to his son. In this letter, he mentions how wise teachers who were persecuted and killed for their teachings were eventually avenged by God. He rhetorically asked what the Athenians gained from putting Socrates to death and then mentioned how famine and plague came upon them, for example. As for Jesus, Mara wrote: *"What did the Jews gain from murdering their wise king? It was after that that their kingdom was abolished."*[3]

About this passage, Josh and Sean McDowell write *"Though Mara never uses Jesus' name, we can be certain he is referring to him because no one else at that point in history would fulfill the requirements of being known as a "wise king" who was killed by the Jews shortly before they were driven from the land. Jesus is obviously in view."* [4]

Source 4: Lucian Of Samosata

Lucian Of Samosata was a second-century Greek satirist. In one of his works, he wrote of the early Christians as follows: *"The Christians . . . worship a man to this day--the distinguished personage who introduced their novel rites, and was crucified on that account. . ."* (Lucian of Samosata, from the book The Passing Peregrinus)

Source 5: The Talmud

Doctor Gary Habermas explains that *"The Jews handed down a large amount of oral tradition from generation to generation. This material was organized according to subject matter by Rabbi Akiba before his death in AD 135. His work was then revised by his student , Rabbi Meir. The project was completed around AD 200 by Rabbi Judah and is known as the Mishnah. Ancient commentary on the Mishna was called the Gemaras. The combination of the Mishnah and the Gemaras form The Talmud. It would be expected that the most reliable information about Jesus from The Talmud would come from the earliest period of compilation -- AD 70 - 200, known as The Tannatic Period."* [5]

A very significant quotation is found in Sanhedrin 43a, dating from just this early period.

"On the eve of the Passover Yeshu was hanged. For forty days before the execution took place, a herald went forth and cried, 'He is going forth to be stoned

because he has practiced sorcery and enticed Israel to apostasy. Any one who can say anything in his favour, let him come forward and plead on his behalf.' But since nothing was brought forward in his favour he was hanged on the eve of the Passover!"

As you may know, "Jesus" is the Greek name for Joshua, which is also Yeshua. Yeshu is shorthand for Yeshua, sort of like how Josh is short for Joshua. Although the Talmud was not officially comprised until about 500 years after the first century, the material contained in the Talmud (i.e the Mishnah and Gemaras) dates early enough for us to consider it trustworthy material when it reports on events in the first century. This passage of The Talmud says that Jesus (Yeshu) was hanged on the eve of The Passover. Now, lest you read this passage anachronistically, allow me to point out that "hanged" in this context doesn't refer to our modern notion of hanging by tying a noose around someone's neck. In the first century, crucified victims were often referred to as having been "hanged". We even see this in The New Testament, such as in Galatians 3:13 and Luke 23:39. What's also interesting about this passage is that it says that Yeshu was leading the people of Israel astray by "sorcery". I'll come back to this point in chapter 12.

Source 6: The Gospel Of Mark

Everyone knows that the synoptic gospels (i.e Matthew, Mark, and Luke) refer to the crucifixion of Jesus, so I don't see any need to unpack this sub-subsection any further. I will clarify one thing though; sometimes I will throw the synoptic gospels together as a single source because many scholars believe that Luke borrowed material from Matthew who in turn borrowed from Mark. There is some good evidence that this is the case, such as the fact that there are passages in the Synoptics that read identically to one another. However, scholars recognize that this is **not always** the case. Sometimes, Matthew and Luke write independently of Mark regarding some event, and sometimes they write independently even of each other! In the case of Jesus' crucifixion, it is believed that Matthew and Luke drew from a source independent of Mark. I'll unpack this in the sub-subsection below.

Source 7: The Gospels Of Matthew and Luke
So, what makes scholars think Matthew and Luke's accounts of Jesus' crucifixion are independent of Mark's? One reason is that Luke 23 says that one of the thieves who was crucified with Jesus repented and asked Jesus to remember him when Jesus entered into His kingdom. Jesus told him that he would be with him in paradise on that very day. This detail is not mentioned by Mark, suggesting that

Luke is relying on a different source. Matthew 27 also mentions the thieves, albeit he omits the repentance of the one. This suggests that whatever source Luke was working on, Matthew was working on that same source. Additionally, Luke records a whole paragraph of Jesus speaking to "the daughters of Jerusalem" (23:27-32). This is completely absent from Mark's passion narrative and therefore, Luke cannot be drawing on Mark as a source here.

Source 8: The Gospel Of John

The gospel of John likewise tells us that Jesus died by Roman crucifixion. Most scholars believe that John was writing independently of the other 3 gospels. Therefore, I treat John as an independent source.

Source 9: The Epistles Of Paul

Paul's epistles mention the crucifixion of Jesus (e.g 1 Corinthians 15:3, Philippians 2).

In all, we have at least 9 early sources that state that Jesus died by Roman Crucifixion. 4 of those sources are secular in nature, 1 of those sources is a non-Christian Jewish source, and 4 of them come from The New Testament.

According to the principle of multiple attestation, this makes it extremely, extremely probable that Jesus' death on a Roman cross at the hands of Pontius Pilate was a real event of history. The principle of multiple attestation says that if you find any event mentioned in two or more independent sources, it is more likely that the event actually occurred. This is because the more and more independent sources an event is mentioned in, the less and less likely it is to be made up. Think about it: how likely is it that **NINE INDEPENDENT SOURCES** all made up the same fictional story? Nine independent historians! Do you honestly expect me to believe that nine independent writers all just happened to make up the same thing? That is statistically impossible! It is statistically impossible for 9 independent writers to **all** make up the same event and treat it as history!

Jesus' death by Roman crucifixion is multiply, multiply, multiply attested, and this makes it extremely probable that the event actually occurred. If this criterion of authenticity were the only one this minimal fact passed, it would be enough to conclude that it occurred.

Paul Maier, retired distinguished professor of ancient history at Western Michigan University said *"Many facts in the ancient world are established on one source. Two or three sources often make an event impregnable."*[6] Two sources?

You can't beat it. That's how source material works in ancient history. Meyer says two independent sources make the historical event "impregnable", but we don't have two sources here, we have **nine!**

Reason 2: Jesus' Crucifixion Is Enemy Attested

Moreover, not only is Jesus' death by crucifixion multiply attested in nine independent documents, but it's also enemy attested. Those who are your enemies are not likely to say things to help your cause. People who are hostile to you are not going to lie to make you look good or to bolster your cause. We have enemy attestation when it comes to Jesus' crucifixion. Neither Tacitus nor Lucian Of Samosata were friendly to Christianity. In Tacitus' account, he calls Christianity a *"pernicious superstition"*! Lucian was ridiculing Christians in the very same passage in which he affirms that Jesus died by crucifixion! The Jewish Talmud accused Jesus of leading Israel astray. So, in addition to multiple attestation in nine independent sources, we have enemy attestation in three of those sources!

Reason 3: The Principle Of Historical Fit

Moreover, the principle of historical fit comes into play here. We know for a fact from the writings of ancient first-century authors like Josephus, Tacitus, and even Archeology (e.g the Yehohannan discovery from 1975), that Romans crucified people back in the first century. And we know that one of those reasons was in the case of treason. Jesus being crucified on the grounds of claiming to be the Messiah fits right in with what we know of Roman executions.

Reason 4: Only Women Had The Guts To Stick With Jesus In His Final Hours

If you were making up a story of any kind, you most likely wouldn't depict yourself, your friends, or people you respected in a bad way. You wouldn't make up lies about them that hurt them or made them look bad. If you were going to lie, you'd make up things to help them or to make them look good. This is why the principle of embarrassment counts in favor of an event's historicity. The principle of embarrassment gives us good grounds to believe the crucifixion of Jesus occurred in three different ways.

John 19 records Jesus' crucifixion. However, John writes *"So the soldiers took charge of Jesus. Carrying his own cross, he went out to the place of the Skull (which in Aramaic is called Golgotha). There they crucified him, and with him two others—one on each side and Jesus in the middle. Pilate had a notice prepared and fastened to the cross. It read: Jesus of Nazareth, the king of the jews. Many of the*

Jews read this sign, for the place where Jesus was crucified was near the city, and the sign was written in Aramaic, Latin and Greek. The chief priests of the Jews protested to Pilate, 'Do not write 'The King of the Jews,' but that this man claimed to be king of the Jews.' Pilate answered, 'What I have written, I have written.' When the soldiers crucified Jesus, they took his clothes, dividing them into four shares, one for each of them, with the undergarment remaining. This garment was seamless, woven in one piece from top to bottom. 'Let's not tear it,' they said to one another. 'Let's decide by lot who will get it.' This happened that the scripture might be fulfilled that said, 'They divided my clothes among them and cast lots for my garment.' So this is what the soldiers did. Near the cross of Jesus stood his mother, his mother's sister, Mary the wife of Clopas, and Mary Magdalene. When Jesus saw his mother there, and the disciple whom he loved standing nearby, he said to her, 'Woman, here is your son,' and to the disciple, 'Here is your mother.' From that time on, this disciple took her into his home." - John 19:16-27

John records that 4 women stayed with Jesus during his final hours; Jesus' mother Mary, Jesus' aunt, Mary Magdalene, and Mary the wife of Clopas (there were a lot of women named Mary in first century Israel). The only male disciple that John records as sticking with Jesus is himself. According to Mark's account, the rest of the disciples all ran away in terror when the Romans came to arrest Jesus (Mark 14:43-52). The fact that most of the disciples abandoned Jesus in his darkest hour is not something the gospel writers would have made up. It gets worse when you consider that **women** are mainly those who stayed behind. In first century Jewish culture, women were considered second class citizens, and Josephus says that they weren't even allowed to witness in a Jewish court of law (more on this in the next chapter). In light of this fact, how remarkable it is that it is women who stay by Jesus' side in his final moments rather than the male disciples! If John were making this up, he would have included at least a few other of the male apostles with him. Yet John puts the women in a good light and most of the men in a bad light! The women are the brave ones and the men are cowards!

Reason 5: Jesus Was Killed In The Most Humiliating Way

As I said above, If you were making up a story of any kind, you most likely wouldn't depict yourself, your friends, or people you respected in a bad way. The gospel writers, whoever they were, clearly respected Jesus. Why would they make up a story about his death that was considered at that time to be the most degrading and humiliating way to die. I mean, these people thought Jesus wasn't just the Messiah, but God incarnate (John 1:1-3, 14)! Why would you write a story about your own God that demeans Him? [7]

As Dr. Gary Habermas said *"Our Lord was killed like a slave? And, he had the best arguments in the universe and he never opened His mouth? .....He might possibly have been crucified nude. May have happened. Didn't always happen. We have a tendency to not add embarrassing things about those we love and there are many."* [8]

Put yourself in the shoes of a first century Jew. If you were going to make up a story of your leader dying and rising, wouldn't you at least have him be killed in a more dignified way? Stoning was one way Jews killed people back in the first century, as we know from the book of Acts (chapter 7) and Josephus' (*Antiquities of The Jews, book 20,* regarding James' martyrdom by stoning). Maybe it's just me, but I think being killed by having a large rock thrown at your head is a far more dignified way to die than being nailed to a stake either half-naked or fully naked. The gospel authors, if they were making up the story of Jesus' death, would most likely have had him die by stoning.

So, once again, the principle of embarrassment gives us good reason to believe the first minimal fact is true.

Reason 6: Multiple Literary Form

These would be different kinds of stories about Jesus' death. Jesus' death is recorded in different books of different genres of the first century. The genres are Miracles, Parables, Creeds, Didactic, Greco-Roman Biography, and Apocalyptic.

The Greco-Roman biographies would obviously be the gospels: Matthew, Mark, Luke, and John.

Apocalyptic genre would be the book of Revelation in which Jesus shows up in Revelation 5 as a wounded lamb, and Jesus was very likely the child born in the wilderness in chapter 12.

Creeds -- We'll talk more about creeds in chapter 5, but Jesus' crucifixion is mentioned in the early resurrection creed cited in 1 Corinthians 15, and in the creed cited in Philippians 2.

Parables -- Jesus' death is told in The Parable Of The Wicked Tenants (Luke 20:9-16).

Didactic - Jesus' crucifixion is mentioned in Peter's sermon in Acts 2. See Acts 2:36

Reason 7: The King Of The Jews and The Principle Of Dissimilarity

When the Romans were crucifying Jesus, they nailed a plaque above his head that read "The King Of The Jews" (Mark 15:26, John 19:19). We know that this is historical on the basis the principle of dissimilarity. "The King Of The Jews" was never a title used for Jesus by the early church. If this title was just made up by the early church and retroactively inserted into the story of Jesus' crucifixion, then we would expect the early church to call Jesus "The King Of The Jews" a lot more frequently than we do, but in fact, the early church never called Jesus by this title. Indeed, Jesus isn't even called "The King Of The Jews" in any other place in the gospels! Additionally, none of the New Testament epistles call Jesus by this title! Therefore, by the principle of dissimilarity, we have good reason to believe that this plaque really was nailed above Jesus' head while he was being crucified, which of course entails that Jesus was actually crucified.

Reason 8: "Why Hast Thou Forsaken Me" -- Principle Of Embarrassment

In Matthew 27, Matthew's account of Jesus' death on the cross, Jesus cries out *"My God! My God! Why have you forsaken me?"*. We can conclude that this is an actual utterance of Jesus on the basis of the principle of embarrassment. Why would Matthew make Jesus ask God why He has forsaken him? It makes it seem as though Jesus doesn't know why he's being crucified even though he's recorded as predicting it earlier (Matthew 20:17-19) and even said why he had to die (Matthew 20:28). Why would Matthew make this saying up? It just raises too many questions. Even today, this saying of Jesus strikes people as something odd for him to say. After all, he predicted his death and even explained why it had to take place. Why is he all of a sudden crying out "Why"?

Now, I do think there's a satisfying explanation for why Jesus said this. It's the first verse of Psalm 22 verbatim. Chapter and verse divisions weren't introduced until around the third century A.D, so when someone wanted to point to a particular biblical passage, they would cite the first line. Most biblical scholars consider Psalm 22 to be a prophecy of the way the Messiah would die. When you compare the contents of Psalm 22 with what happened to Jesus in the gospels, there are striking similarities, but I won't go into them now. I'll leave it up to you to look into that yourself. Jesus was calling attention to this Psalm in order to proclaim to the people that he was fulfilling yet another messianic prophecy. By the way, this gives further evidence that Jesus saw himself as Israel's Messiah (as we talked about in chapter 2).

Nevertheless, even though an explanation exists for this cry of Jesus', wouldn't it be easier for Matthew to just omit it altogether rather than go through the trouble of explaining it? Certainly. And that's why we can conclude that Jesus actually made this statement. Of course, since the context of this statement is Jesus dying by crucifixion, that logically entails that the crucifixion actually occurred as well.

A Possible Objection: A skeptic may rebut "Perhaps Matthew included this statement of Jesus precisely **because** it was the first verse of Psalm 22. Matthew was trying to convince his readers that Jesus was the Messiah. So I would say that far from having a motivation to **ex**clude this saying of Jesus, he had a strong motivation to **in**clude this statement. Especially considering that Matthew's gospel is widely believed to be directed at a Jewish audience, and the fact that Matthew cites fulfilled prophecy in various other places in his gospel."

I don't disagree that Matthew included the "Why have you forsaken me?" phrase in his gospel because he wanted his readers to know that Jesus was fulfilling another prophecy, however, I don't think this means that the principle of embarrassment can't apply to this. First, in all of the instances in which Matthew points to Jesus fulfilling prophecy, he explicitly points out that Jesus is fulfilling what was foretold in scripture. He would add "this happened to fulfill the scripture that says…".This saying of Jesus would still be awkward given that it makes it look like He's doubting God, but Matthew could have his cake and eat it too by including the statement and then tell his readers that Jesus' was fulfilling what was written in a messianic Psalm. Matthew never does that, which is why many Bible readers even today miss the connection. Moreover, even if Matthew's original audience would have made the connection between Psalm 22 and Jesus' statement, what would they have likely thought? That The Old Testament prophesied faithlessness on the part of the anointed one? It's still awkward even in the case of messianic apologetics. Even if the Jewish audience would have said "Hey! Jesus is fulfilling Psalm 22!" they would have still been prompted to ask "Why did scripture predict that the Messiah would lose faith in God?" Making the messianic connection by itself does nothing to remove the awkwardness of this saying.

Moreover, there were other messianic death prophesies Matthew could have had Jesus allude to, such as Isaiah 53 or Zechariah 12:10. If Matthew were making this up, why didn't he allude to these less awkward messianic death prophecies? Psalm 22 wasn't the only one he could have drawn on.

Summary and Conclusion

We've seen that the historical evidence for Jesus having been executed via Roman crucifixion is overwhelming. Jesus' death by Roman crucifixion is multiply, multiply, *multiply attested* in 9 independent sources. 4 of those sources are secular,

1 of them Jewish, and 4 of them are from The New Testament. It is statistically impossible for 9 different writers to all fabricate the same fictional event and then treat it as history. Moreover, Jesus' crucifixion is *enemy attested* by two secular sources (Tacitus and Lucian) and by the Jewish Talmud. These sources were actually ridiculing Christianity in the same context that they affirm the historicity of Jesus' crucifixion. Moreover, Jesus' death is coherent with the well-established facts of Roman history. In addition to these, Jesus' crucifixion meets the criterion of embarrassment in three different ways; (1) John makes women the brave ones to stay by Jesus' side during his final hours while the disciples abandoned him, and (2) If you're going to make up a story about someone you cherish dying, you'd make the specific way he died much more dignified. Roman crucifixion was not only an extremely painful way to die, but it was an extremely shameful way as well. (3) Additionally, "My God! My God! Why Have You Forsaken Me" is an awkward saying of Jesus, so it's unlikely to be made up. Also, Jesus' death is told in multiple literary forms. Finally, the principle of dissimilarity supports the historicity of the crucifixion because a title is ascribed to Jesus that isn't ascribed to him anywhere else, in The New Testament or in the writings of the early church fathers.

Of the 5 minimal facts, the death of Jesus on a cross is the one that I don't think I'll ever doubt. The evidence for it is so overwhelming and so plenteous, it passes so many of the criteria of authenticity in so many different ways, that I am baffled how anyone could possibly deny it. In fact, no one does, at least not among scholars. The only people who deny that Jesus existed and died via Roman crucifixion are your internet infidel types.

The agnostic historian Bart Ehrman states that "*One of the most certain facts of history is that Jesus was crucified on orders of the Roman prefect of Judea, Pontius Pilate.* ".[9] The highly critical scholar of the Jesus Seminar, John Dominic Crossan, writes, *"That he was crucified is as sure as anything historical can ever be."* [10] Like Ehrman, Crossan is not a Christian. Yet both Ehrman and Crossan agree that Jesus' death by crucifixion is a historical fact. Gerd Ludemann, an atheist historian said: *"Jesus' death as a consequence of crucifixion is an indisputable fact."* [11]

Now, why did I go to such lengths to establish the historicity of Jesus' crucifixion? One reason is that you have to have a death before you can have a resurrection. Additionally, most of the people who will be reading this book are not scholars or trained historians, but laymen, and many of them deny that Jesus even existed altogether, much less died on a cross. But among **scholars**, both Christian and non-Christian, the crucifixion of Jesus is just taken for granted.[12] It isn't even debated among Christian and Non-Christian scholars. I think that's why Dr. William Lane Craig, in his presentations on the evidence for the resurrection, skips this minimal fact entirely and goes right to Jesus' burial or the empty tomb. Which, by the way, is the next minimal fact in our case.

Notes

1: Origen, Contra Celsum, 1:47

2: From the online article "Did Josephus Refer To Jesus?" by Christopher Price ----
http://bede.org.uk/Josephus.htm

3: British Museum, Syriac Manuscript, Additional 14,658

4: McDowell, Josh; McDowell, Sean. Evidence That Demands a Verdict: Life-Changing Truth for a Skeptical World (p. 150). Thomas Nelson. Kindle Edition.

5: Gary Habermas, "The Historical Jesus: Ancient Evidence For The Life Of Christ", pages 202-203, College Press.

6: Paul L. Maier, In the Fullness of Time: A Historian Looks at Christmas, Easter, and the Early Church (San Francisco: Harper Collins, 1991), 197.

7: The American Biblical Scholar John P. Meier makes this same argument in "How do we decide what comes from Jesus" in The Historical Jesus in Recent Research by James D. G. Dunn and Scot McKnight 2006 ISBN 1-57506-100-7 pages 126–128

8: Dr. Gary Habermas, transcribed from the lecture "Evidence For The Minimal Facts", given at The National Conference On Christian Apologetics, October 14th 2017.

9: A Brief Introduction to the New Testament by Bart D. Ehrman 2008 ISBN 0-19-536934-3 page 136

10: See John Dominic Crossan, Jesus: A Revolutionary Biography (San Francisco: HarperCollins, 1991), 145; see also 154, 196, 201.

11: Dr. Gerd Ludemann, "The Resurrection Of Christ: A Historical Inquiry", 2004, page 50.

12: See RE Brown, *The Death Of The Messiah,* 1994, page 1373

Chapter 4

Fact 2 - The Empty Tomb

I remember one Easter week, I was scrolling through my Facebook timeline, and I came across a comic made by someone in the organization *Answers In Genesis*. The comic featured four panels with four children. Three of the four children were in dismay over empty Easter baskets, screaming "Empty!" The child in the last panel was reading his Bible, a smile on his face, and a thought bubble above his head featuring the empty tomb of Jesus. The boy smiled and said "Empty!" A smile broke out upon my face as well, for I realized the message the comic sent across. The resurrection of Jesus is what Easter is truly about. If it really happened, and Jesus left an empty grave behind, then Easter should be a joyous occasion for us regardless of whether we get any goodies in our Easter Baskets or not.

So far, we've established the first minimal fact to be explained: Jesus definitely died as a result of Roman crucifixion. Now the really interesting question needs to be raised: what happened **after** Jesus died? Was Jesus' grave really found empty? Let's look at the evidence for the empty tomb.

Reason 1: The Jerusalem Factor

Jesus' resurrection was first publicly proclaimed in Jerusalem. This is according to the early sermon summary in Acts 2[1] and Tactitus'[2] independent report that Christianity got its start in Judea (the region the city of Jerusalem existed in). Given that both the book of Acts and Tacitus independently report that Christianity got its start in this part of the world, it is multiply attested and therefore is a historical fact.

Now, given that Jesus was crucified in that very same city, if Jesus' body were still in the tomb, preaching on the resurrection could never have gotten off the ground. Christianity had a lot of enemies. If anyone wanted to disprove the resurrection, all they would have had to do would be to go down to the tomb, pluck the body out of the tomb and parade it down the streets for all to see. They could even go so far as to string Jesus' corpse up in a high place so that even more people could get a glimpse at it. Everyone who got a look at Jesus' body would have known that the disciples' message was false. If the enemies of Christianity had done this, Christianity would have died before it even got off the ground. However, Christianity **didn't** die. It's still one of the most prominent religions today. How is this to be explained? Why didn't the enemies of Christianity (such as the Pharisees) go down to Jesus' tomb and exhume his corpse for all to see, dismantling Christianity from the get go? I think the reason they didn't take Jesus' body out of the tomb is because there was no body **to be** taken out.

They would have plucked His body out of the tomb and paraded it down the street if they could have, but they were unable to. Why? Because the tomb was empty. There was no body **to be** exhumed. That's the only reasonable explanation I can come up with for why they didn't do that.

Objection: Jesus' Body Was Unrecognizable By The Time The Disciples Started Proclaiming The Resurrection, So Producing The Corpse Would Have Done No Good.

Some skeptics have responded to this argument by saying that Jesus' body was unrecognizable by the time the disciples started running around telling folks that He rose from the dead, so it wouldn't really have the effect of demolishing the Christian faith after all. Consequently, the enemies of Christianity either didn't produce the body, or they did but people just responded with "That's not really Jesus".

There are some problems with this objection. First of all, in the arid climate of Jerusalem, a corpses' distinctive wounds, stature, hair color, and hair style would have been identifiable even after 50 days (the time when the book of Acts says the disciples started proclaiming Christ's resurrection).[3] Therefore, it would have been no trouble to figure out whether a corpse belonged to Jesus or not. A person could examine the corpse' physical stature, weight, distinctive wounds ("does this corpse bear the wounds consistent with a crucified victim?"), and hair color and style to see if it was consistent with what one would expect Jesus' corpse to be like. You don't even need to be a trained forensic pathologist to do this. Anyone of any education level could check these things out.

Secondly, even if Jesus' body truly was unrecognizable, we should still have expected **any body at all** to have created a mass exodus from the Christian church, even if a small number of adherents remained. Such an exodus would surely have been picked up by Lucian of Samosata, who was ridiculing Christianity in his work and would surely have loved to use such an incident as evidence against the

Christians' claims. Moreover, we would expect the early church apologists like Justin Martyr to try to respond and explain this mass exodus and why there was a body in Jesus' tomb if Jesus had really risen. We would especially expect The Apostle Paul to address such an incident in his epistles. Yet, history is silent on such an exodus. None of the non-Christian historians say anything about it, Paul says nothing about it, and none of the early church fathers feel compelled to address it.

Reason 2: All Four Gospels Feature Women As Witnesses To The Empty Tomb

All four gospels feature women as the first witnesses to Jesus' empty tomb. Now, why is that significant? As I briefly mentioned in the previous chapter, women were considered second class citizens in the first century. Talmud Sotah 19a says *"Sooner let the words of the law be burnt than delivered to women"*! The Talmud also contains a rabbinic saying that goes like this: *"Blessed is he whose children are male, but woe to him whose children are female"*! And according to the Jewish historian Josephus, their testimony was considered so untrustworthy that they weren't even permitted to serve as witnesses in a Jewish court of law (accept as a last resort, when no male witnesses were available)! Josephus wrote: *"But let not the testimony of women be admitted, on account of the levity and boldness of their sex, nor let servants be admitted to give testimony on account of the ignobility of their soul; since it is probable that they may not speak truth, either out of hope of gain, or fear of punishment."* (Antiquities, 4.8.15).

Women were (A) second class citizens, and (B) considered to be so untrustworthy that no one wanted them to even stand as witnesses in a court of law! In light of this fact, how remarkable it is that it is women who are said to be the chief witnesses to the empty tomb. If the gospel authors were playing fast and loose with the facts, they surely would have made male disciples such as Peter or John the chief witnesses to the empty tomb. The fact that it is women instead of men who are said to be the first witnesses to the empty tomb is best explained by the fact that the empty tomb narratives in the gospels are true!

To make women your first witnesses to the empty tomb would be to insert words into the mouths of witnesses who would not be believed! Therefore, by the principle of embarrassment, we have good reason to believe the tomb was empty.

Reason 3: The Enemies Of Christianity Presupposed The Vacancy Of The Tomb When They Said That The Disciples Stole The Body

When a child tells his teacher that the dog ate his homework, that presupposes that the homework is not in the child's possession. When the enemies of Christianity had to resort to accusing the disciples of stealing the body, that presupposes that there was no body in the tomb.

"While the women were on their way, some of the guards went into the city and reported to the chief priests everything that had happened. When the chief priests had met with the elders and devised a plan, they gave the soldiers a large sum of money, telling them, 'You are to say, 'His disciples came during the night and stole him away while we were asleep.' If this report gets to the governor, we will satisfy him and keep you out of trouble.' So the soldiers took the money and did as they were instructed. And this story has been widely circulated among the Jews to this very day." - Matthew 28:11-15

This is powerful evidence due to The Principle Of Enemy Attestation. Now, you might be wondering why we should view this as good evidence for the empty tomb, since it's comes from Matthew's gospel and not directly from the Jewish leadership themselves. It's not like it's coming out of a book written by Caiaphas where he writes "The tomb was empty because the disciples took his body" or anything like that. Couldn't Matthew have made this up simply to make the empty tomb story seem more credible? Well, no. I don't think so. I say that for three reasons.

First, consider the fact that Matthew says *"This story has been widely circulated **to this very day"**.* Now, what does **"to this very day"** mean? Clearly, Matthew is saying that the opponents of Christianity were running around spreading this story even at the very time period that he was penning these words! They were making this claim to potential converts even during the very time period that Matthew was writing his gospel. If the anti-Christian Jews were **not** making that accusation, then Matthew could have easily been falsified. People could have gone to the Jewish leadership and asked them "We read in the gospel of Matthew that you deny Jesus rose from the dead. You explain his empty tomb by saying they stole the body. Is this true?" If it wasn't true, the Jewish leadership could have said "What? We said no such thing! What are you talking about?" Would Matthew really open himself up to such easy falsification?

Secondly, people don't usually respond to accusations unless someone actually made that accusation of them. Imagine you walk into your front yard and discover that your car is missing. In a panic, you cry out "My car is gone! My car is gone! What happened to it!? Dude, where's my car!?" and then your friend shows up and says "Gee, that's a shame. I don't know what happened to your car, but it's not like I stole it or anything!!!" You would look at your friend funny and say "I never said that you stole my car. Wait a minute, is there something you're not telling me?" People simply don't respond to accusations unless there is truly an accuser. In those rare moments that they do respond to non-existent accusations, they cause themselves to look guilty of the very thing they're denying.

Thirdly, the claims of the opponents of Christianity is multiply attested. In Justin Martyr's "Dialogue With Trypho", he responds to this accusation from the Jews, and Tertullian rebuts it as well in his work "De Spectaculous". This implies that the enemies of Christianity really were making this claim. It originated in the first century, and persisted throughout the second and third.

Reason 4: The Empty Tomb Is Multiply Attested

Earlier in this book, I said that most scholars believe that Matthew and Luke used a lot of material from Mark, and in those particular instances, we don't have independent attestation among the synoptics. That said, I also said that this wasn't always the case. With regards to certain incidents, the synoptics aren't borrowing from one another at all. The empty tomb is one such case. Matthew is clearly working with an independent source, for he includes the story of the guard at the tomb, which is unique to his gospel. Neither Mark nor Luke mention a guard at the tomb, so one would be hard pressed to make a case that Luke and Matthew are copying off of Mark here. Luke also has an independent source, because he tells the story of two disciples visiting the tomb to check out Mary Magdalene's report. This is not found in Mark or Matthew. And again, like I said before, everyone agrees that the gospel of John is independent from all of the synoptics given how different John is from the other 3. So, in this case, the empty tomb is reported in 4 independent sources. Remember from the last chapter that I quoted Paul Maier as saying that most historical incidents are confirmed on the basis of only one source, and if you can find two independent sources, that makes an event impregnable. Regarding the discovery of the empty tomb, we have, not just **two** independent sources, but **four!**

You have another source when you consider the early Pauline creed cited in 1 Corinthians 15. Now, some may object "Wait a minute! Paul never mentions the empty tomb in 1 Corinthians 15!" This is a half truth. While the empty tomb is not **explicitly** mentioned in the creed, it is **implicitly** mentioned. Dr. William Lane Craig explains that *"The old tradition cited by Paul in I Cor. 15.3-5 implies the fact of the* *empty tomb. For any first century Jew, to say that of a dead man 'that he was buried and that he was raised' is to imply that a vacant grave was left behind."* [4]

Adding the Pauline creed to the 4 gospels, we have a total of 5 independent sources attesting that Jesus' tomb was found empty. What are the odds that 5 independent sources would **all** make up the same lie?

Reason 5: The Phrase "On The Third Day" Is Best Explained By The Historicity Of The Empty Tomb

The expression "on the third day" implies the empty tomb. Since no one was actually sitting in the tomb, saw Jesus' body begin to glow and radiate, saw Jesus stand up, fold his garments and walk out of the tomb, why did the early disciples date the resurrection "on the third day"? Why not the fourth day? Why not the fifth day? Why not the eleventyseventh day? I think the most reasonable inference is that this was the amount of time after Jesus' execution that his women followers found the sepulcher vacant. So, the resurrection naturally came to be dated itself to that point in time.

Reason 6: Mark's Account Is Simple And Lacks Signs Of Embellishment

Dr. William Lane Craig explains that *"All one has to do to appreciate this point is to compare Mark's account to the accounts which are found in the later apocryphal gospels. These are forgeries that arose during the centuries following the appearance of the New Testament. These do contain all sorts of wild, legendary accounts about the resurrection. For example, in the so-called Gospel of Peter, which is a forgery from the second half of the second century after Christ, the tomb is surrounded not only by a Roman guard, but also by all of the chief priests and the Pharisees, as well as a huge crowd of people from the surrounding countryside who have come to watch the tomb. Suddenly, during the night, a voice rings out from heaven, and the stone over the door of the tomb rolls back by itself, then two men are seen descending out of heaven and entering into the tomb, then three men, gigantic figures, come out of the tomb, the heads of two of the men reach to the clouds, the head of the third man overpasses the clouds, and then a cross comes out of the tomb, and a voice from heaven asks, "Hast thou preached to them who sleep?" and the cross answers, "Yea." Now, these are how real legends look. They are colored with all sorts of theological and apologetical motifs, motifs which are conspicuously lacking from the Markan account which by comparison is stark in its simplicity."* [5]

Reason 7: Multiple Literary Forms

Repeated as miracle (John 20), creed (1 Corinthians 15:4), didactic (see Acts 2:24-32), and apocalyptic.

Reason 8: The Reason The Women Went To The Tomb - Historical Fit/Coherence

The reason the gospels say the women even went down to the tomb to begin with lends credence to the accounts. It was a standard practice of Jews to anoint the bodies of dead friends and family members. Why the women didn't go on Saturday is very likely due to the fact that it was the Sabbath, the shops were closed, and they couldn't buy perfumes and ointments with which to anoint the body. They would have had to wait until Sunday when the shops were open before they could get the perfumes to anoint Jesus' body. See Mark 16:1-5, Luke 23:56-24:1-3.

So, the principle of historical fit (also known as The Principle Of Coherence) is applicable here.[6]

Reason 9: The Nazareth Decree

Dr. Norman Geisler wrote: *"A slab of stone was found in Nazareth in 1878, inscribed with a decree from Emperor Claudius (A.D. 41-54) that no graves should be disturbed or bodies extracted or moved. This type of decree is not uncommon, but the startling fact is that here "the offender [shall] be sentenced to capital punishment on [the] charge of violation of [a] sepulchre" (Hemer, BASHH, 155). Other notices warned of a fine, but death for disturbing graves? A likely explanation is that Claudius, having heard of the Christian doctrine of resurrection and Jesus' empty tomb while investigating the riots of A.D. 49, decided not to let any such report surface again. This would make sense in light of the Jewish argument that the body had been stolen (Matt. 28:11-15). This is early testimony to the strong and persistent belief that Jesus rose from the dead."[7]*

Why would Claudius issue the death penalty for disturbing graves? That seems like an extreme overreaction. However, as Geisler said in the citation above, it makes sense if Claudius knew of the Jewish polemic against Jesus' empty tomb and was trying to prevent any alleged resurrections from occurring again.

This is not, by itself, conclusive proof of Jesus' empty tomb, but it is strongly indicative. Claudius hearing the Jewish explanation for why Jesus' tomb was empty, and then putting the strongest deterrent he could for disturbing graves to prevent any more Christianities popping up seems like the best explanation to me. I really can't think of another reason why Emperor Claudius would treat so mild a crime as grave robbing so seriously.

-

Reason 10: Jesus' Tomb Was Never Venerated As A Shrine

The philosopher and apologist J.P Moreland explains that: *"In Palestine during the days of Jesus, at least fifty tombs of prophets or other holy persons served as sites of religious worship and veneration. However, there is no good evidence that such a practice was ever associated with Jesus' tomb. Since this was customary, and since Jesus was a fitting object of veneration, why were such religious activities not conducted at his tomb? The most reasonable answer must be that Jesus' body was not in his tomb, and thus the tomb was not regarded as an appropriate site for such veneration. . . . It seems, then, the lack of veneration at the tomb of Jesus is powerful evidence that the tomb was empty."* [8]

Summary and Conclusion

We have seen 10 good reasons to believe that Jesus' tomb was empty the Sunday morning following his execution. For one thing, if Jesus' body were still in the tomb, Jesus' enemies would have exhumed the body and paraded it down the street for all to see. Anyone who looked upon the dead body of Jesus as it was being carried down the streets of Jerusalem would have been persuaded that the disciples were lying about the resurrection. Christianity would have died before it even got off the ground. The best explanation for why it didn't die is that the opponents of Christianity **did not** exhume His body. The reason they did not exhume his body is that there was no body **to be** exhumed. Secondly, the fact that all 4 gospels feature women as the chief witnesses to the empty tomb makes it highly probable that Jesus' tomb was found empty. This conclusion is on the basis of the principle of embarrassment. If the gospel authors were simply fabricating the empty tomb story, they would have made male disciples like Peter or John discover the empty tomb, given that the testimony of women was considered so unreliable that people didn't even want them to testify in a court of law. Thirdly, the enemies of Christianity, rather than exhume the body and show it to everyone, said that the disciples stole Jesus' body, which implies an empty tomb. Fourthly, there's good reason to believe that Matthew and Luke are using independent sources for their empty tomb accounts and aren't relying on Mark, given the different material they include. This leads to a reasonable inference that Matthew, Mark, and Luke are each recording the empty tomb narrative independently of one another, giving us multiple attestation in 4 sources, when John's gospel is included. If you add Paul's implicit mention of the empty tomb in 1 Corinthians 15, we have a total of 5 independent sources. The odds that 5 independent sources would all make up the same lie is fantastically improbable. Fifthly, the fact that the resurrection was dated "on the third day" indicates the factuality of the tomb. Sixth, Jesus' empty tomb is found in multiple literary forms. Seventh, The Nazareth Decree, while not conclusive proof of the empty tomb, is highly suggestive. Eighth, The Principle Of Historical Fit applies. Ninth, Mark's account is stark in its simplicity. Finally, the fact that Jesus' tomb was never venerated is a good reason to believe there was no one in the tomb **to** venerate.

According to Jacob Kremer, a New Testament critic who has specialized in the study of the resurrection: *"By far most scholars hold firmly to the reliability of the biblical statements about the empty tomb."* [9] Former Oxford University church historian William Wand writes, *"All the strictly historical evidence we have is in favor of [the empty tomb], and those scholars who reject it ought to recognize that they do so on some other ground than that of scientific history."* [10]

Do we have enough evidence to conclude that Jesus rose from the dead? No. If the empty tomb were all the evidence we had, we would not be justified in concluding that Jesus rose from the dead. After all, an empty tomb can be accounted for in any number of ways. It will only be when the empty tomb is combined with the 3 other minimal facts we'll look at in this book (the postmortem appearances to the disciples, Paul, and James), that we'll see that the inference to the resurrection is justified.

Notes

1: Acts 2 -- https://www.biblegateway.com/passage/?search=Acts+2&version=NIV

2: *"Consequently, to get rid of the report, Nero fastened the guilt and inflicted the most exquisite tortures on a class hated for their abominations, called Christians by the populace. Christus, from whom the name had its origin, suffered the extreme penalty during the reign of Tiberius at the hands of one of our procurators, Pontius Pilatus, and a most mischievous superstition, thus checked for the moment, again broke out **not only in Judea, the first source of the evil**, but even in Rome, where all things hideous and shameful from every part of the world find their centre and become popular. Accordingly, an arrest was first made of all who pleaded guilty; then, upon their information, an immense multitude was convicted, not so much of* *the crime of firing the city, as of hatred against mankind."* - Tacitus, Annals 15:44 (emphasis mine)

3: Gary Habermas and Michael Licona responded to this objection in their book "The Case For The Resurrection Of Jesus" and in the footnotes, they said they got this information from the Medical Examiner's Office for the Commonwealth of Virginia. Habermas and Licona said *"The physician in charge said that even in Virginia, which has a climate warm and damp enough to promote quick decomposition, an unprepared corpse undergoing a normal rate of decomposition should still after fifty days have its hair and an identifying stature. The wounds would 'definitely' be identifiable. Thus, a corpse in a much worse state than what would be expected for arid Jerusalem would still be identifiable after fifty days."* -- Habermas, Gary R.; Licona, Michael R.. The Case for the Resurrection of Jesus (p. 287). Kregel Publications. Kindle Edition.

4: William Lane Craig, "The Resurrection Of Jesus",
https://www.reasonablefaith.org/writings/popular-writings/jesus-of-nazareth/the-resurrection-of-jesus/

5: William Lane Craig, "Evidence For Jesus' Resurrection", from a lecture given at Southhampton Civic Hall UK,
https://www.reasonablefaith.org/videos/lectures/evidence-for-jesus-resurrection-southampton-uk/

6: Byron R. McCane, "Burial Practices in First Century Palestine", n.p. [cited 16 Nov 2017]. Online:
http://www.bibleodyssey.org/en/people/related-articles/burial-practices-in-first-century-palestine

7: Norman Geisler, When Skeptics Ask: A Handbook on Christian Evidences (1990), p. 206. The exact same paragraph appears even more recently in Geisler's Baker Encyclopedia of Christian Apologetics (1998), p. 48.

8: J.P Moreland, "Scaling The Secular City", Bakerback Academic, pages 161–162

9:Jacob Kremer, Die Osterevangelien—Geschichten um Geschichte (Stuttgart: Katholisches Bibelwerk, 1977), 49–50

10: William Wand, Christianity: A Historical Religion? (Valley Forge, Pa.: Judson, 1972), 93– 94.

Chapter 5

Fact 3 - The Postmortem Appearances To The Disciples

In the last 2 chapters of this book, we saw that the evidence that Jesus died by Roman crucifixion is overwhelming to the point that even atheist historians say that it's an indisputable fact. Then, we saw 10 pieces of historical evidence pointing to the reality of Jesus' empty tomb which was found by a group of His women followers the Sunday following His execution.

However, if we just stopped there, we wouldn't have enough evidence to justifiably infer that Christ had gloriously returned to life. After all, an empty tomb by itself, says nothing. An empty tomb can be explained in a dozen different ways. But, Jesus' death by crucifixion and His empty tomb aren't the only minimal facts in need of explanation. We also have the facts of Jesus' postmortem appearances to His disciples and His postmortem appearances to Paul and James.

In this chapter, we will examine the historical evidence for the third minimal fact: Jesus' disciples believed that He appeared to them alive after His death.

Reason 1: The Early Creed Cited In 1 Corinthians 15.

The first piece of evidence in favor of postmortem appearances I want to look at is Paul's list of appearances in 1 Corinthians 15. Most scholars of all theological stripes agree that Paul is citing an early creed in verses 3-8 and that this creed dates to within 5 years of the crucifixion of Jesus. They also believe that Paul received this creed from the apostles Peter and James just a few years after his conversion. If these scholars are right, this provides us with early and eyewitness testimony to the resurrection of Jesus. But what does the creed say? How do we know it's a creed? How do we know it dates to within 5 years of the crucifixion? How do we know that Paul got it from Peter and James? Let's look at the reasons why historians have reached these conclusions.

This is what the creed says: *"For what I received I passed on to you as of first importance: that Christ died for our sins according to the Scriptures, that he was buried, that he was raised on the third day according to the Scriptures, and that he appeared to Cephas, and then to the Twelve. After that, he appeared to more than five hundred of the brothers and sisters at the same time, most of whom are still living, though some have fallen asleep. Then he appeared to James, then to all the apostles, and last of all he appeared to me also, as to one abnormally born."* - 1 Corinthians 15:3-8

How do we know that this is a creed? Maybe this is just doctrine that Paul is teaching in his own words. Scholars have come to believe that this is a creed on the basis of the following reasons

1: Paul Alerts Us That He's Not Writing In His Own Hand Here.

In verse 3, Paul says outright that his words are not his own. He writes *"For **what I received, I passed on to you** as of first importance."* Paul essentially says "I received this information from someone else. It's not a list of things I came up with. Now, I'm going to pass on what I've received to you." So, he's outright telling us that the information he's about to cite is something he himself received and is about to pass on to his readers. Additionally, "received" and "passed on" were typical terms used by rabbis who were passing along holy tradition.[1]

2: The Language In Verses 4-7 Are Non-Pauline

Joachim Jeremias, a leading authority on this issue, notes that phrases such as "For our sins", "According to the scriptures", "The Twelve", "The Third Day", and "He was raised", are non-Pauline.[2] That is to say, Paul doesn't usually talk like this, employing these phrases. This implies that Paul is quoting something rather than teaching resurrection facts in his own words.

3: Parallelism Is Apparent In The Text.[3]

Parallelism is a type of wording that was commonly found in oral traditions. The purpose of parallelism was to aid memorization. Parallelism involves writing several lines that go by the pattern of the first line being long followed by a short line followed by another long line and then another short line. Long sentence, short sentence, long sentence, short sentence. When you examine 1 Corinthians 15, this is exactly what you find.

"Christ died for our sins according to the Scriptures," (long)
"and that He was buried" (short)
"and that He was raised on the third day in accordance with the scriptures" (long)
"and that He appeared to Cephas, then to the twelve..." (short)
"After that, he appeared to more than 500 brothers and sisters at the same time, most of whom are still living, though some have fallen asleep." (long)

4: The Repeated Use Of The Phrase "And That" Suggests This Is A Creed[4]

Just as Parallelism was a wording style to make memorization of creeds easier, putting a common repetitive phrase in creeds also helped aid memorization. In this case, the repetitive phrase is "and that". Depending on the English translation, you'll sometimes just see the word "that", but "and that" is what's found in the Greek.

   *"**and that** he was buried, **and that** he was raised on the third day according to the Scriptures, **and that** he appeared to Cephas, and then to the Twelve."*

For these reasons, we have good grounds for affirming that the material cited in verses 4-7 are part of a creed. Paul received the creed somewhere and then proceeded to cite it to his Corinthian readers. What this means is that the material in 1 Corinthians 15:4-7 predates the actual writing of 1 Corinthians, which virtually all scholars date to around 55 A.D.

   But how much earlier does this material date? Well, first of all, it certainly has to predate Paul's first visit to the Corinthian church. Why? Because in verse 3, he uses the past tense "I pass**ed** on to you." *"For what I received, I pass**ed** on to you."* In the latter part of that sentence, Paul uses the past tense of "pass". This implies that the information he's about to cite in his epistle is information that he already cited to the Corinthians. And since he "receiv**ed**" this creed from someone else, this means the creed predates even Paul's first visit there in AD 51.

   If this were as far back as we could go, it would still be extremely early information since the creedal data would date no later than 20 years after Jesus' death.

   But, as I said earlier in this chapter, most scholars believe that Paul got this creed directly from the apostles Peter and James, just 5 years after his conversion. In Galatians 1, Paul is recounting his conversion from skepticism. He describes how he persecuted the church (verses 13-14) that God revealed his son to him (verses 15-16), and then he says that he went away into Arabia and then went to Damascus (verse 17). Paul then writes *"Then after three years, I went up to Jerusalem to get acquainted with Cephas and stayed with him fifteen days. I saw none of the other apostles—only James, the Lord's brother."* (verses 18-19). This seems like the most likely place and time for Paul to have received the 1 Cor. 15 creed. First of all, two of the explicitly named individuals that appear in the creed (Peter and James) are also the two individuals Paul was talking to. Secondly, As New Testament Historian Dr. Gary Habermas pointed out; *"Paul's use of the verb historesai (1:18), is a term that indicates the investigation of a topic.*[5] *The immediate context both before and after reveals this subject matter: Paul was inquiring concerning the nature of the Gospel proclamation (Gal. 1:11-2:10), of which Jesus' resurrection was the center (1 Cor. 15:3-4, 14, 17; Gal. 1:11, 16)."* [6]

These seem like very good indications that this was indeed when and where Paul received the creed. In that case, the information in the creed dates to within just a few years of Jesus' death! By the principles of early attestation, this makes 1 Corinthians 15:3-8 extremely reliable material. This is because there was no time whatsoever for legend or embellishment to creep in. The apostles were proclaiming that Christ rose from the dead within a measly 5 years of His crucifixion!

The creed cited in 1 Corinthians 15 dates back so early, well within the lifetimes of the eyewitnesses, that anyone curious about whether or not Paul was telling the truth could have traveled over to Jerusalem and interviewed the people mentioned in the creed to see if they really did believe Jesus appeared to them. If Paul were lying about these people and they really hadn't seen Jesus, the cat would have been out of the bag and the resurrection would have been exposed as a falsehood. Given how fragile a faux resurrection would be in this case, the best explanation is that the twelve disciples, James, and 500 people actually did have postmortem Jesus experiences.

In fact, some have argued that Paul is essentially daring the Corinthians to interview these people if they are in doubt by mentioning that *"some of them are still living, though some have fallen asleep."*[7] It's as if Paul is saying "If you don't believe that Jesus appeared to these individuals, go talk to them yourselves! Some of them have died, but others are still around to affirm what I've said."

Reason 2: Paul Had Direct Contact With The Twelve Disciples And Affirmed That They Claimed Jesus Rose From The Dead

Let's say you don't think that the two arguments which are given in favor of Paul receiving the creed during the trip mentioned in Galatians 1:18-20 are sufficient. Nevertheless, the creed still dates to no later than 50 A.D, just 20 years after the death of Jesus. The creed could have been received 2 years or 20 years, but no earlier and no later. So my arguments above still stand that this is an early source within the lifetimes of the eyewitnesses who could have falsified the postmortem appearances if they hadn't occurred.

Secondly, even if Paul didn't receive the creed in the Galatians 1 trip, we still know that he had firsthand contact with the original twelve disciples and were therefore in the perfect position to know what they believed.

Paul makes 2 trips to Jerusalem. The first trip occurs 5 years after his conversion (Galatians 1:18-20), and the second one takes place more than 14 years after (Galatians 2:1-2). Paul makes two trips, and he's there at +5 years and +18 years after the cross. Both trips are very early and he talks to the eyewitnesses. What are they discussing? The gospel. In 2:2 he specifically says *"I went in response to a revelation and, meeting privately with those esteemed as leaders, I presented to them the gospel that I preach among the Gentiles. I wanted to be sure I was not running and had not been running my race in vain."* In other words, Paul is essentially saying "I just wanted to double check and make sure that I'm preaching the same message as my fellow apostles are. I gave them the gospel I preached and wanted to cross-reference it with the one they preach." What was the result of such an inquiry? Paul says in 2:6 *"They added nothing to my message."* Then he said *"On the contrary, they recognized that I had been entrusted with the task of preaching the gospel to the uncircumcised, just as Peter had been to the circumcised. For God, who was at work in Peter as an apostle to the circumcised, was also at work in me as an apostle to the Gentiles. James, Cephas, and John, those esteemed as pillars, gave me and Barnabas the right hand of fellowship when they recognized the grace given to me. They agreed that we should go to the Gentiles, and they to the circumcised."* (verses 7-10)

Probably the best thing Paul contributes to our case is interviewing the other eyewitnesses and giving us the data. Paul said that he and the other apostles preached the same message. In Galatians 1 and 2, he's talking with the twelve disciples and in Galatians 2:6-10, he affirms that what he's teaching is what they're teaching. If the disciples were not claiming that Christ had risen from the dead and had appeared to them, that would not be the case. Also, in 1 Corinthians 15:11, just after citing the creed, he basically says "I don't care if you go to them, I don't care if you go to me, we are preaching the same message about Jesus' appearances."

Reason 3: The Disciples Of The Disciples Affirmed That They Preached Jesus' Resurrection

The early church fathers lived and wrote in the first, second, third, and fourth centuries. When you investigate the writings of these guys, you find that some of them had physical contact with the apostles. Given this fact, just as we can trace the disciples' teachings back to them through Paul, we can trace the teachings of the disciples back to them through the church fathers!

The early church father Clement (c. 30– 100) wrote to the Corinthian church in 95 AD. Around 185, Irenaeus gave us some extra info about this Corinthian epistle. Irenaeus wrote: *"Clement was allotted the bishopric. This man, as he had seen the blessed apostles, and had been conversant with them, might be said to have the preaching of the apostles still echoing, and their traditions before his eyes. Nor was he alone, for there were many still remaining who had received instructions from the apostles. In the time of this Clement, no small dissension having occurred among the brothers at Corinth, the Church in Rome dispatched a most powerful letter to the Corinthians."*[8] Around 200, the African church father, Tertullian wrote, *"For this is the manner in which the apostolic churches transmit their registers: as the church of Smyrna, which records that Polycarp was placed therein by John; as also the church of Rome, which makes Clement to have been ordained in like manner by Peter."* [9] According to Irenaeus and Tertullian, Clement engaged in fellowship with the apostles. Clement writes of their belief in the resurrection thusly; *"Therefore, having received orders and complete certainty caused by the resurrection of our Lord Jesus Christ and believing in the Word of God, they went with the Holy Spirit's certainty, preaching the good news that the kingdom of God is about to come."* [10] Clement said that the apostles believed in the resurrection of Jesus! If he knew the apostles (as Irenaeus and Tertullian say he did), Clement would be in the best position to know whether or not they were truly teaching that Christ got out of His grave. Irenaeus wrote that Polycarp (c. 69– c. 155) knew the disciples. He said: *"But Polycarp also was not only instructed by apostles, and conversed with many who had seen Christ, but was also, by apostles in Asia, appointed bishop of the Church in Smyrna, whom I also saw in my early youth, for he tarried [on earth] a very long time, and, when a very old man, gloriously and most nobly suffering martyrdom, departed this life, having always taught the things which he had learned from the apostles."*[11]

Irenaeus wrote a letter to a person named Florinius. In this letter, Irenaeus also talked about Polycarp. Unfortunately, the letter that Irenaeus wrote to Florinius was annihilated by the sands of time, but while the letter itself is gone, the early church historian Eusebius quoted a portion from it; *"When I was still a boy I saw you in Lower Asia with Polycarp when you had high status at the imperial court and wanted to gain his favor. I remember events from those days more clearly than those that happened recently . . . so that I can even picture the place where the blessed Polycarp sat and conversed, his comings and goings, his character, his personal appearance, his discourses to the crowds, and how he reported his discussions with John and others who had seen the Lord. He recalled their very words, what they reported about the Lord and his miracles and his teaching—*

things that Polycarp had heard directly from eyewitnesses of the Word of life and reported in full harmony with Scripture." [12]

Given the fact that Polycarp knew the apostles personally, he would have been in the best position to know what the disciples believed. Polycarp mentioned the resurrection 5 times in his letter to the church in Phillipi.

So, through Polycarp and Clement, we can trace the claims of the resurrection right back to the disciples themselves.

"But!" the skeptic may object "Just because the disciples were <u>claiming</u> that Jesus rose from the dead, that doesn't mean that He actually did. Maybe the disciples were making the whole thing up! Maybe they were lying about having seen the risen Jesus". I have never found any attempt by non-Christians to make the disciples out to be bald faced liars very convincing. This is because church history is unanimous in claiming that all of the disciples (with the exception of John) died brutal martyrs deaths. Why would they die for a lie? Why would they die for something that they knew wasn't true? I could believe someone would die for a lie that they believed was true, but I can't bring myself to believe that someone would willingly die for something they knew was false.

Some of the sources that record the disciples' martyrdoms are:

*Clement Of Rome – reported sufferings and martyrdoms of Peter and Paul.[13]

*Polycarp – Reported the sufferings and martyrdom of the disciples in general.[14]

*Tertullian – Reported the martyrdom of Peter and Paul (and specifically says that Peter was crucified and that Nero beheaded Paul). [15]

*Book Of Acts -- Reports martyrdom of James the son of Zebedee (beheaded by Herod Agrippa).[16]

*Eusebius -- Says in his *Ecclesiastical History* that all of the apostles were martyred, and says that Peter was crucified upside down.

At this point, skeptics usually respond by saying "Well that doesn't prove anything. Other religions have martyrs. Does that mean their religious beliefs are true? Think of the terrorists who flew planes into the World Trade Center, for example. Does the fact that these terrorists were willing to die for their religious beliefs prove that Islam is true?" This rebuttal simply shows that the objector has misunderstood the argument. I am not arguing that because the disciples died martyrs deaths that this proves that Jesus rose from the dead. What I'm arguing is that their willingness to suffer and die proves that they sincerely believed what they were claiming rather than trying to pull the wool over peoples' eyes. No one would say the terrorists who took down the World Trade Center consciously thought that Islam was false. If they believed Islam was false, those 3,000 people would still be alive today. Martyrdom doesn't prove a claim is true, it simply proves sincerity on the part of the one making the claim. Since almost all of the disciples were willing to die (some in horrible, slow, torturous, and gruesome ways), only an idiot would continue to say "Nah, they were simply spouting bald face lies." I mean, can you imagine St. Peter lying upside down on the cross, having been beaten to a pulp, having had nails driven through his hands and feet, and bleeding and suffocating thinking to himself "Jesus is dead. He didn't really rise. We stole his body and hid it at the bottom of a lake. He's still dead, and soon I will be too! This torture was worth it!"

It's also worth pointing out that the apostles differ from modern day martyrs in that they were in a unique position to know for sure whether or not Jesus rose from the dead. The resurrection proclamations originated with them. If it's made up, then they're the ones who made it up. And yet, they died horribly for making this claim. Most martyrs, including Christian martyrs of today, die on the basis of secondary evidence (e.g the minimal facts approach) or no evidence (blind faith). The disciples came to believe Jesus rose from the dead because they claimed that He appeared to them personally, that is, primary evidence! They claimed to have **seen** him! This places their martyrdom in a totally separate category than all of the ones you read about in "Voice Of The Martyrs".

What all of this means is that through Paul and the church fathers Polycarp and Clement, we can affirm that the twelve disciples of Jesus claimed Jesus rose from the dead and appeared to them. Through the fact that they all died brutal deaths when they could have saved themselves by recanting means that they really believed what they were claiming.

Reason 4: The Postmortem Appearances To The Disciples Are Multiply Attested

Jesus' after-death appearance to the apostle Peter is independently mentioned by Paul and Luke (1 Corinthians 15:5; Luke 24:34). Virtually all scholars agree that Paul and Luke are independent sources. Therefore, the appearance to Peter is multiply attested. The appearance to the Twelve disciples is recorded by Paul, it's recorded by Luke, and it's recorded by John (1 Corinthians 15:5; Luke 24:36–53; John 20:19–31). Therefore, we have 3 independent sources recording the postmortem appearance to the disciples as a group. Again, what are the odds that 3 independent sources are all going to make up the same lie? On the basis of the principle of multiple attestation, we should conclude that the postmortem appearances are a fact, however you want to explain them.

Reason 5: Doubting Thomas Gives Us Reason Not To Doubt

John 20:24-29 records the postmortem appearance to Thomas. All of the other disciples had seen Jesus alive and were rejoicing at his resurrection, but Thomas was so skeptical of the resurrection that he said that he wouldn't believe it until he placed his fingers in Jesus' hands and side. Verses later, we read that Jesus appeared to Thomas and Thomas was convinced. However, why would the writer of the gospel of John depict Thomas in such a bad light? John 20 doesn't depict one of the apostles in a very good light by making him out to be a hard-headed skeptic, disbelieving the testimony of the rest of the apostles. It seems to me that Thomas' skepticism is unlikely to be a Christian invention on the basis of the principle of embarrassment. Therefore, this passage is very likely to be telling us a historical fact.

Now, perhaps I can play devil's advocate and propose an objection to this particular point: maybe the reason John puts Thomas in a bad light is that he disliked Thomas. Perhaps, later on, they got into heated arguments causing a rift between them. John 20's depiction of Thomas, therefore, is slander. However, this is a possibility that has no historical evidence behind it. If the skeptic wants to undermine this fifth argument, he'll have to do more than just propose an alternative possibility. He'll have to back up that possibility with evidence. We have no reason to believe that the writer of John's gospel (be he the apostle John or whoever) had any dislike of St. Thomas. No church historian hints at any tension between the apostle John and Thomas, nor do any of Paul's writings indicate that such tension existed. We have no reason to believe that John had anything but the utmost respect for Thomas as he did the other apostles.

Reason 6: Brave Women, Cowardly Disciples

Before the appearance to St. Thomas, the gospel of John reports that the risen Jesus appeared to Mary Magdalene before He appeared to anyone else (John 20:11-17), and Jesus told her to tell the twelve disciples that He had risen (verse 18). We then read that Mary went and told the disciples what Jesus told her to tell them, but we also read in verse 19 that they were hiding in fear of the Jews!

Now, the principle of embarrassment has got a lot to go on here. First of all, remember that women were second-class citizens back in that culture and their testimony was so worthless that they weren't even permitted to serve as witnesses in a Jewish court of law. In light of this fact, it is astonishing that not only is a woman the first to witness the empty tomb, but the first to see the risen Christ as well! If John were simply making this narrative up, wouldn't he have had a man be the first witness of the risen Christ? Oh, no, but he couldn't do that because he wrote that the men were locked up somewhere hiding in fear of the Jewish leadership. This is also a shocking thing to mention if you're just making up a narrative. Why would John make the men (which would include John himself if he's really the author of this book) be hiding like a bunch of wusses and write that only a woman follower of Christ had the guts to go down to the tomb? This paints the disciples in an embarrassing light and exalts a person who, back then, had low social status. By the principle of embarrassment, we can conclude that this account is historical.

But it gets even better! For the specific words Jesus said to Mary were *"Go instead to my brothers and tell them, 'I am ascending to my Father and your Father, to my God and your God.'"* (verse 17). John's gospel puts more emphasis on the deity of Christ than any of the other 3, yet he says that God the father is "His God". When you've told your readers from verse 1 that Jesus is God, it's odd to have him say that The Father is His God, as though Jesus is somehow an inferior being. If Jesus has a God, how can he be God? Now, just like with "Why have you forsaken me" which we examined in chapter 3, I think a plausible explanation for this sentence can be given (e-book readers can click the hyperlink to see what that explanation is). I don't think Jesus' words here in any way diminish His deity. However, the point here is that **they seem to**. Therefore, rather than having to go through the trouble of explaining this saying, it would have been much easier for John if he had just omitted that part altogether. The fact that it's in here gives us reason to believe that John is not making this up, this is actually what Miss Magdalene heard the postmortem Jesus say. Once again, the principle of embarrassment gives us reason to believe this account is historical.

The principle of embarrassment applies to John 20 in three different ways:

1: A Woman is the first to see the risen Jesus. She sees him before **any** of the twelve do.

2: The disciples are hiding like cowards because they're afraid the big bad Pharisees are going to get them.

3: Jesus calls The Father "My God" which prima facie suggests he isn't God, in a gospel that emphasized His divinity since literally verse 1.

This gives us yet another reason to believe that the 12 disciples had a postmortem appearance experience of Jesus. Again, you can try to explain this postmortem appearance by appeal to a naturalistic theory if you want to, but the fact that they believed they saw Jesus post-crucifixion seems well grounded historically.

Conclusion

We've seen that as with Jesus' death by crucifixion and Jesus' empty tomb, there is an astounding amount of historical evidence for the postmortem appearances to the disciples. Now, you can try to explain these appearances in some way other than to say Jesus really rose from the dead, but you have no grounds on which to deny that the disciples really believed they saw Him post-crucifixion.

As the agnostic historian, Bart Ehrman said *"We can say **with complete certainty** [emphasis added] that some of his disciples at some later time insisted that he soon appeared to them. . . . Historians, of course, have no difficulty whatsoever speaking about the belief in Jesus' resurrection, since it is a matter of public record"*[17]

The atheist historian Gerd Ludemann put it this way: *"It may be taken as historically certain that Peter and the disciples had experiences after Jesus' death in which he appeared to them as the risen Christ."* [18] For a historian, who is an atheist no less, to say that something like this is historically certain speaks volumes!

The atheist scholar E.P Sanders said *"That Jesus' followers (and later Paul) had resurrection experiences is, in my judgment, a fact. What the reality was that gave rise to the experiences I do not know."*[19]

Do we have enough evidence now to infer that Jesus rose from the dead? Actually, I think we do. In my experience, skeptics have a hard time coming up with a naturalistic theory that can account for both Jesus' empty tomb and Jesus' post mortem appearances to the disciples. However, I think we can make our case for the resurrection even stronger by examining post mortem appearances of Jesus to two specific individuals: Paul and James. It is these appearances that we will examine in the next chapter.

Notes

1: See Reginald Fuller, "Resurrection Narratives", page 10; Wilkens, "resurrection", page 2; Rudolph Bultmann, "Theology", vol. 1, p. 293; C.H Dodd, "Apostolic Preaching", pp. 13-14; "Risen Christ", p. 125; Neufeld, "Confessions", p. 27

2: Joachim Jeremias, "The Eucharistic Words", Hymns Ancient and Modern ltd, April 30th 2012, pp. 101-102

3: See especially Fuller, "Resurrection Narratives", pp. 11-12; Weber, "The Cross", p. 59, Jeremias, "The Eucharistic Words", pp. 102-103

4: Pinchas Lapide, "Resurrection", pp. 101-102

5: Several studies on the meaning of historesai in Gal. 1:18 have reached similar conclusions. See William Farmer, *"Peter and Paul, and the Tradition Concerning `The Lord's Supper' in I Cor. 11:23-25,"* Criswell Theological Review, Vol. 2 (1987), 122-130, in particular, and 135-138 for an apostolic, Petrine source for the pre-Pauline tradition. Also helpful is an older but still authoritative study by G.D. Kilpatrick, *"Galatians 1:18 historesai Kephan"* in New Testament Essays: Studies in Memory of Thomas Walter Manson, A.J.B. Higgins, editor (Manchester: Manchester University, 1959), 144-149. Paul Barnett reports that this same term appears in Herodotus, Polybius, and Plutarch, for whom it meant to inquire (41). Similar ideas are contained in J. Dore, *"La Resurrection de Jesus: A L'Epreuve du Discours Theologique,"* Recherches de Science Religieuse, Vol. 65 (1977), 291, endnote 1

6: Gary Habermas: "Experiences of the Risen Jesus: The Foundational Historical Issue in the Early Proclamation of the Resurrection", Originally published in Dialog: A Journal of Theology, Vol. 45; No. 3 (Fall, 2006), pp. 288-297; published by Blackwell Publishing, UK.

7: See the online article "Authenticating The Resurrection Of Jesus: The Corinthian Creed", May 3rd, 2012, http://www.thefaithexplained.com/blog/authenticating-the-resurrection-of-jesus-the-corinthian-creed/

8: Irenaeus, Against Heresies, 3.3.3, c. 185. Taken from A. Roberts, J. Donaldson, and A. C. Coxe, eds. and trans., The Ante-Nicene Fathers: Translations of the Writings of the Fathers Down to A.D. 325 (Oak Harbor, Ore.: Logos Research Systems, 1997).

9: Tertullian, The Prescription Against Heretics, 32. In ibid.

10: Irenaeus, Against Heresies, 3.3.4.

11: Ibid.

12: Irenaeus, To Florinus, cited by the fourth-century church historian, Eusebius, who regarded Irenaeus as a reliable source (Ecclesiastical History 5.20). See To Florinus in Roberts, Donaldson, and Coxe, eds. and trans., The Ante-Nicene Fathers. See Eusebius, Eusebius: The Church History, Paul L. Maier, ed. and trans. (Grand Rapids: Kregel, 1999), 195–96.

13: *"Because of envy and jealousy, the greatest and most righteous pillars have been persecuted and contended unto death. Let us set the good apostles before our eyes. Peter, who because of unrighteous envy endured, not one or two, but many afflictions, and having borne witness went to the due glorious place. Because of envy and rivalries, steadfast Paul pointed to the prize. Seven times chained, exiled, stoned, having become a preacher both in the East and in the West, he received honor fitting of his faith, having taught righteousness to the whole world, unto the boundary on which the sun sets; having testified in the presence of the leaders. Thus he was freed from the world and went to the holy place. He became a great example of steadfastness."* - Clement Of Rome, First Clement 5: 2– 7,

14: *"They are in the place due them with the Lord, in association with him also they suffered together. For they did not love the present age. . . ."* - Polycarp, "To The Philippians", 9.2

15: *"That Paul is beheaded has been written in their own blood. And if a heretic wishes his confidence to rest upon a public record, the archives of the empire will speak, as would the stones of Jerusalem. We read the lives of the Caesars: At Rome Nero was the first who stained with blood the rising faith. Then is Peter girt by another, when he is made fast to the cross. Then does Paul obtain a birth suited to Roman citizenship, when in Rome he springs to life again ennobled by martyrdom."* - Tertullian,

16: Acts 12:1-2

17: Bart Ehrman, Jesus: Apocalyptic Prophet of the New Millennium (New York: Oxford University, 1999), 230-231.

18: Gerd Lüdemann, What Really Happened to Jesus?, trans. John Bowden (Louisville, Kent.: Westminster John Knox Press, 1995), p. 80.

19: E.P. Sanders, The Historical Figure of Jesus, page 280

Chapter 6

Facts 4 and 5 -

The Postmortem Appearances To Paul and James

I remember when I first read the book of Acts as a new Christian. I strongly disliked Saul Of Tarsus for what he did to innocent Christians, including Stephen. I just wanted to get in a time machine, and go kick the guy in the underwear area. But then I read of his dramatic experience on the road to Damascus. As I continued to read Acts, the person I originally disliked was a person I grew really fond of. The change in Paul's life by his encounter with Christ was dramatic.

In the previous chapter, we looked at the historical evidence for the post-mortem appearances of Jesus to the twelve disciples. In this chapter, we will focus on Jesus' appearances to two specific individuals: Paul and James.

The Church Persecutor Paul

It's pretty obvious that Paul claimed to be an eyewitness of the resurrection. In 1 Corinthians 15:8, immediately after citing the early resurrection creed, he said: *"last of all, as to one untimely born, he appeared to me also."* Earlier in that same letter, he asked rhetorically *"Am I not free? Am I not an apostle? Have I not seen our Lord?"* (1 Corinthians 9:1). So, from Paul's own pen he tells us that he had a postmortem appearance experience.

However, some skeptics may balk and say "Yeah, he **said** he saw Jesus raised from the dead. But anyone can claim anything. I can claim I saw Santa Claus leaving toys under my Christmas tree last December. That doesn't make it true. How do we know Paul isn't just lying?" This is a fair question. This is why in prior writings, instead of merely pointing to where Paul says he saw Jesus, I made an inferential case for his postmortem appearance experience. There are several historical facts about Paul which only make sense if Paul actually had a postmortem appearance experience.

*Before Paul Was A Christian, He Was A Persecutor Of The Church

We have good historical evidence that prior to becoming a Christian, Paul was a persecutor of Christians. In 1 Corinthians 15:9, Paul said *"For I am the least of the apostles and do not deserve to even be called an apostle because I persecuted the church of God"*, likewise in Galatians 1:13-14, Paul said *"For you have heard of my previous way of life in Judaism, how intensely I persecuted the church of God and tried to destroy it. I was advancing in Judaism beyond many of my own age among my people and was extremely zealous for the traditions of my fathers."*. In 1 Timothy 1:13, Paul said *"Even though I was once a blasphemer and a persecutor and a violent man, I was shown mercy because I acted in ignorance and unbelief."*
Now, I am inclined to believe that Paul is telling the truth here on the basis of three reasons.

1: The Principle of Embarrassment. People make up lies to make themselves look good, they don't make up lies to make themselves look bad. Paul is mentioning details about himself that cast him in a pretty bad light.
Think about it for a moment; if you were writing a letter to someone, would you lie about having a drug abuse problem that you don't actually have? If you were writing a letter to some friends, would you make up lies about how you terrorized your local neighborhood? I don't think so! You probably wouldn't even admit something like that **even if it were true!** But you **especially** wouldn't say that if were **not** true. People don't make up lies that make themselves look bad! Paul would never say that he was a persecutor of the church if it wasn't true.

2: The Principle Of Multiple Attestation. Not only does Paul say that he was a persecutor of the church, but Luke mentions it as well in the book of Acts (8:1-4, 9:1-2). Paul and Luke are independent sources, and therefore, there is multiple attestation to Paul being a persecutor. It is highly unlikely that both Paul and Luke independently fabricated the same lie. On the basis of the principle of multiple attestation, we have good reason to believe that Paul persecuted the church.

3: Paul Had A Reputation

Let's keep something in mind here: in all of the epistles, Paul is writing **to** someone. And in Galatians 1:13, Paul said ""***For you have heard of my previous way of life in Judaism, how intensely I persecuted the church of God and tried to destroy it.***" (emphasis mine). Paul says that he had a reputation for being a persecutor of the church, and tells his readers that they knew of that reputation. Now, if Paul wasn't really a persecutor of the church, his readers would have immediately called him out for lying. You don't say "You know about that bad stuff I did. You've heard about it." unless you did the thing you're talking about.

*Paul Became A Christian, And Then Suffered And Died For Preaching The Gospel

Paul obviously became a Christian sometime after persecuting Christians. Like with the disciples, we know that Paul actually believed the message he was preaching because he endured terrible suffering throughout his life for the sake of the gospel, and was eventually killed for his Christian faith. Seven Independent sources attest to Paul's suffering and martyrdom.

Paul himself recounts instances of his suffering. *"Five times I received from the Jews the forty lashes minus one. Three times I was beaten with rods, once I was pelted with stones, three times I was shipwrecked, I spent a night and a day in the open sea, I have been constantly on the move. I have been in danger from rivers, in danger from bandits, in danger from my fellow Jews, in danger from Gentiles; in danger in the city, in danger in the country, in danger at sea; and in danger from false believers. I have labored and toiled and have often gone without sleep; I have known hunger and thirst and have often gone without food; I have been cold and naked. Besides everything else, I face daily the pressure of my concern for all the churches."* - 2 Corinthians 11:24-28

Some of the specific sufferings mentioned by Paul in 2 Corinthians are also reported by Luke. One of the shipwrecks was recorded in Acts 27:14-44, Paul was stoned in Acts 14:19, and Acts 16:22-24 records an instance of Paul being scourged. The book of Acts records several other hardships Paul endured for being a Christian, but I won't mention them here.

Clement of Rome[1], Tertullian[2], and Dionysius of Corinth[3] (cited by Eusebius) mention his martyrdom. Polycarp[4] and Origen[5] record it as well. Paul was beheaded during the harsh persecution of Emperor Nero in the A.D 60s.

In all, we have 7 independent sources that testify that Paul suffered and died for preaching the gospel. On the basis of the principle of multiple attestations, we, therefore, have good grounds for affirming that Paul actually did suffer and die for the gospel.

*The Best Explanation: Paul Actually Saw Jesus

Now, how do we account for Paul's radical, sudden change from Christian destroyer to Christian leader? From someone who caused martyrs deaths to someone who died a martyr's death himself? I can think of no other explanation than the one Paul himself gave, "*Then he appeared to me also, as to one untimely born.*" (1 Corinthians 15:8).

The Skeptic James

We now come to our fifth and final minimal fact: the conversion of the skeptic James. The Gospels tell us that Jesus had several siblings. Jesus' siblings included James, Jude, Simon, plus some unnamed sisters. Most skeptics I've conversed with love to go after this minimal fact because they say it has the least amount of evidence for it. After all, it's not mentioned anywhere except in one line, and that line is in the creed cited by Paul in 1 Corinthians 15. Nevertheless, I still think we have good grounds for affirming that this appearance occurred. First of all, as I said in the previous chapter, we have good reason to believe Paul got the creed from James himself. Secondly, the creed is extremely early, just 5 years after the death of Jesus, so had James not really experienced a postmortem appearance, he could have publicly rebuked Paul for lying. The severe earliness of the creedal tradition and the probability that Paul got the creed from James has to count for something, right?

However, I think that just as with Paul, we can make an inferential argument.

*James Was A Skeptic During Jesus' Lifetime

James and his other brothers, we are told, were not believers during Jesus' lifetime. We know this based on:

<u>1: The Principle Of Embarrassment</u>

It was embarrassing for a rabbi's family to not accept him back in those days.[6] So this isn't very flattering for Jesus, but it gets worse! In fact, Mark 3:20-35 tells us that Jesus' family thought he was crazy and that they had come to seize him and take him home! This doesn't paint Jesus or His family in a very good light, given the stigmatism back then. Therefore, it's highly unlikely that the gospel writers would have invented skepticism on the part of Jesus' brother James.

In fact, John 7 recounts a rather nasty story where Jesus' brothers try to goad him into a death trap by showing himself publicly at a feast when they knew that the Jewish leaders were trying to kill him! Why in the world would John place Jesus' brothers in such an ugly light if such an event never took place?

2: The Principle Of Multiple Attestation

Not only does Mark mention it (chapter 3), but John mentions it as well (chapter 7). Mark and John are independent sources and therefore, James' skepticism is multiply attested. So, we've established that James was a skeptic.

*Just A Short Time After Jesus' Death, James Came To Believe That Jesus Had Risen From The Dead.

Even though James was a skeptic, we know that later in the early church, James emerges as one of the pillars of the New Testament church, and one of the leaders of the church. Moreover, he was eventually martyred.

Multiple Attestation
This is mentioned in both the book of Acts (21:17-20) as well as by Paul in his letter to the Galatians (2:9). Again, Paul and Luke are independently reporting this. Thus, we know this on the principle of multiple attestations.

*James Was Martyred For His Christian Faith

Multiple Attestation
We have the testimony of Flavius Josephus, Hegesippus, and Clement Of Alexandria[7] that James was martyred for his belief in his brother as the risen Christ. James' martyrdom is multiply attested in these three sources.

*The Most Likely Explanation For Why James Went From Being A Skeptic To Being A Believer Virtually Overnight Is That The Risen Jesus Appeared To Him As 1 Corinthians 15:7 says.

I think the best explanation for James' rapid conversion is that he believed the risen Jesus appeared to him.

New Testament critic Reginald H. Fuller says *"Even if there were not an appearance to James mentioned by Paul, we should have to invent one to explain the transformation that occurred in James between the time of his unbelieving days when Jesus was alive and his time of leadership in the early church"* [8]

That's exactly the argument I'm making here. 1 Corinthians 15:7 aside, we have historically established that James was (1) a skeptic prior to Jesus' death, (2) became a Christian shortly after Jesus' death, and was willing to die for his Christian faith. How can we explain James' overnight transformation if not that James had an experience which he perceived to be a visitation of the risen Jesus? I don't think we can.

Conclusion

We have come to the end of the first step. We have historically established 5 facts which will undergird our inference to Jesus' resurrection.

The 5 minimal facts that undergird the inference to the resurrection are:

1: Jesus died by crucifixion.
2: Jesus' tomb was empty the following Sunday.
3: The disciples experienced postmortem appearances.
4: A church persecutor named Paul converted to Christianity on the basis of what he perceived to be an appearance of the risen Jesus.
5: The skeptic James converted on the basis of what he perceived was a postmortem appearance of Jesus.

In the next chapter, we'll see what the best explanation of these 5 facts is. At face value, it seems like The Resurrection Hypothesis is how we should explain them. However, perhaps we should examine other alternatives before we appeal to the supernatural.

Notes

1: Clement Of Rome, 1 Clement 5:2-7

2: Scorpiace, 15, in Roberts, Donaldson, and Coxe, eds. and trans., The Ante-Nicene Fathers.

3: H.E. 2.26;

4: Polycarp, "To The Philippians", 9.2

5: Origen, as cited by Eusebius in *Ecclesiastical History*

6: See J.P Moreland's Interview with Lee Strobel in "The Case For Christ", Zondervan, page 248

7: Josephus, *Antiquities Book 20, Chapter 9*, Hegesippus as cited in *"Eusebius. Church History Book II Chapter 23. The Martyrdom of James, who was called the Brother of the Lord"*, Clement Of Alexandria, also cited by Eusebius in ibid.

8: Reginald H. Fuller, The Formation of the Resurrection Narratives (New York: Macmillan, 1980), 10.

Chapter 7

Reasoning To The Resurrection

In chapters 3, 4, 5, and 6, we saw that powerful historical evidence exists for the following 5 facts:

1: Jesus died by Roman crucifixion.

2: His tomb was found empty by a group of His women followers the following Sunday Morning.

3: The 12 Disciples believed they saw Jesus alive shortly after His death.

4: A church persecutor named Paul converted to Christianity on the basis of what he perceived to be an appearance of the risen Jesus.

5: A skeptic named James converted to Christianity on the basis of what he perceived to be an appearance of the risen Jesus.

These are the 5 facts that are granted by nearly every historian and scholar who studies the subject, even the non-Christian ones (e.g Ehrman, Ludemann, Sanders). These are the minimal facts. In chapter 1 of this book, I said that the case for Jesus' resurrection involved two steps. The first step is figuring out what the facts are, and the second step is discerning what the best explanation of those facts are. We accomplished the first step in chapters 3-6 of this book. Now we come to the second step; what is the best explanation for the 5 aforementioned facts?

Over the two millennia, skeptics have proposed dozens of naturalistic theories to try to account for the minimal facts. Let's look at them and see if any of them work. I've opted to address these naturalistic theories in the order in which these theories started appearing in the literature throughout history. I'll address the very earliest proposal and then end with the most recently proposed theories.

Theory 1: The Stolen Body Theory (Disciples Version)

You'll recall from chapter 4 that this is the explanation the Jewish leadership came up with to account for the empty tomb in Matthew 28. The Jewish leaders paid off the Roman guards to tell people that the disciples came in the middle of the night to steal the body. That's the explanation being given here: The disciples stole the body, hid it somewhere, and then ran around telling everyone "Oh! Oh! He's alive! He's risen from the dead!" if anyone skeptical wanted to check it out for themselves, they'd go down to the tomb and find the body gone. Then the disciples could say "See? I told ya." Hermann Samuel Reimarus popularized this theory in the 1760s.[1]

Of all the naturalistic theories, this is one of the weakest.

Recall from chapter 5 that church history is unanimous in that all 12 disciples died horrible, gruesome deaths for proclaiming that Jesus rose from the dead. James, the brother of John, was beheaded by decree of King Herod Agrippa, Peter was crucified upside down, Thomas was speared to death in India, Matthew died by being dragged by a horse, and Phillip was crucified on an X shaped cross.[2] They could have saved themselves simply by recanting, yet they proclaimed the resurrection of Jesus despite agonizing, brutal torture, despite forfeiting their lives. Why would they do that? Why would they die for a lie?

Now, again, when you bring this point up to skeptics, they'll say "But that doesn't prove the resurrection is true any more than Muslims giving up their lives in acts of Jihad proves that Islam is true". And they're right. I totally agree with them. But, they're missing the point. I'm not saying the disciples' martyrdoms prove that Jesus rose from the dead. I'm saying it proves that **they believed** he rose from the dead. Martyrdom doesn't prove the disciples were right, it just proves they sincerely believed what they were saying. To put it another way: while people will die for a lie they **think** is **true**, no one will die for a lie they **know** is **false**.

And that is the fatal flaw in the Stolen Body Theory. It posits that the disciples stole Jesus' body and deliberately tried to deceive the masses, and then they willingly endured beatings, torture, and executions for preaching what they consciously believed wasn't true.

The late Charles Colson, who did prison time for being an accomplice in Watergate but who later became a Christian, wrote:

"Watergate involved a conspiracy to cover up, perpetuated by the closest aids to the President of the United States—the most powerful men in America, who were intensely loyal to their president. But one of them, John Dean, turned states

evidence, that is, testified against Nixon, as he put it, "to save his own skin"—and he did so only two weeks after informing the president about what was really going on—two weeks! The real cover-up, the lie, could only be held together for two weeks, and then everybody else jumped ship in order to save themselves. Now, the fact is that all that those around the President were facing was embarrassment, maybe prison. Nobody's life was at stake. But what about the disciples? Twelve powerless men, peasants really, were facing not just embarrassment or political disgrace, but beatings, stonings, execution. Every single one of the disciples insisted, to their dying breaths, that they had physically seen Jesus bodily raised from the dead. Don't you think that one of those apostles would have cracked before being beheaded or stoned? That one of them would have made a deal with the authorities? None did." [3]

As if the unreasonableness of positing that the disciples willingly suffered and died for a lie wasn't bad enough, this theory has other issues. For one, we've seen that Paul and James converted to Christianity because they believed they **saw** the risen Jesus. This theory cannot account for their conversion experiences.

This theory fails because
1: The disciples died for preaching the resurrection. Liars make poor martyrs.
2: It doesn't explain why Paul believed he saw Jesus post-crucifixion.
3: It doesn't explain why James believed he saw Jesus post-crucifixion.

Theory 2: Stolen Body Theory (Other Person Version)

People who realize you can't implicate the disciples in stealing Jesus' body (since it's impossible for hoaxers to sincerely believe their own hoax) modify the stolen body theory a bit. Instead of saying the disciples stole the body, they say that someone else stole the body. Who? They never specify. Maybe the butler did it.

The problems with this theory are numerous. First, we've seen that the disciples sincerely believed they **saw** the risen Jesus appear to them. Second, Paul of Tarsus went from Christian killer to Christian maker because he thought he **saw** the risen Jesus appear to Him on the road to Damascus. Thirdly, the skeptic James converted because he believed he **saw** Jesus alive after his death. This modified version of The Stolen Body Theory (called Fraud B by Habermas) can't explain **any** of the postmortem experiences. The **only** minimal fact that it can account for is the empty tomb.

Besides that, who would have a motive to steal the body of Jesus anyway? We already know we can't implicate the disciples. Liars make poor martyrs. Was it the Romans? What business would they have plucking Jesus' body out of the tomb and hiding it somewhere? Was it the Pharisees? The body being snatched is precisely what they were trying to stop! That's why they had guards situated outside the tomb! Who exactly is supposed to be the culprit here? Moreover, even though grave robbers are a thing, I don't know of any grave robbers who would steal a person's corpse. They want valuable things buried with the corpse, but they don't want the corpse itself.

Theory 3: The Wrong Tomb Theory

This naturalistic theory comes to you courtesy of Kirsopp Lake. This theory states that on that first Easter morning, the women went down to the wrong tomb and concluded on that basis, that Jesus had risen from the dead. The whole thing was really a simple misunderstanding! Jesus' tomb wasn't empty! They just went to the wrong tomb. This tomb never had a body in it at all.

There are a quite a few problems with this view. First off, The Wrong Tomb Theory expects us to believe that everyone who would have been interested in the tomb totally forgot where it was! Not only did the women go to the wrong tomb, but later John and Peter went to the wrong tomb, and then the Pharisees also went to the wrong tomb, followed by the Romans who also went to the wrong tomb, and of course Joseph of Arimathea went to the wrong tomb. He must have forgotten where the tomb that he owned was located.

This is beyond implausible. But even more devastating to the theory is that it doesn't explain the beliefs of the disciples, James, or Paul that they had **seen** the risen Jesus. We've already seen in chapters 5 and 6 that there's good evidence that the disciples, James, and Paul believed that they saw the risen Jesus appear to them!

This theory fails because;
1: Tomb's location was well known. Extremely unlikely everyone interested in the tomb forgot where it was.
2: The disciples didn't believe because the tomb was empty, but because they believed Jesus appeared to them.
3: Paul was convinced on the basis of an appearance.
4: James was convinced on the basis of an appearance.

Theory 4: The Swoon Theory.

Friedrich Schleiermacher put this theory forth in his book *"On Religion: Speeches to its Cultured Despisers"* in 1799. This theory says that maybe Jesus didn't actually die on the cross. Maybe he merely fainted on the cross and then the cool damp air of the tomb sort of roused him around into consciousness. He later appeared to his disciples, not because he had risen from the dead, but because he never died in the first place. This theory seeks to explain minimal facts 2-5 by denying minimal fact 1. Crucified? Yes. Dead? No.

What are the problems with this theory? The following descriptions are very graphic; reader's discretion is advised.

First of all, given the nature of pre-crucifixion scourging, and of the crucifixion itself, it is extremely unlikely that a crucifixion victim could walk away alive.

When a to-be-crucified person was scourged, they would be given 40 lashes. History tells us that the Roman 40 lashes were from a whip of braided leather thongs, with metal balls, broken pieces of sheep bone, broken glass, and basically anything sharp that would cut a person. These sharp pieces of sheep bone, metal, and broken glass were woven into the braided leather thongs. When the whip would strike the flesh, the metal balls would cause severe bruising, and the sheep bone and broken glass would cut the flesh severely. You can easily imagine how shredded a person's back would be after being cut in 40 different places with multiple blades!

According to Dr. Alexander Methrell, the cuts and force of the beating could shred the back so much that the spine of the victim was sometimes exposed![4] The whipping would have gone all the way down the shoulders to the back, and the back of the legs. One physician who has studied Roman beatings said: *"As the flogging continued the lacerations would tear into the underlying skeletal muscles and produce quivering ribbons of bleeding flesh."*[5]

Eusebius, a third-century historian, described scourging with the following words: *"The sufferer's veins were laid bare, and the very muscles, sinews, and bowels of the victim were open to exposure."*

The result of such a hellish beating would mean that Jesus would very likely go into Hypovolemic shock.[6] Hypovolemic shock is caused by severe blood loss. It causes four symptoms to occur. First, the heart races in a desperate attempt to replace all the blood that was lost, second, the blood pressure plummets bringing about fainting or collapsing, third, the kidneys stop making urine in an attempt to preserve what little liquid is left in the body, and fourth, the person gets very, very thirsty.

When you read the gospel accounts of Jesus' execution, all of the symptoms of hypovolemic shock are present. At one point, Jesus falls while carrying his cross, and Simon of Cyrene is forced to help Jesus carry his cross the rest of the way. Later, when Jesus was on the cross, He said "I thirst", and then a Roman soldier dipped a sponge in vinegar and stuck it up to Jesus' mouth for him to drink (see John 19:28-29). Jesus was in critical condition even before He was crucified!

Jesus then carried His cross to the site of the crucifixion, and the Romans nailed Him to it.

Now, how does crucifixion kill its victims? Scientific experiments have been done on volunteers to test what the effects of hanging on a cross would have. These were controlled circumstances, so there was no real danger of these people being harmed. While these volunteers were hanging on the cross, they would mention having difficulty breathing. They would have to push up and down in order to breathe. Eventually, they'd get too exhausted to push up and down anymore, so the scientist would take the person down off the cross at the volunteer's request.

What these experiments showed was that crucifixion victims die from suffocation. Once Jesus was hanging vertically, the weight of his body and the position of his arms put great stress on the diaphragm, and would put his chest in an inhaled position. So in order to exhale, Jesus would have had to push up on his feet and take a breath. Finally, with the pressure on his chest eased he'd be able to exhale. He would push up to exhale and then come back down to inhale. Over, and over, and over. Eventually, exhaustion would take over and he could no longer push himself up to breathe. He would die of asphyxiation. The Roman soldiers would have known when a crucified person was finally dead because they would notice that the victims weren't pushing up to breathe any longer. "Well, maybe Jesus stopped pushing up on purpose in order to fool the soldiers!" you might respond. That's not plausible. You can't do that for very long, and the Romans were no fools. If anyone tried to fake death by not pushing up, they'd know it. They'd wait to see whether the person was playing possum or not.

When the Romans wanted to speed up death, they'd break the legs of the people on the crosses with a massive club. Then they wouldn't be able to push up to breathe, and death would come quickly. However, they didn't do this to Jesus because they saw that He was already dead, but just to make sure, they drove a spear through him. It punctured both his heart and his lung. The gospel of John tells us that when the soldier did that, blood and water gushed out (John 19:34). This single fact proves that not only was Jesus dead, but it also tells us what He died of; heart failure, due to shock and constriction of the heart detected by the presence of fluid in the pericardium. In this instance, the heart has ceased beating. This brought about an accumulation of fluid in Jesus' heart, which is called "pericardial effusion". In addition to this, it also brought about a collection of fluid in the lungs, which is called "pleural effusion". These two fluids cannot be present if the person's heart is still beating.

By the way, for those who want to doubt John's description of the blood and water, I have this to say to you: we have excellent reason to believe that John is telling the truth here. For one thing, John was an uneducated fisherman. Do you think he would know about "pericardial effusion" and "pleural effusion"? Of course not! While anyone would expect to see a pierced body gush blood, not many even today would expect clear fluid to come out. Yet, that's exactly what occurs in the case of heart failure due to shock and constriction of the heart. I didn't even know about this phenomenon until I read about it in Lee Strobel's *The Case For Christ.* Given John's lack of medical knowledge, having water come out of Jesus' side would make as much sense to him as having Skittles pour out. So, despite being mentioned in only one source, we still have reason to believe this description is true. In addition, a Roman author named Quintilian records an instance of Romans piercing a crucified body to check if it was dead, so that increases the plausibility of John's account even more.

This theory fails because:
It was impossible for Jesus to survive this whole ordeal.

1: Jesus was in hypovolemic shock from the pre-crucifixion scourging alone! Jesus was in critical condition even on his way to the cross so he would have bled out.

2: But if bleeding out didn't kill him, He would have eventually died of suffocation.

3: If neither of those two things got him, we can be sure Jesus was dead because (A) you can't survive a spear jab to the heart and (B) that spear jab revealed Jesus' heart and lungs collected pericardial effusion and pleural effusion, which isn't possible if the heart is still beating.

But let's suppose the impossible did occur. Let's suppose that against all odds, Jesus somehow survived the aforementioned Hell on Earth. Non-Christian David Strauss explains that *"It is impossible that a being who had stolen half dead out of the sepulchre, who crept about weak and ill and wanting medical treatment… could have given the disciples the impression that he was a conqueror over death and the grave, the Prince of life: an impression that lay at the bottom of their future ministry."*[7] Habermas comments, *"Every once in a while, the swoon theory appears again. But it has not really been very popular since Strauss's devastating critique in 1835. By the turn of the century, it was declared to be only a curiosity of the past."*[8]

The first minimal fact stands: Jesus died by crucifixion.

Theory 5: The Hallucination Theory

David Strauss rightly thought The Swoon Theory was untenable, so he sought to explain Jesus' postmortem appearances by means of hallucinations. This is probably the most popular naturalistic theory today. Gerd Ludemann holds it, Bart Ehrman holds it, a lot of skeptical scholars hold it.

The biggest problem with this theory is that, as any psychologist will tell you, hallucinations are occurrences that happen in the minds of individuals. They're like dreams in this way. Imagine a group of your friends came up to you one day and said: "Boy, we all had one nice dream last night, didn't we?" You would probably think that they were pulling a practical joke on you. You would never take seriously their claim that they all simultaneously had the exact same dream. This is because dreams are individual occurrences. By the very nature of the case, they cannot be shared experiences. Hallucinations are the same way.

Now, the extremely early creed I talked about in chapter 5 of this book tells us that Jesus appeared to several **groups** of people. He appeared to all of the original disciples, then to James, then 500 individuals at the same time, and finally to Paul. Do Ludemann and Ehrman honestly expect me to believe that they **all** hallucinated? They **all** had the exact same hallucination!? Impossible! It's impossible for 500 individuals to have the same hallucination at exactly the same time! This would be just as likely as the entire city of New York having the same dream on the same night! But not only did Jesus appear to 500 people at the same time, he also appeared to multiple groups on different occasions. Do Ludemann and Ehrman expect me to believe that multiple groups of people on multiple different occasions all had the exact same hallucination?

Lee Strobel, during his investigation of the historical evidence for Jesus' resurrection, asked a medical expert on the possibility of 500 people hallucinating the risen Jesus. This expert said that for a group of 500 people to witness the exact same hallucination of a raised Jesus would *"be a bigger miracle than the resurrection itself!"*[9]

Moreover, not only are group hallucinations statistically impossible, but hallucinations of any kind are uncommon. Hallucinations are usually induced by sleep deprivation, drugs, a high fever, or mental instability. If none of these 4 factors are present, it's highly unlikely that you're going to have a hallucination. As far as we know, none of the disciples, Paul, or James were insomniacs, sick, crazy, or druggies.

Moreover, even if the impossible did occur, and the minds of all these different groups of people produced hallucinations of Jesus, that would still leave the empty tomb unaccounted for. What happened to Jesus' body? Why is it gone?

This theory fails because
1: Jesus appeared to The Twelve Disciples, Paul, James, and 500 individuals. There were multiple group appearances. It is statistically impossible that all of these

people would have the exact same hallucination, even if they were in the frame of mind to hallucinate, which isn't likely either.

2: It doesn't account for the empty tomb.

Theory 6: The GroupThink Theory

Some skeptics have considered that perhaps the disciples were so in anticipation of Jesus' return from the dead that they talked themselves into it. One day they went to the tomb and John was like "Peter, I think I see Jesus! Over there! Do you see him?" and Peter was like "Oh, yeah! Yeah! Yeah! I think I do! I think I do!" and they just kind of talked themselves into it. Well, this couldn't be the case either. Why? Because you have to be in anticipation that you're going to experience something like that. You have to be primed for it. They weren't! There are four reasons why the groupthink theory is untenable.

1: Jesus died. Jews weren't expecting a dying messiah, but a messiah who would be a conquering warrior king, one who would throw off the yoke of Rome.[10]

2: According to the Old Testament (which Jews call the "Tanakh"), anyone hung on a tree was under God's curse. This is mentioned in Deuteronomy 21:23. Since Roman crosses were made out of wood, they were technically trees, so people would often speak of the crucified as "being hung on a tree". And since this was in the minds of Jews, the way in which Jesus died would have only served to convince the disciples that Caiaphas and the others were right in condemning Jesus as a blasphemer and a heretic.

3: Jews believed that all people would rise from the dead at the end of the world, but they never expected any isolated person to get out of their grave right smack dab in the middle of human history.

4: Some of the people who experienced a sighting of the risen Jesus were skeptics…James and Paul. These two were not in any way expecting Jesus to come back to life.

Theory 7: The Pauline Conversion Disorder Theory

This theory is one I found out about in Habermas and Licona's *"The Case For The Resurrection Of Jesus"* and this theory argues that Paul's conversion from skepticism was a result of conversion disorder. Conversion Disorder is a neurological malfunction that occurs whenever a major change comes into someone's life. Habermas and Licona write: *"Let us suppose that the year is 1968. A young American named Rick has been drafted into the U.S. Army for a tour in Vietnam. Shortly after he receives his letter from the Department of Defense, Rick begins to feel a sharp pain all the way down his right leg. The pain worsens, and by the time he goes for his military physical he is limping severely. In this case, Rick is not faking the pain in order to get out of going to Vietnam. He may have conversion disorder. Typical symptoms of conversion disorder are blindness, paralysis, loss of voice, pain, uncontrolled vomiting, tics, and seizures."*[11]

All of these are temporary of course, as conversion disorder does not last forever. Could Paul have experienced something like this? He experienced temporary blindness at the moment he saw a bright light and thought he saw Jesus (see Acts 9). Could Paul have experienced a neurological malfunction?

This theory is plagued with problems. Not the least of which is that it only addresses Paul's conversion and nothing else. It doesn't explain the empty tomb, the appearance to the disciples, or the appearance to James. The resurrection hypothesis explains all of these.

But moreover, Paul is unlikely to have experienced conversion disorder anyway. According to the *Diagnostic and Statistical Manual of Mental Disorders: DSM-IV*, women are more likely to have conversion disorder than men by as much as a 5-1 ratio. Adolescents, military combatants, and those with a low IQ are also more likely to experience the disorder. Paul doesn't fall into any of these categories. Paul is not a woman, teenager, warrior, or dummy. This doesn't mean he couldn't have experienced the disorder. It just means it's unlikely. However, when you look at the other problems associated with The Pauline Conversion Disorder theory, it makes it even more unlikely.

Not only must we employ conversion disorder to explain Paul's experience, but we must also say that Paul experienced an auditory hallucination, as well as a Messiah Complex. Why? Because Paul not only saw a bright light and went blind, but he also heard a voice that told Him to spread the gospel message. Now, it is possible to find people who have experienced conversion disorder, people who have had auditory hallucinations, as well as people who have a messiah complex, but it's extremely rare to find people who have simultaneously experienced all 3.

This theory fails because

1: It has an inadequate explanatory scope. At best, it gives a natural explanation for Paul's conversion. But it doesn't account for the postmortem appearances to the disciples or James. It certainly doesn't account for the empty tomb.

2: Paul isn't a likely candidate for conversion disorder.

3: It's extremely rare to find someone who has conversion disorder, has experienced an audible hallucination and has a messiah complex all at the exact same moment.

Theory 8: The Legend Theory

Could the resurrection have been a legend that developed over time? No. Why? Because, as we saw in chapter 5 of this book we can trace the claims of the resurrection to the lips of the original disciples! In Paul's letters, he says he had access to the original disciples and had fellowshipped with them. I'm sure Peter told Paul whether or not he had seen Jesus when he visited them in Galatians 1, and he certainly told Paul that in Galatians 2 as the whole purpose of Paul's second visit was to determine if he and the other apostles were preaching the same gospel. And of course, the creedal tradition dates to within five years after the death of Jesus. It's likely he got the creed from Peter and James when he visited them three years after his conversion, this is well within the lifetimes of the twelve disciples who could have corrected this oral tradition if He really hadn't appeared to them. Moreover, the early church fathers Tertullian and Irenaeus attest that the church fathers Polycarp and Clement were students of the apostle John and that they knew several other apostles as well. This is significant because Polycarp and Clement say that the original disciples were claiming that Jesus rose from the dead. Since they knew and fellowshipped with Jesus' twelve disciples, they would certainly be in the position to know what the disciples believed.

The above comprise nine ancient sources that attest to the original disciples' claims to have seen Jesus. And with the seven independent sources that attest to their martyrdom, we can conclude that they didn't just merely **claim** that Jesus appeared to them, they really **believed** it.

We saw earlier that the 1 Corinthians 15 creed dates to within five years after the crucifixion! A.N Sherwin White of Oxford University did a study of the rates at which legend develops in the ancient world, and he discovered that two generations weren't even enough time for legend to build up and eliminate a core of historical truth.[12] But we don't have two generations of time here; we don't even have an entire decade! We only have five years!

Theory 9: The Copy Cat Theory

This theory has, in terms of popularity, an extreme contrast between academia and lay circles. While it is extremely popular among internet infidels and atheist bloggers, hardly any historian who studies ancient Palestinian history gives it any merit. This theory was popular among scholars in the 19th century, but was thoroughly discredited and abandoned at the turn of the 20th. It was killed by scholarship but its ghost lives on in the realm of atheistic blogs. What is this theory?

This theory says that the story of Jesus as we find it in The New Testament was essentially plagiarized from various stories of dying and rising gods in pagan religions that predate Christianity. Sometimes the skeptic will say "I'm going to describe someone and I want you to tell me who it is. This man was born on December 25th to a virgin. A star in the east signaled his birth. He had 12 disciples. He walked on water. He was killed, but then rose from the dead 3 days later." And the other person goes "You're obviously talking about Jesus." and the atheist goes "No! I'm not! I'm talking about the tale of Horus who predated Jesus! You see, Christians just took the story of Horus and put a new spin on it! In fact, Horus is not the only example. There are many examples of pagan gods who match the description of Jesus. You, Mr. Christian, don't believe any of these. Why would you put stock in the story of Jesus? Can't you see that the story of Jesus is just the myth that took hold?" Often times in these discussions, the Christians are raddled. They had never heard any of this before and it does a major dent in their faith. Many atheists don't just argue that the story of Jesus' miracles and resurrection were plagiarized from these pagan deities, but they infer that these similarities disprove that Jesus of Nazareth even existed as a historical figure!

Was Jesus just a plagiarized Horus? Given that this theory is so extremely widespread among lay atheists, I will devote a good amount of time to debunking this.

First: You Still Have To Explain The Minimal Facts.
In one sense, this argument is merely a red herring. The Red Herring fallacy occurs when someone brings up an argument that is irrelevant in the debate at hand. The fallacy occurs when someone, either knowingly or unknowingly, tries to throw you off the trail. When you think about it, whether there are stories predating Jesus doesn't really tell us anything as to whether or not Jesus rose from the dead. Jesus' death by crucifixion is multiply, multiply, multiply attested in **NINE INDEPENDENT ACCOUNTS**, 4 of those accounts are secular in nature (i.e Josephus, Tacitus, Mara Bar Serapion, Lucian Of Samosata), 1 of them is Jewish, and 4 of them are from the New Testament (i.e The Gospel Of Mark, The Gospels Of Matthew and Luke, The Gospel Of John, and The Apostle Paul's Epistles). On the basis of the principle of multiple attestation alone, we can have the utmost certainty that a man named Jesus existed, and died on a Roman Cross at the command of Pontius Pilate, the prefect of Judea during the reign of Tiberius Caesar at the request of the Jewish Sanhedrin. It is statistically impossible for 9

independent sources to **all** make up the same lie and then treat it as though it were a historical event. Moreover, we have enemy attestation to the crucifixion of Jesus, as Tacitus and Lucian Of Samosata were mocking Christianity in the very same contexts in which they affirm the historicity of Jesus and his death on the cross. If the story of Jesus' death were a myth, Tacitus and Lucian would have gladly pointed that out. Instead, Lucian said in a nutshell "Those silly Christians. The god they worship is a crucified criminal" and Tacitus said *"Christus, the founder of the name [Christian] suffered the extreme penalty at the hands of one of our procurators, Pontius Pilate during the reign of Tiberius".* They are hostile sources who affirm the historicity of Jesus' existence and Jesus' death by Roman crucifixion. Moreover, there are many details in the gospel accounts about Jesus' death that the disciples or the early church just would not make up, such as Jesus crying out "My God! My God! Why have you forsaken me!" even though in the same book, Jesus repeatedly predicted his death and gave the reason for why he had to die. Not to mention that it looks awkward for God to cry out to himself and seemingly have no faith in him. In John's gospel, women are the only ones who have the guts to stay with Jesus during his final hours while all the men are in hiding because of fear of the religious leaders. Additionally, crucifixion wasn't just an excruciatingly painful way to die, it was a humiliating way to die. Crucifixion victims were sometimes crucified fully nude, and even in cases in which they weren't they were crucified in their undergarments. Imagine how you'd feel if you were strung up in town square wearing nothing but your Fruit Of The Loom briefs. Why would the early church make up a story that demeans their God in such a way? If they were going to make up a fake story about a death of Jesus, why not have him die by stoning? A Much more dignified death. The principle of embarrassment applies to the gospel crucifixion accounts in 3 different ways.

The first minimal fact passes so many of the historian's principles of authenticity that it is futile to try to dispute its historicity.

What about the empty tomb? Again, pointing to parallels between "dying and rising pagan gods" doesn't explain the empty tomb. Like the crucifixion, the empty tomb is established on multiple lines of historical evidence. The principle of embarrassment applies to the empty tomb accounts because women were second class citizens back then whose testimony was so worthless that they weren't even permitted to serve as witnesses in a court of law. Women did sometimes testify, but only when there was not a single male witness at the crime. It's not that women weren't allowed to testify at all, but they were only allowed to testify as a last resort. Given that womens' testimony was so lowly regarded, it's highly unlikely that the disciples or the early church would depict them as being the chief witnesses to the empty tomb, for to do that would be to put words in the mouths of witnesses who would not be believed. If the gospel authors were making up the empty tomb story, they would have made male disciples like Peter or John discover the empty tomb. The fact that it is women rather than men who are the chief witnesses to the empty tomb is best explained by the fact that, like it or not, they were indeed the first witnesses to the empty tomb, and the gospel writers faithfully recorded, what was for them, an awkward and embarrassing fact. The principle of embarrassment gives us good reason to believe the historicity of the empty tomb narratives. Pointing to supposed parallels to Jesus and "dying and rising gods" does nothing to either refute the historicity of the empty tomb, nor explain it. The empty tomb also meets the principle of multiple attestation, for it is recorded by Matthew, Mark, Luke, and John, and it is implied in the 1 Corinthians 15 creed. It is statistically impossible for 5 independent sources to all make up the same lie. Further, regardless of whether or not the disciples were merely plagiarizing pagan deity stories, the Jewish leadership would have gladly gotten Jesus' body out of the tomb, showed it to everyone, and the hoax would have been squashed before it gained any traction. The fact that Christianity is still alive today is a strong indicator that the enemies did not exhume his corpse, and the reason for that is that there was no corpse to be exhumed. The tomb was empty.

Moreover, the historical evidence that Jesus' disciples both claimed to see the risen Jesus and that they really believed it is not refuted or addressed by pointing to similarities between Jesus and pagan gods. In chapter 5, we saw that we can trace the claims of the resurrection to the lips of the original disciples! In Paul's letters, he says that he had access to the original disciples and had fellowshipped with them. In Galatians 2, Paul says that his purpose in meeting the apostles was to make sure that they were preaching the same message. Paul says they were (2:6). In 1 Corinthians 15:11, Paul essentially says it doesn't matter whether you talk to the 12 disciples or him, they preach the same message. Moreover, the creedal tradition (1 Cor 15:3ff) dates to within five years after the death of Jesus This is well within the lifetimes of the twelve disciples who could have corrected this oral tradition if He really hadn't appeared to them. Moreover, the early church fathers Tertullian and Irenaeus attest that the church fathers Polycarp and Clement were students of the apostle John and that they knew several other apostles as well. This is significant because Polycarp and Clement say that the original disciples were claiming that Jesus rose from the dead and appeared to them. Since they knew and fellowshipped with Jesus' twelve disciples, they would certainly be in the position to know what the disciples believed.

With the seven independent sources that attest to their martyrdom, we can conclude that they didn't just merely claim that Jesus appeared to them, they really believed it. They really believed that Jesus rose from the dead and appeared to them.

Then we have the conversion of the two skeptics, Paul and James. If the story of Jesus' resurrection were merely a plagiarized tale, how on Earth did these two skeptics get involved? What caused Paul to go from persecuting Christians, whom he believed were leading Jews away from worship of the one true God, to being a Christian himself? Why is it that James didn't believe His brother was the messiah until sometime after His death? As I argued in the previous chapter, the best explanation is that they had experiences of seeing the risen Jesus.

The major point I am trying to emphasize in rehashing the minimal facts and the historical evidence for them is this: You need to explain the experiences of the disciples, Paul, and James if you're going to adequately explain Christianity. If you don't explain the disciples' experiences, if you don't explain Paul's conversion, and if you don't explain James' conversion, you haven't explained Christianity's origin. The historical evidence establishes that the 5 minimal facts **are indeed** facts. And these facts are neither refuted nor explained by saying "Look! The story of Jesus looks a lot like the story of Adonis!" or "Look! The story of Jesus looks a lot like the story of Horus!" or "Look! Jesus and Mithras are really similar!" I don't care. Explain the empty tomb, explain why the disciples believed they saw Jesus after his death, explain what caused Paul and James to believe they saw Jesus alive after his death, or shut up.

Secondly, Parallels Between Stories Is No Indication Of Non-Historicity

Just because two stories may be a lot alike does not entail that one of them isn't historical. We have some strange examples in history of two very similar stories, but no one doubts their historicity. I'll give you one example.

A long time ago, there was an incredible tragedy that occurred. A huge passenger ship, which people said was unsinkable, on a cold night in the North Atlantic about 200 miles off of Newfoundland, struck an iceberg and sank. Many people died because there weren't enough lifeboats. Now, you believe I'm talking about The Titanic, right? Nope. I'm talking about a ship called Titan, in a novel written in 1898, fourteen years before the wreck of the Titanic, called *The Wreck of the Titan* written by a person named Morgan Robertson.

The parallels between the fiction of The Wreck Of The Titan and the historical event of The Titanic are actually striking! However, I don't know of anyone who would argue that there never really was a ship called The Titanic that sank. If the novel *The Wreck Of The Titan* doesn't disprove the historicity of the accounts of The Titanic, why would similarities between Horus and Jesus or Mithras and Jesus disprove the accounts of Jesus' miracles, death, and resurrection?

As I pointed out in the previous sub-subsection, Jesus' resurrection is well attested. On the other hand, the stories of Horus, Mithras, Attis, etc. have next to no historical evidence in their favor.

Thirdly, Jews Were Committed To An Exclusive Faith

Jews were adamantly committed to their religious beliefs and traditions and refused to blend their religious ideas and traditions with that of others (a view known as syncretism). Mystery religions were inclusive. They would adopt any doctrine or theological concept that they wanted to. They were very loose and didn't have a measure of orthodoxy, but Judaism and Christianity were exclusive. In general, Jewish people adamantly resisted outside religious ideas, most likely due to the fact that they had, by the time of the first century, learned from The Old Testament that God did not tolerate mingling with other nations.

In Antiquity of the Jews, the Jewish historian Josephus talks about an event in which the Romans try to force something on the Jews and how the Jews responded to it.:

"But now Pilate, the procurator of Judea, removed the army from Cesarea to Jerusalem, to take their winter quarters there, in order to abolish the Jewish laws. So he introduced Caesar's effigies, which were upon the ensigns, and brought them into the city; whereas our law forbids us the very making of images; on which account the former procurators were wont to make their entry into the city with such ensigns as had not those ornaments. Pilate was the first who brought those images to Jerusalem, and set them up there; which was done without the knowledge of the people, because it was done in the nighttime; but as soon as they knew it, they came in multitudes to Cesarea, and interceded with Pilate many days, that he would remove the images; and when he would not grant their requests, because it would tend to the injury of Caesar, while yet they persevered in their request, on the sixth day he ordered his soldiers to have their weapons privately, while he came and sat upon his judgment seat, which seat was so prepared in the open place of the city, that it concealed the army that lay ready to oppress them; and when the Jews petitioned him again, he gave a signal to the soldiers to encompass them round, and threatened that their punishment should be no less than immediate death, unless they would leave off disturbing him, and go their ways home. But they threw themselves upon the ground, and laid their necks bare, and said they would take their death very willingly, rather than the wisdom of their laws should be transgressed; upon which Pilate was deeply affected with their firm resolution to keep their laws inviolable, and presently commanded the images to be carried back

from Jerusalem to Cesarea." (Josephus, Works Of Flavius Josephus, 18:55–59)

It is undeniable that Christianity sprung up out of a thoroughly Jewish culture. The idea that a group of devout Jews would see ideas in other religions and then adopt them into their own religious views is incredibly implausible in light of what we know about ancient Jews.

Fourth, The Similarities Between Jesus And The Pagan Deities Are Very Vague

One of the reasons why The Copy Cat Theory lost its standing among scholars is that the more they compared Jesus' story to the stories of these pagan gods, the more they found it implausible that any copying had been done. The similarities that were touted were very vague and stretched. The differences among the accounts were jarring and far outnumbered the vague similarities.

Let's look at just a few examples: One example is that Dionysius is said to have died and risen again like Jesus. But when you examine the stories, you find that Dyonisis wasn't miraculously raised from the dead by his deity Father, but that his mother pieced him back together. Other stories say that Dionysus was killed by Zeus swallowing his heart and his heart was made into a potion given to Semele. Does this sound like Jesus at all? Dionysis was born on December 25th just like Jesus. This proves plagiarism, right? Well, first of all, it isn't strange for multiple people to share the same birthday. I share a birthday with actor Zachary Quinto, but that doesn't mean that if biographies were written about our lives that you could claim one copied the other. Secondly, The Bible never says that Jesus was born on December 25th. That date for Christmas was chosen by The Pope hundreds of years after Jesus was born.[13] Most modern scholars believe Jesus was born in the summer, sometime between June and September.[14]

It is said that Mithras was born of a virgin, just like Jesus. Newsflash: Mithras was born out of a rock. Now, I guess technically one could say that since rocks can't have sex, the rock was a virgin, and therefore you do have a virgin birth. But by that logic, Frosty The Snowman was also born of a virgin since I'm pretty sure that old soot hats don't engage in copulation! This is ridiculous. The birth of Mithras was nothing like the birth of Jesus. Jesus was born of a human woman, not a rock.

What about Horus? During his battle with Set, he lost an eye, but he never died. Since he never died, he couldn't be resurrected. Death is a prerequisite to resurrection.

Osiris was killed by his brother, chopped up into 14 pieces and the pieces were scattered all over Egypt. The goddess Isis retrieved all of these pieces (except for one) and put him back together again. Moreover, Osiris wasn't resurrected but merely given the status as god of the gloomy underworld. Now, does this sound like Jesus' death and resurrection? Sure, you have a guy who is killed, and he's brought back to life in a sense, but Jesus wasn't chopped up into 14 pieces by one of his brothers and had his body parts scattered all over Israel, He was crucified by the Roman government. Moreover, when Jesus rose from the dead, He had all of his parts (unlike Osiris). The only thing Jesus and Osiris have in common is that they both died and came back to life, but the skeptics aren't taking the various differences between these two into account.

These are just a few of the not-so-similarities between Jesus and pagan gods.

As Bart Ehrman, agnostic professor of Religious Studies at UNC, has said:

"The alleged parallels between Jesus and the "pagan" savior-gods in most instances reside in the modern imagination: We do not have accounts of others who were born to virgin mothers and who died as an atonement for sin and then were raised from the dead (despite what the sensationalists claim ad nauseum in their propagandized versions)."[15]

Finally, There Are No Story's Of Dying And Rising Pagan Gods Until AFTER The First Century

If all of this weren't enough to discredit The CopyCat theory, consider the fact that most of the alleged parallels don't emerge until well after the establishment of the Christian church! Therefore, if any borrowing were done, it would be in the opposite direction! The pagan religions would have copied from Christianity!

The earliest cases of resurrection myths came after Jesus. For example, the story of Adonis dates to the 2nd Century A.D and the story of Attis dates to the 3rd century A.D. So, even if you could make a case for plagiarism, the plagiarism would be on the part of the pagan authors, not the New Testament writers![16]

Much more could be said on why The Copy Cat Theory is a failure to refute the historicity of Jesus' resurrection, but I think enough has been said to show that The Copy Cat Theory is complete rubbish. First, even if all of the claims of mythicists were true, that would do nothing to refute the historical arguments **for** 5 minimal facts (i.e Jesus died, tomb was empty, disciples, Paul, and James thought they saw him afterwards). Simply noting parallels does nothing to account for the empty tomb and the postmortem appearances of Jesus. Secondly, if you're going to say that similarities in stories is a hallmark of non-historicity, you would have to conclude that there was never a ship named the Titanic. Thirdly, it's highly improbable that first century Israelite Jews would have incorporated any elements from outside religions, given how exclusive they were. Fourthly, the similarities that are present are vague and strained. The differences far outbalance the similarities. Finally, most of the cases in question come after the rise of Christianity. You can't copy from sources that didn't exist yet.

Theory 10: The Twin Theory

This theory says that Jesus had an unknown identical twin brother who saw Jesus hanging on the cross one day and decided to prank the disciples by stealing the body, hiding it somewhere, and then appearing before the disciples telling them that He was the risen Lord.

This theory is silly. Aside from the blatant ad-hoc nature of this hypothesis, it has several problems.

For one thing, are we expected to believe that no one was smart enough to figure out that this person was not Jesus? The twin would not have known the disciples very well. As a result of that, he would not have been able to copy Jesus' mannerisms and personality. The disciples would very likely have gotten suspicious. "Jesus, you okay? You're not acting like yourself". Moreover, the twin would not have been able to walk through walls, nor could the twin have been able to ascend to Heaven.

Theory 11: The Alien Theory

I've saved the silliest theory for last. I'm addressing this theory, not because I take it seriously, but as a sci-fi fan, I love aliens and besides, I want to cover **all** the bases. I want to refute **every** naturalistic theory there is, even the silly ones hardly anyone posits. This theory says that Jesus was an alien from outer space, and that as a member of his species, he had special powers that, while natural to him, seemed like miracles to everyone around him. He fooled a lot of people into thinking that He was the messiah that their holy book promised would come, but his prank got him into hot water with the religious leaders, leading to his execution. While in the tomb, Jesus used his special alien powers to heal himself and walk out of the tomb, appear before the disciples and wow them for a while before Jesus "ascended" (i.e was beamed up into an invisible spaceship that took him back to His home planet).

As a Whovian, I like to put my own spin on this theory and say that Jesus was a Time Lord from the planet Gallifrey. I call this the "Time Lord Jesus" view. Gallifreyans look exactly like humans on the outside, so Jesus could spend 3 years here without anyone knowing his true origins. He pranked the people into thinking He was their promised Messiah, but then was unfortunately crucified because he didn't know when to back off. If you watch Doctor Who, you know Time Lords have the ability to "regenerate" when they're on the brink of death. Maybe, while in the tomb, Time Lord Jesus regenerated. Then he got up and walked out of his tomb. This would explain not only his empty tomb and postmortem appearances, but it would also explain why Mary Magdalene didn't recognize Him at first nor did the disciples on the road to Emmaus. Tom Baker looks a lot different than John Pertwee, after all.

Was Jesus a Time Lord from Gallifrey? Did He not resurrect but regenerate? This theory is plagued with issues. There's a reason why hardly anyone holds it.

1: The amount of time spent by the Jesus alien convincing people that he was their Messiah is absurd.

What alien would spend three years just to pull a prank on some unsuspecting Earthlings? Three years? This is like the longest episode of Punk'd ever! Are we seriously expected to believe that this Jesus Alien would waste three years of his life fooling these Earthlings into thinking that He was their promised Messiah? Why not just put some whoopee cushions under peoples' seats, or put some fake snakes in peoples' cabinets? Why such a long-lasting prank? I know of no prankster who is that dedicated to his hoaxes. Even if you have a long lifespan of thousands of years, I would think you'd still get bored. There's simply too much time and effort put into Jesus' 3 year ministry for me to believe that He was some extraterrestrial playing a practical joke. At what point does trolling the pharisees, wowing crowds with miracles, and giving long sermons get boring and you want to "phone home"?

2: Liars Make Poor Martyrs, No Matter What Planet You're From

Again, we have to ask "Why would anyone die for a known lie?" People will die for a lie only if they **think** it is true. No one will die for a lie that they **know** is false. Jesus' crucifixion is the best attested fact of history. Why would Jesus willingly die a horrible, slow, torturous death unless He really believed that He was God incarnate and Israel's Messiah? Jesus could have easily have cleared up the whole misunderstanding at his trial when Caiaphas asked "Are you the messiah? The son of the living God?" It would be obvious to anyone in Jesus' shoes that he was in big trouble. If Jesus were a prankster, he would have denied the whole thing and tried to escape. According to the gospel records, he had many chances to avert his death. He could have fled under the blanket of night instead of praying in the Garden of Gethsemane. By the way, we have good reason to believe that Jesus actually did pray in the Garden of Gethsemane prior to His crucifixion on the basis of the principle of embarrassment. Jesus didn't face His death boldly and courageously at first. He appeared to be asking The Father not to allow it if it be possible. That's not something the early church would make up. Given that Jesus willingly went to crucifixion for his divine and messianic claims, it is untenable to say that he was an extraterrestrial prankster. Jesus really believed His claims about Himself.

3: All This Theory Gets You Is A Dead Alien

Recall from earlier in this chapter, the medical evidence we examined for crucifixion. It was impossible for anyone to survive the rigors of scourging and crucifixion, and the Romans had good indicators to tell when someone had actually died on the cross (e.g they weren't pushing up anymore to breathe). All this theory gets you is a dead alien. Jesus would have actually had to have been alive after he was taken off the cross to heal himself. A Time Lord can only regenerate if there's still some life left in him.

What About A Combination Of Naturalistic Theories?

Some skeptics have argued "Okay, so none of these theories can explain the 5 minimal facts **on their own**, but maybe the right explanation is more complex than that. Maybe more than one naturalistic theory needs to be invoked to account for the data." For example, the skeptic might try to explain all 5 minimal facts by saying that perhaps the postmortem appearances to the disciples were hallucinations, and the appearance to Paul was a result of conversion disorder. This would account for Jesus' appearances. However, the reason the tomb was empty was that someone other than the disciples stole the body and hid it somewhere. Seeing Jesus' tomb empty and then seeing hallucinations of Him later together convinced them that He had risen from the dead. We could call this Fraud B-Hallucination-conversion-disorder Theory.

There are a number of issues with trying to combine naturalistic theories. First, appealing to multiple scenarios this way smacks of the ad-hoc fallacy. In other words, it appears as though the skeptic is just grabbing at anything he can to avoid concluding that Jesus was raised from the dead. The ad-hoc fallacy occurs when one makes up explanations simply to keep his own view from being falsified even though he has no evidence whatsoever that these explanations are actually true. Now, of course, if one could produce good evidence that someone had stolen Jesus' body, that Jesus' disciples could have group hallucinations, and that Paul really suffered conversion disorder, then the ad-hoc nature of the combination theory would disappear. However, no such evidence exists.

Secondly, some of the problems that plague the theories when considered by themselves remain even when they're combined with other naturalistic theories. For example, Paul is still a highly unlikely candidate for conversion disorder, group hallucinations are statistically impossible, and there's still no reason to believe that any Joe Schmoe would have any motivation at all to steal Jesus' corpse. So even this combination of theories proves to be untenable.

The point is this: combining 3 bad theories does not add up to 1 good theory. Instead, when you combine bad theories, you just end up with an even worse one. A bad theory + a bad theory + a bad theory = a **really** bad theory!

The Best Explanation: He Is Risen!

In his book "Justifying Historical Descriptions", CB McCullagh[18] puts forth several criteria which historians use for assessing historical theories. These criteria are (1) explanatory scope, (2) explanatory power, (3) plausibility, (4) not being ad hoc/contrived, (5) being in agreement with established beliefs, and (6) outstripping its' rival theories. The "He Is Risen" hypothesis passes every single one of these tests with flying colors. The same cannot be said about the various naturalistic theories we looked at.

Explanatory Scope: It explains why the body of Jesus was not in His tomb, why hundreds of people on different occasions believed they saw Jesus alive after His crucifixion, and it also explains the conversion of the church persecutor Saul Of Tarsus (i.e Paul). It also explains the conversion of the skeptic James. It explains every single piece of data that requires an explanation. The **best** of the naturalistic theories explain only **one** minimal fact **at most**. But the majority don't even explain that many.

Explanatory Power: It explains why the tomb of Jesus was vacant, why folks kept seeing Jesus alive on numerous occasions, in spite of the fact that He was killed days before on a Roman cross.

Plausibility: Given the background of Jesus' life and claims, the resurrection is an authentication of those claims.

Ad Hoc: You know a theory is ad hoc if it requires the making of quite a few other theories to save itself from being proven to be erroneous. The resurrection hypothesis is not that kind of explanation. It only requires the subsequent declaration to be true: it is possible that God exists.

In accord with accepted beliefs: I can hear the voice of the skeptic now screaming "People who die stay dead, stupid! Science has proven that dead people don't come back to life!" This is not a valid objection. The hypothesis isn't that Jesus rose from the dead by natural causes, but that God raised Jesus from the dead via a miracle. This does not conflict with the conventional belief that people cannot and do not rise from the dead, naturally.

Outstripping Rival Theories: We've seen that none of the naturalistic theories can adequately explain all of the data. Only the resurrection hypothesis succeeds in criteria 1-4 above, and should, therefore, be preferred.

The best explanation of the five minimal facts is that "He Is Risen"! There are no naturalistic theories that can explain the 5 minimal facts. The only theory that **can** explain all of them is a **super**naturalistic theory.

Using abductive reasoning, we took our two "E Lists" and arrived at the conclusion that Jesus rose from the dead. Our first E List (our Evidence List) listed the facts to be explained (e.g Jesus died by crucifixion, Jesus' tomb was empty, Jesus' disciples believed they saw Him alive afterwards, etc.). Our second E List (our Explanation List) listed all of the possible explanations that could account for what was on the first E List. We kept crossing out explanations until only one remained: Jesus rose from the dead. Of the 13 explanations, we ruled out 12 of them. Only the last one can adequately account for all of the evidence.

Notes

1: See Gary Habermas. "The Resurrection Of Jesus Workbook", Credo Courses, page 60.

2: To see some of the sources reporting these, check out the footnotes in chapter 5.

3: Charles Colson, "An Unholy Hoax? The Authenticity of Christ," BreakPoint syndicated column 020329, (29 March 2002).

4: See Dr. Alexander Methrell's interview with Lee Strobel in "The Case For Christ", chapter 11, page 195, published by Zondervan

5: Lumpkin R: The physical suffering of Christ. J Med. Assoc Ala 1978,47:8-10,47.

6: No, I'm not a trained medical professional. I'm getting all of this information from sources who are qualified to speak on this matter; Medical Doctor Alexander Methrell, from his interview with Lee Strobel in The Case For Christ, the 1986 edition of The Journal Of American Medical Assosiation, the documentary "Crucifixion" which I saw on The History Channel a few Good Fridays ago. While I'm not an expert in this field, I'm drawing on the expertise of those who are, so don't try to argue with me ad hominem.

7: Strauss, David. The Life of Jesus for the People. Volume One, Second Edition. London: Williams and Norgate. 1879. 412.

8: Habermas, Gary. "The Late Twentieth-Century Resurgence of Naturalistic Responses to Jesus' Resurrection." Trinity Journal 22NS (2001) 190.

9: Strobel, Lee. 1997. God's Outrageous Claims: Discover What They Mean for You. p. 215, Zondervan

10: The Jews of the first century got their prophecies mixed up. Jesus will indeed get rid of all the evil in the world, He will overthrow Israel's oppressors, but He'll do this in His second coming. In His first coming, He was to be an atoning sacrifice for our sins (1 John 2:2 cf. Isaiah 53).

11: Habermas, Gary R.; Licona, Michael R.. The Case for the Resurrection of Jesus (p. 113). Kregel Publications. Kindle Edition.

12: A. N. Sherwin-White, Roman Society and Roman Law in the New Testament (Oxford: Clarendon Press, 1963), pp. 188-91.

13: https://www.whychristmas.com/customs/25th.shtml

14: To see my sources to back up what I'm saying, check out the following sources. My sources for this information:
https://www.apologeticspress.org/apcontent.aspx?category=10&article=186 , and https://www.reasonablefaith.org/writings/question-answer/jesus-and-pagan-mythology/ , and http://i.stack.imgur.com/29UE7.jpg , and "The Case For The Resurrection Of Jesus" by Gary Habermas and Michael Licona, pages 90-91, Kregle. "Zeitgeist Debunked: Jesus Is Not A Copy Of Pagan Gods", by Stephen Bancarz, May 26th 2017,
http://reasonsforjesus.com/zeitgeist-debunked-jesus-is-not-a-copy-of-pagan-gods/

15: Bart Ehrman, "Did Jesus Exist?" May 20th, 2012, The Huffington Post,
https://www.huffingtonpost.com/bart-d-ehrman/did-jesus-exist_b_1349544.html

16: Bruce Metzger, Historical and Literary, pp. 11 20-22, cf. Edwin Yamauchi, "Easter: Myth, Hallucination, Or History", Christianity Today, vol. XVIII, no. 12, March 15 1974, pp. 4-7 and vol. XVIII no. 13, March 29th, 1974, pp 12-16

17: C. Behan McCullagh, Justifying Historical Descriptions (Cambridge: Cambridge University Press, 1984), p. 19.

Chapter 8

Jedi Jesus?

In the previous chapter, we looked at a dozen naturalistic theories that non-Christian scholars developed to try to account for the minimal facts, and we found that every single one of them had numerous holes in them. The only explanation that could adequately account for all of the minimal facts is the explanation that Jesus was miraculously raised to life.

However, even if one concedes that Jesus was resurrected, does it have to be a physical resurrection? Maybe Jesus was "resurrected" in the sense that his spirit left his body, appeared to the disciples, Paul, and James for a little while and then departed to the Kingdom of God.

This theory was introduced by Karl Theodor Keim, a German professor who wrote, *Jesus of Nazareth and the National Life of Israel* (1867-1872). Keim provided refutation to David Strauss' Hallucination Theory and then went on to claim that Jesus was raised from the dead all right, but he wasn't raised in a physical, bodily manner.

Dr. Gary Habermas whimsically refers to this theory as "The Jedi Jesus" theory. Why? Well, in the original *Star Wars* trilogy, Obi Wan Kenobi is struck down by the movie's antagonist, Darth Vader. Later on, the ghost of Obi Wan appears to Luke Skywalker to mentor and comfort him. Obi Wan's body was destroyed. He didn't rise from the dead and appear before Luke. Rather, it was his spirit that appeared to him. At the end of the first *Star Wars* trilogy, after the rebellion had defeated The Empire, everyone was celebrating. Luke again sees Obi Wan Kenobi's spirit along with the spirits of Yoda and Anakin Skywalker, who had "a deathbed conversion" so to speak, before he passed away as Darth Vader.

Could Jesus' post mortem appearances have been something like this? Could Jesus have appeared to the disciples like Obi Wan appeared to Luke Skywalker?

Notice that this is an alternative **super**naturalistic theory, not a naturalistic theory. Karl Keim would agree that Jesus actually "rose from the dead". Jesus was actually there in front of His disciples. These weren't hallucinations, a previously swooned Jesus, or anything like that. Keim would say Jesus was really there, just not in a physical body.

If Keim is right, then while we do have evidence for a supernatural event, the exclusivity of Jesus is undermined. After all, the ancient world (as well as the modern, by the way) is littered with ghost stories and tellings of loved ones appearing after their death to say goodbye before departing to the afterlife. As a Christian theist, I'm inclined to believe some of these accounts may very well be true. Some of them may be false. Some of them may be due to "a bout of indigestion". But in any case, if Keim is right, Jesus' resurrection just becomes another ghost story, albeit a very well attested one. Only if Jesus was raised **bodily**, can we say that God truly vindicated His claim to deity, and ergo the rest of His teachings as well.

What is the evidence against Keim's theory?

The Gospels Depict A Physically Raised Jesus

All 4 gospel accounts depict a physically raised Jesus. In Luke's account (24:39-43), we're told that Jesus told his disciples that he wasn't "a bodiless demon" and to prove it to them, he took some fish and chowed down on it right in front of them. Ghosts can't eat fish. Jesus ate fish again with His disciples later, on a beach. This is recorded in John's gospel (John 21). Luke and John are independent sources, and both attest that the Jesus that appeared to the twelve disciples was a physical Jesus, capable of eating.

The Word "Resurrection" Always Means A Physical Resurrection In The Ancient Literature

World renowned New Testament scholar N.T Wright wrote a 800-something page book called *The Resurrection Of The Son Of God* (2003), and in the first half of the book, he spends an enormous amount of time surveying ancient pagan, Jewish, and Christian literature from a variety of geographical locations. He concludes that in the ancient world, Pagans, Jews, and Christians alike understood the Greek word "anastasis" (resurrection) to mean bodily resurrection. Space obviously does not permit me to delve into all of those sources here, but you can check out Tom Wright's book for yourself if you want to fact check me.

The Apostle Paul Taught A Physical Resurrection

Those who try to advocate for the non-physical resurrection view typically ignore the blatant descriptions of Jesus eating fish in the gospel accounts and dismiss them as evolved theology. In other words, the resurrection doctrine started out as non-physical, and then it turned into a doctrine of a physical resurrection later on. Okay, for one thing, I think scholars like Craig Blomberg make a compelling case that the 4 gospels and Acts were written between 50 A.D and 62 A.D, and literally all scholars agree that Paul penned his epistles in the 50s, so there's very little time for that sort of embellishment to occur. But given that the dating of the gospels is not a part of the minimal facts approach, I'll merely leave this as an informational footnote.

The physicality is still multiply attested, being recorded in both Luke's account and John's account. The physicality of the resurrected Jesus in both accounts involve very different incidents (though both involve fish), so one cannot say that John was borrowing from Luke. They are independently reporting a physical Jesus.

But let's leave the gospels to the side. If the apostle Paul taught a physical resurrection, then there's no way this kind of embellishment explanation is going to fly. Let's examine Paul's writings to see whether he had a physical or non-physical resurrection in mind.

Paul Says Jesus "Was Buried" and "Was Raised"

In the pre-Pauline creed that Paul cites in 1 Corinthians 15, we have a strong indication of a physical resurrection. "...*Christ died for our sins according to the scriptures, and that he was buried, and that he was raised on the third day according to the scriptures*". Whoa! Stop right there! Christ "was buried" and "was raised"? If Paul had a ghostly non-physical resurrection in mind, and if those whom he got this creed from had that in mind, what is the importance of mentioning the burial? Creeds had to be short in order to contribute to easy memorization, so the odds that they put Jesus' burial in there, if the burial were an unimportant detail are not good. It had to have been important.

Jesus "died", "was buried", "was raised". The creed contra-juxtaposes Jesus' burial with His resurrection. This contra-juxtaposition implies that the thing that went down in burial came up in resurrection. The body of Jesus was buried, but then it got up and walked out of the tomb. Died → Buried → Raised. I think this heavily implies that a physical resurrection was in view.

Paul Says Jesus' Resurrection Is A Model Preceding Our Own

Paul taught that when God raises us from the dead, we will be raised in the same way that Jesus was raised. If our resurrection will be bodily, then that means Paul saw Jesus' resurrection as bodily as well. In Romans 8:11, Paul says *"And if the Spirit of him who raised Jesus from the dead is living in you, he who raised Christ from the dead will also give life to your **mortal bodies** because of his Spirit who lives in you."* (emphasis mine). Paul explicitly says that the same Spirit who raised Jesus from the dead will likewise give life to our mortal bodies. He specifically uses the word "bodies". Now, lest you think this is a mistranslation or a quirk of English, let's look at the original Greek. The word translated as "bodies" in this verse is *Soma*. According to Thayer's Greek Lexicon, *"σῶμα, σώματος, τό (apparently from σῶς 'entire' (but cf. Curtius, § 570; others from the root, ska, sko, 'to cover', cf. Vanicek, p. 1055; Curtius, p. 696)), the Sept. for בָּשָׂר, גְּוִיָּה, etc.; נְבֵלָה (a corpse), also for Chaldean שֶׁגֶּם; a body; and: 1. the body both of men and of animals (on the distinction between it and σάρξ see σάρξ, especially 2 at the beginning; (cf. Dickson, St. Paul's use of 'Flesh' and 'Spirit', p. 247ff));"* [1] Elsewhere in The New Testament where this word is used, it undoubtedly refers to a physical body. For example, in Matthew 26, we read that Martha's sister Mary was anointing Jesus with perfume. In verse 12, Jesus says *"When she poured this perfume on my body* [soma]*, she did it to prepare me for burial."* The Greek there is "ἐπὶ τοῦ σώματός μου πρὸς" The author clearly doesn't intend for us to think Mary was pouring perfume on a ghost!

The same Spirit who raised Jesus from the dead will give life to our mortal bodies/soma. Paul clearly envisions our resurrection as bodily. That means he saw Jesus' resurrection as bodily as well.

Paul writes that when Christ returns, he *"will transform our lowly **bodies** so that they will be like his glorious **body"** (Philippians 3:21). Again, the Greek word Paul uses is "soma" and everywhere in the New Testament (not to mention other Greek works) where soma is used, it refers to a physical body. The apostle could easily have said we would be like Jesus' glorious **spirit** (Greek → Neuma). But instead, he used the word **body (soma)**.

The Empty Tomb Must Still Be Explained

Any theory, naturalistic or supernaturalistic, must explain **all** of the facts. If they fail to explain any of the minimal facts, they must be rejected on the basis of inadequate explanatory scope. The "Jedi Jesus" theory can't account for the empty tomb. The empty tomb is multiply attested in Matthew, Mark, Luke, and John. The principle of embarrassment establishes it as a fact because they wouldn't have wanted to make women the chief witnesses to the tomb given that their testimony was generally deemed worthless, and the enemies of Christianity tried to explain the empty tomb away by saying that the disciples stole the body. The empty tomb is a historical fact that must be explained. A bodily resurrection can account not only for Jesus' appearances but His empty tomb as well. Therefore, the bodily resurrection theory should be preferred over the non-bodily resurrection theory.

But What About Texts Used To Deny A Bodily Resurrection?

Some have suggested that a few biblical passages describe the appearances of the risen Jesus in a non-bodily manner. Let's take a gander at a few of these passages.

"Galatians 1:16 seems to say Paul's experience was not physical."

Paul writes that God was pleased *"to reveal His Son in me."* Wait a minute! Hold the phone! "**In** me"? "Revealed his son **in** me?" Some have used the language that Paul employs here to argue that Paul considered Jesus' appearance to Him as something of an inward experience rather than an objective reality.

This is not the best explanation of this verse, since Paul elsewhere strongly teaches bodily resurrection (see Romans 8:11, Philippians 3:21, 1 Corinthians 15:3), and N.T Wright's lengthy word study in *The Resurrection Of The Son Of God* (2003) showed that no matter where you look in the ancient literature, be it Jewish sources, pagan sources, or Christian sources, everyone unanimously agreed that when you say a dead man was resurrected (anastasis) from the dead, you meant his spirit came back to his corpse and as a result, his corpse was re-animated. Most scholars seem to think that what Paul is talking about here is how he learned about Christ and grew spiritually during the 3 years after his Road-To-Damascus experience.

"First Peter 3:18 says Jesus' spirit was made alive, not his body."

Peter writes that Jesus died for our sins, *"having been put to death in the flesh, but made alive in the spirit."* Some hold that Peter is saying that Jesus' spirit was made alive, not his body.

Dr. Norman Geisler explains why this verse doesn't support the spiritual resurrection view in his book *When Critics Ask: A Popular Handbook On Bible Difficulties* which he co-wrote with Thomas Howe. He writes *"First of all, the passage can be translated, 'He was put to death in the body but made alive by the [Holy] Spirit' (niv). The passage is translated with this same understanding by the nkjv and others.*

Second, the parallel between death and being made alive normally refer to the resurrection of the body in the NT. For example, Paul declared that 'Christ died and rose and lived again' (Rom. 14:9), and 'He was crucified in weakness, yet he lives by the power of God' (2 Cor. 13:4).

Third, the context refers to the event as 'the resurrection of Jesus Christ' (3:21). But this is everywhere understood as a bodily resurrection in the NT (cf. Acts 4:33; Rom 1:4; 1 Cor. 15:21; 1 Peter 1:3; Rev. 20:5).

Fourth, even if 'spirit' refers to Jesus' human spirit (not to the Holy Spirit), it cannot mean He had no resurrection body. Otherwise, the reference to His 'body' (flesh) before the resurrection would mean He had no human spirit then. It seems better to take "flesh" in this context as a reference to His whole condition of humiliation before the resurrection and "spirit" to refer to His unlimited power and imperishable life after the resurrection." [2]

"First Corinthians 15:37–50 contrasts the natural physical body with the spiritual"

Paul declares that the resurrection body is a "spiritual body" (1 Corinthians 15:44), but a spiritual body is an immaterial body, right?

First, remember that this is the very same chapter in which Paul hinted at bodily resurrection in verse 3, where he says Christ "died", "was buried", and "was raised". Paul puts Jesus' resurrection in contra-juxtaposition with his burial, implying that the resurrection that occurred was physical. Also, Paul explicitly taught bodily resurrection in Romans 8:11 and Philippians 3:21. Given these facts, we must infer that what Paul means by "natural body" and "spiritual body", he probably doesn't mean a contrast between a physical and ghostly body. Since the resurrection was the centerpiece of Paul's theology (in fact, in 15:4, he says if it didn't happen, our faith is futile), and given that he strongly taught bodily resurrection elsewhere, we must look for another explanation than "Paul is teaching a spiritual resurrection here". What, exactly, is Paul saying here?

To really get a feel of what Paul is talking about, we need to get down into the original Greek words employed in this passage. Those words are *psychikos* and *pneumatikos*. The former is what's translated as "natural" and the latter is what's translated as "spiritual". *"it is sown a natural [psychikos] body, it is raised a spiritual [pneumatikos] body"* (1 Corinthians 15:44). Whatchu talkin' bout, Paul? In order to answer this, let's first look at something he said earlier in the exact same epistle. In 1 Corinthians 2:14–15, Paul wrote, *"But a natural [psychikos] man does not accept the things of the Spirit of God, for they are foolishness to him; and he cannot understand them, because they are spiritually appraised. But he who is spiritual [pneumatikos] appraises all things, yet he himself is appraised by no one."* In this verse, the apostle contra-juxtaposes the natural man and the spiritual man. By "natural man", Paul means the unsaved person who follows his sinful desires and is in rebellion against God. By "spiritual" Paul means, well....the opposite of that. Someone whose life and conduct is guided by The Holy Spirit.

Now these same two words (natural/psychikos and spiritual/pneumatikos) are the words Paul uses in 15:44. So what does Paul mean here? We die in a state of sinfulness. We die in the state of being predisposed to wrongdoing because of our "sinful nature". But, when we're resurrected, we won't have a sin nature anymore. Right now, we're oriented towards "the flesh" (i.e the sin nature). At the resurrection, we'll be oriented towards The Holy Spirit.

Now, If Paul wanted to convey a comparison between a meaty body and a ghostly body, he had a much better Greek word at his disposal; Sarkikos. In 9:11 Paul writes, *"If we sowed spiritual [pneumatikos] things in you, is it too much if we reap material [sarkikos] things from you?"* Sarkikos means fleshly, material, physical. It's derivative of the Greek word "sarx" which literally means "flesh", skin.

"Paul Says That Flesh And Blood Cannot Inherit The Kingdom Of God"

Another popular proof-text that supporters of The Jedi Jesus view use is 1 Corinthians 15:50, *"I declare to you, brothers and sisters, that flesh and blood cannot inherit the kingdom of God, nor does the perishable inherit the imperishable."* He then goes on in the proceeding verses to talk about the resurrection of believers. If the context indicates that Paul is talking about the resurrection of believers, and Paul explicitly says that flesh and blood cannot inherit the Kingdom Of God (i.e Heaven), doesn't that mean that Paul had a non-physical resurrection in mind? How can the resurrection be physical if flesh and blood cannot inherit the Kingdom?

First of all, we need to remember that elsewhere Paul explicitly taught bodily resurrection (see 1 Corinthians 15:3, Romans 8:11, Philippians 3:21), and the survey of ancient literature done by N.T Wright shows that virtually everyone in the ancient world understood the term anastasis (resurrection) to be referring to a bodily resurrection. They had stories of ghosts appearing to people, but they never used the word anastasis to describe those events. All of this makes a non-physical resurrection interpretation of 1 Corinthians 15:50 suspect. We should always interpret the unclear verses in scripture in light of the clear verses.

So, if Paul isn't saying that physical beings can't inherit the Kingdom, what is he saying? First of all, notice that the very next thing Paul says is *"nor does the perishable inherit the imperishable"*. This suggests that Paul is saying, not that the resurrection body won't have flesh, but that it won't have **corruptible** flesh. Moreover, a look at other places in which the phrase is used suggests that it was a figure of speech to denote mortality. The phrase "flesh and blood" is used 5 times in

The New Testament and twice in the Old Testament apocrypha.[3] It was *"a common Jewish expression referring to man as a mortal being"*[4] So, to say that a man was "flesh and blood" was simply to say that he was mortal. It would be like today if we said a man is a "red blooded American". No one would think we were contrasting him with someone who had green blood or blue blood. Likewise, the original recipients of Paul's letter would not have interpreted Paul as contrasting a body of "flesh and blood" with an immaterial body lacking flesh and blood.

Conclusion

We have seen that the non-physical resurrection interpretation is untenable. Given that no naturalistic explanation can explain the 5 minimal facts and given that this supernatural explanation fails, the only remaining explanation is that Jesus was miraculously and physically raised from the dead.

Are you convinced yet? If not. Why not? Maybe you still have some lingering questions about this topic that have yet to be answered. I shall address those in the next chapter.

Notes

1: See → https://biblehub.com/greek/4983.htm

2: This excerpt is from *When Critics Ask: A Popular Handbook on Bible Difficulties* (Wheaton, Ill.: Victor Books, 1992). © 2014 Norman Geisler and Thomas Howe.

3: The expression occurs in the New Testament in Matthew 16:17; 1 Corinthians 15:50; Galatians 1:16; Ephesians 6:12; and Hebrews 2:14. Its use in the LXX Apocrypha text of Ecclesiasticus is interesting: *"As the green leaf on a thick tree, some fall, and some grow: so is the generation of flesh and blood, one cometh to an end, and another is born"* (Ecclus. 14:18); *"What is brighter than the sun? Yet the light thereof faileth: and flesh and blood will imagine evil (17:31)."* Ecclesiasticus quotations are from Lancelot C. L. Brenton, translator, The Septuagint with Apocrypha: Greek and English (London: Samuel Bagster and Sons, 1851)

4: See comments on Matthew 16:17 in Carson, Matthew.

Chapter 9

Some Unanswered Questions

In chapters 3, 4, 5, and 6 of this book, we've seen powerful historical evidence that (1) Jesus died by Roman crucifixion, that (2) His tomb was found empty the following Sunday morning, that (3) the twelve disciples believed they saw Jesus alive after His death, that (4) a church persecutor named Paul converted to Christianity on the basis of what he perceived to be an appearance of the risen Jesus, and (5) a skeptic named James converted to Christianity on the basis of what he perceived to be appearance of the risen Jesus.

In chapter 7, we looked at various ways that skeptics have tried to account for the minimal facts and we saw that they all fail. No naturalistic theory can account for all 5 of the minimal facts. In the previous chapter, we looked at one supernatural theory and saw that it was also untenable. The only theory that **can** account for the facts is that God physically raised Jesus from the dead. The hypothesis that God The Father miraculously raised Jesus to life explains **all** of the data perfectly. The resurrection explains every piece of data that is in need of explanation, but even the best of the naturalistic theories could explain **one** of the five facts **at most**. The majority didn't even explain that many. The "He Is Risen" hypothesis has exhaustive explanatory scope and power and ergo outshines any other proposed explanation.

So Why Do People Still Deny It?

In fact, In a lecture titled "Evidence For The Minimal Facts" given on October 14th, 2017 at The National Conference On Christian Apologetics in Charlotte, North

Carolina,[1] Dr. Gary Habermas said that in scholarship today, the vast majority of non-Christian historians affirm the 5 minimal facts as true, and they will also admit that they can come up with no naturalistic explanation to account for them. Their attitude can basically be summed up in this sentence: "We admit these 5 facts are true, and we admit that we cannot come up with a good alternative to explain them, but we will not conclude that Jesus rose from the dead."

Why is that? If you have an empty tomb, and various people claimed and believed that they saw Jesus alive after his death, and every single naturalistic theory that can be posed is an abject failure, why would you not conclude that the best explanation is that Jesus rose from the dead? I mean, it has the ability to explain all of the data, it meets C.B McCullagh's 6 tests for being a good historical theory[2], why would you just dig in your heels and say "I don't know how to account for this data, but I know that Jesus didn't rise from the dead"?

For Some, It Could Be A Heart Issue, Not A Head Issue

I don't think there's a one size fits all answer. I think the reason why skeptical scholars today reject the historicity of Jesus' resurrection differs from individual to individual. For some, it could be what I said in the introduction of this book; namely that this is not merely a matter of whether the evidence is sufficient, this is a moral and/or emotional issue for them. As I said in the introduction, if Jesus rose from the dead, the entire Christian worldview is vindicated. For some non-Christians (scholars and laypeople alike), they just don't **want** Christianity to be true. If Christianity is true, then they know that they'll either have to change the way they're living so they can have a nice afterlife or else face God's judgment for living in rebellion against Him. Atheism is a crutch for these people; if they can make themselves believe there's no God, then they can live however they want and not have to worry. If there's no God, there's no soul. If there's no soul, there's no afterlife. If there's no afterlife, there's no Hell. If there's no Hell, then they can sin, sin, sin away and have a perfectly clear conscience about it. It may also be that they had family or friends die who weren't Christians, and they know that if Christianity is true, those people are in Hell now, so it's more comforting for these people to just continue believing it isn't true.[3]

Read this candid statement from a famous atheist, for example:

"[A fear of religion] has large and often pernicious consequences for modern intellectual life. [...] I speak from experience, being strongly subject to this fear myself: I want atheism to be true and am made uneasy by the fact... that some of the most intelligent and well-informed people I know are religious believers. It isn't

just that I don't believe in God and, naturally, hope that I'm right in my belief. It's that I hope there is no God! I don't want there to be a God; I don't want the universe to be like that." - Thomas Nagel [4]

Of course, this applies to atheists and agnostics. For other non-Christians, like Muslims or Mormons, their non-intellectual aversion is slightly different. Ask any Christian who has been converted out of Islam and he or she will tell you that it's hard. Your family turns their back on you, perhaps they'll try to murder you in an honor killing, your friends will leave you, every loved one you had who was also a Muslim will shun you and maybe even try to kill you.

Let me just quickly say something to those of you who may fall into the above category; having a relationship with Jesus Christ is worth more than anything you could ever have in this world. The apostle Paul, who, as we saw earlier, endured severe hardships for being a Christian, wrote; *"But whatever were gains to me I now consider loss for the sake of Christ. What is more, I consider everything a loss because of the surpassing worth of knowing Christ Jesus my Lord, for whose sake I have lost all things. I consider them garbage, that I may gain Christ."* (Philippians 3:7-8). According to Paul, having a relationship with Jesus Christ is worth so much, that everything else is **garbage** by comparison! The late Nabeel Qureshi, whose had some people turn their back on him when he converted to Christianity wrote; *"All suffering is worth it to follow Jesus. He is that amazing."* [5]

Speaking as a Christian myself, I wholeheartedly agree with Paul's and Nabeel's statements. My relationship with God means more to me than anything this world has to offer. Yahweh is the best thing that has ever happened to me, and the happiest part of my day is when I spend time talking to Him in prayer. For my Muslim readers, I probably don't even need to tell you about the things you could lose if you became a follower of Christ. You likely know already. You may be resisting the evidence put forth in this book for that reason. You don't want Christianity to be true because you don't want to follow Christ for fear of everyone turning their backs on you. But listen, if Jesus really is the one true God, wouldn't you want to worship Him? Don't you really want to know who the true God is? Whatever you may lose, it doesn't even compare to what you will gain. Take it from Nabeel Qureshi. Take it from Paul, who got his butt handed to him on more than one occasion for preaching the gospel. He says everything is garbage in comparison to knowing Christ! Think about that, **everything** is **garbage** when contrasted with having a relationship with Jesus! And this is coming from a man who lived a life of constant persecution! That ought to tell you something. Moreover, you should take comfort from Psalm 27:10. In this psalm, King David wrote *"Though my father and mother forsake me, The Lord will receive me."* Your earthly father may abandon you and call you an infidel for following Christ, but you'll have a Heavenly Father who will receive you into His loving arms. If you accept Christ, God will be your Father. John 1:12 says *"For those who received Him [Christ] to those who believed in his name, He gave the right to be called children of God".*

Jesus Himself promised *"And everyone who has left houses or brothers or sisters or father or mother or wife or children or fields for my sake will receive a hundred times as much and will inherit eternal life."* (Matthew 19:29)

Unanswered Questions May Linger

Of course, for others, it may not be an emotional or moral issue. It may be the case that unanswered questions still linger. Some readers may be thinking "Gosh, there sure is a lot of evidence for Jesus' resurrection, but I still have unanswered questions. Why didn't Jesus appear to any of His enemies after He rose, such as Pontius Pilate or Caiaphas? This would have convinced them that they were wrong to crucify Him, they would repent and become Christians. Also, why is it that Mark's gospel records no appearances? If Mark's gospel is the earliest gospel as most scholars say, does this imply that the appearances were legendary embellishments? And besides, doesn't Darwinian Evolution establish that atheism is true and that Genesis 1 is false? I don't think I can commit my life to Christ when there are still so many unanswered questions."

Dealing With Unanswered Questions

First of all, you shouldn't need to have **all** of your questions answered before you can make a decision for Christ. We will never have every question answered in this life. What you should do is weigh the evidence. Imagine a scale with the evidence for Jesus' resurrection on one side and your unanswered questions on the other. Does the totality of the evidence tip in favor of Jesus' resurrection? If so, then you should conclude that Jesus rose from the dead, despite there being a few unanswered questions about it. Would your question, if left unanswered, affect the weight of the arguments in any way? If not, then you should be comfortable with it being left unanswered.

J. Warner Wallace, cold case homicide detective and Christian Apologist said this about unanswered questions:

"After a long career as a cold-case detective, I've learned to get comfortable with unanswered questions. In fact, I've never investigated or presented a case to a jury that wasn't plagued with a number of mysteries. As much as I wish it wasn't so, there is no such thing as a perfect case; every case has unanswered questions. In fact, when we seat a jury for a criminal trial, we often ask the prospective jurors if

they are going to be comfortable making a decision without complete information. If potential jurors can't envision themselves making a decision unless they can remove every possible doubt (and answer every possible question), we'll do our best to make sure they don't serve on our panel. Every case is imperfect; there are no cases devoid of unanswered questions. Every juror is asked to make a decision, even though the evidential case will be less than complete. As detectives and prosecutors, we do our best to be thorough and present enough evidence so jurors can arrive at the most reasonable inference. But, if you need 'beyond a possible doubt,' rather than 'beyond a reasonable doubt,' you're not ready to sit on a jury. The standard of proof is 'beyond a reasonable doubt' for a good reason; no case is evidentially complete; no case maker can eliminate every possible reservation." [6]

I think the evidence is sufficient to warrant the conclusion that Jesus rose from the dead and Christianity is true, even in spite of some unanswered questions. Think about it for a moment; would the absence of an answer to the question "Why didn't Jesus appear to Pilate and the Pharisees?" undermine the powerful historical evidence that He **did** appear to the disciples, Paul, and James? How would an inability to answer that question undermine the evidence for those 3 minimal facts? Would it undermine the evidence for the empty tomb? Would it mean that the resurrection isn't the best explanation for the 5 minimal facts? Certainly not. I think we could say "Why didn't He appear to his enemies? It's kind of weird that he didn't do that. But the evidence that he **did** appear to the disciples, Paul, and James is strong enough, and since no naturalistic theory can account for them, I'm still justified in concluding that Jesus rose from the dead."

Answering The Unanswered Questions

But do answers to these questions exist? Yes. Let me take the time to address these one by one.

Question 1: Why Didn't Jesus Appear To Pilate And The Pharisees?

This is a common question that skeptics and believers alike have asked. In fact, my Dad asked me this question one evening when we were watching the 1977 mini series *Jesus of Nazareth*, starring Robert Powell. If Jesus really rose from the dead, then why didn't he appear to Pontius Pilate, the Pharisees, and all who doubted him? Surely He would have done this for scripture teaches that God wants all people to be saved (2 Peter 3:9, 1 Timothy 2:4) and that Christ died for the entire world (John 3:16, 1 John 2:2), and that confession of Jesus' lordship and in His resurrection are requirements for salvation (Romans 10:9), so then why didn't Jesus appear to Pilate and the Pharisees so that they could believe in Him so that they could be saved? I propose several answers.

1: Who Says He Didn't Appear To Them?

This is often overlooked, but there's a passage in the book of Acts that suggests that Jesus did appear to at least a few of the religious leaders, resulting in their conversions. Acts 6:7 says *"So the word of God spread. The number of disciples in Jerusalem increased rapidly, **and a large number of priests** became obedient to the faith."* (emphasis mine). Now, granted, it could be that these might not be the same Pharisees who were constantly trying to trip Jesus up and voted to condemn him to death, but they **could** be. It's possible that some of the people who ridiculed Jesus, opposed him throughout his ministry, and voted for his death were among the 500 individuals whom Jesus appeared to in 1 Corinthians 15. But, it also could be that these priests converted through the preaching of the apostles. So, while this verse isn't irrefutable proof that Jesus appeared to those who opposed him throughout his ministry, it does at least open the door to it.

2: It's Possible That It May Have Done No Good

People who don't want to believe something, won't believe it, no matter how strong the evidence is. It could have been the case that had Jesus appeared to Caiaphas, he would have said that Satan was trying to deceive him. After all, the religious leaders appealed to demonic forces to try to explain away his other miracles, like his exorcism in Mark 3:20-30, for example. Pilate might have explained his appearance away as a hallucination or a vision, and blamed it on a guilty conscience. Only God knows how these people would have responded to a postmortem appearance of Jesus. If it would have done no good, then Jesus would have just been wasting his time appearing to them. In the book of Exodus, Pharaoh had more than enough evidence to know that Yahweh existed and wanted him to let the Israelites go free. Yet, it took about a dozen plagues over a period of time before he finally consented. But even after consenting, Pharaoh changed his mind again and chased after the Israelites who were on their way to The Red Sea. People who truly desire not to believe and repent, won't.

Question 2: Why Are There No Appearances In Mark's Gospel?

According to most scholars, Mark's gospel is the earliest gospel to have been written. Matthew and Luke were written sometime later, and John's gospel was written last. However, Mark's gospel contains no appearances. There is a longer ending to Mark which does include appearances, but most scholars agree that these were added by a scribe later on. Most are in agreement that Mark's gospel ends at verse 8 of chapter 16. If this is true, then the earliest gospel contains no appearances while the later ones do. Is this a sign of theological embellishment over time?

1: Mark Doesn't Include Appearances, But He Does Predict Them

While it's true that the ending to Mark's gospel includes no narrative where Jesus shows up and says "Hi, y'all. I'm back!", Mark includes predictions that there **will be** appearances. The young man told the women "*Don't be alarmed, You are looking for Jesus the Nazarene, who was crucified. He has risen! He is not here. See the place where they laid him. But go, tell his disciples and Peter, 'He is going ahead of you into Galilee. **There you will see him**, just as he told you.'*" (Mark 16:4-5, emphasis mine).

So, certainly, Mark believed there would be appearances. He just didn't record any interactions between the risen Jesus and his apostles.

2: The 1 Corinthians 15 Creed Predates Mark

Secondly, remember that in chapter 5, we saw that the earliest tradition of Jesus' postmortem appearances is the creed cited in 1 Corinthians 15. This creed contains several appearances, including appearances to the twelve disciples, and this creed dates to within 5 years of Jesus' death. Moreover, all scholars, Christian and non-Christian alike affirm that all of Paul's letters predate the gospels. So, if any embellishment went on, it was going in the opposite direction; appearances to non-appearances!

3: The Evidence From Paul and The Church Fathers Let Us Trace The Claims Of Resurrection Back To The Disciples

Even if we threw out the gospels entirely, we could still affirm that the disciples **claimed** they saw Jesus alive and that they really **believed** it through the writings of Paul and the church fathers. I talked about this in chapter 5 of this book. Paul says that the disciples were claiming that Jesus appeared to them since he took two trips to Jerusalem to meet with them. One of these trips is recorded in Galatians 1, the other in Galatians 2. In Galatians 1, Paul says he spent 15 days with the apostles Peter and James. It's unthinkable that the resurrection wouldn't have come up in conversation at some point during that visit. Indeed, in Galatians 2, he specifically says that the specific reason he went to Jerusalem was to compare the gospel that he and the other apostles were preaching. He wanted to make sure that the gospel he was preaching was the same gospel the twelve disciples were preaching, and he said: *"They added nothing to my message"*. After citing the 1 Corinthians 15 creed, he says in verse 11 *"Whether it is I or they, this is what we preach"* (i.e Jesus' postmortem appearances). Paul gives us a direct link to what the disciples were claiming. Paul preached that Jesus died an atoning death on the cross, was buried, and then rose from the dead and appeared to His disciples and His brother James. Paul laid out the gospel he preached before the disciples and asked "Is this the true gospel or am I preaching a false gospel?" and the disciples said "You're preaching the right gospel."

Moreover, the early church fathers Irenaeus and Tertullian said that Polycarp and Clement were students of the apostle John. Polycarp and Clement wrote in their writings that the disciples claimed that Jesus rose from the dead. Polycarp and Clement are a direct link to what John and the other disciples believed. They say that the disciples were preaching Jesus' resurrection.

Additionally, church history is unanimous that all of the disciples were brutally killed for making this claim. No one would ever die for something they consciously believed is a lie. The fact that they died for preaching that Jesus rose from the dead proves they really believed it. Why did they believe it? Because they **saw** him.

In conclusion, the fact that Mark doesn't report any postmortem appearances doesn't hurt my case one little bit.

Question 3: Don't Miracle Stories In Other Religions Discredit The Resurrection?

It has been argued by skeptics, both scholars and layman, that miracle stories in other religions disprove or cast doubt on the resurrection of Jesus and the other miracles reported in The Bible. Sometimes this is posed in the form of this question "You reject all of these other miracles as being credible or true, so why do you accept the resurrection of Jesus as being a fact of history? Aren't you being inconsistent? Aren't you cherry-picking which miracles you want to believe and which you want to disbelieve? Moreover, if you're going to accept the miracles of The Bible, you should accept the miracles of Islam and Buddhism, and Mormonism."

What should the Christian Apologist say in response to this objection? I can give 3 reasons why this objection doesn't carry any weight

1: The Historical Evidence Establishes That Jesus Rose From The Dead

Most people who make this objection don't even realize that there is any evidence for the resurrection of Jesus. But as we saw in chapters 3, 4, 5, 6, and 7 of this book, there is excellent evidence for the resurrection of Jesus. Just using the standard criteria of authenticity that historians use, we've determined that (1) Jesus died by crucifixion, (2) His tomb was empty, (3) his twelve disciples believed they saw him alive after his death, (4) that a church persecutor named Paul converted on the basis of what he perceived to be a postmortem appearance of Jesus, and (5) a skeptic named James became a Christian because of what he perceived to be a postmortem appearance of the risen Jesus. In chapters 7 and 8, we saw that no theory can account for these 5 facts other than that Jesus physically rose from the dead, and therefore we are within our rational rights in coming to this conclusion.

Now, by contrast, other miracle claims in other religions tend to be rather poorly attested. Sometimes the sources come centuries after the alleged event the sources describe (such as the miracles of Buddha and Krishna)[7], and/or is found in only one source (like Islam's Hadith, which report the miracles of Muhammad). This isn't the case with The New Testament records. Even the most skeptical liberal scholars date all of them to within the first century, only mere decades after the event.[8]

The fact that other miracles are poorly attested or are made up cannot be used as an argument that the resurrection of Jesus is likewise poorly attested and made up. In fact, each miracle claim has to be examined on an individual, case-by-case basis.

2: If Christianity Is True, We Need Not Necessarily Explain Away Or Reject Other Miracle Claims

If the Christian worldview is true (and we've seen good evidence throughout this book to believe that it is), then we should expect to find at least a few miracle claims in other cultures at different points in time. Even in Scripture, God acted supernaturally among unbelievers, such as healing Naaman's leprosy (see 2 Kings 5). According to The Bible, demons can perform actual supernatural wonders or counterfeit miracles intended to confound people, such as the magi of Pharaoh (in Exodus 7-8) and the fortune teller who harassed the apostle Paul (in Acts 16:16-18), for examples.

Thus, Christians have no obligation to disprove miracle claims in other religious traditions and writings. In fact, I've sometimes conjectured whether an actual angel appeared to Muhammad, but that it was a demon. This would be plausible given the fact that The Bible says that Satan can disguise himself as an angel of light (2 Corinthians 11:14). If The Bible is correct that demons exist and wander the Earth, looking for souls to devour (1 Peter 5:8), it isn't a wonder that every culture throughout human history has had a belief in evil spirits.

3: Miracle Claims In Other Religions Can Usually Be Explained By A Naturalistic Theory

Often times, these supposed miracles can be explained by a natural explanation. For example, legendary embellishment can account for the miracles of Muhammad and Buddha. But this explanation fails for Jesus since (1) The epistles of Paul which mention the resurrection only dates to within a few decades after Jesus' death (1 Corinthians being dated to A.D 55), (2) There's good evidence, as we saw in chapter 5, that the creed contained in 1 Corinthians 15 dates to within only 5 years after the death of Jesus (WAY too early for legend to develop), and (3) through the apostle Paul, and the church fathers Clement and Polycarp, we can trace the claim that Jesus rose from the dead back to the very lips of the apostles, as explained above and in chapter 5. Since the claim that Jesus rose from the dead can be traced to the very lips of the apostles, the resurrection of Jesus isn't a legend that developed over time.

Question 4: Isn't This Whole Approach Dishonoring To God's Word? I Mean, You're Scrutinizing It and cross-examining The New Testament documents like a witness on trial.

This objection comes, not from skeptics or seekers, but Christians. Isn't The Minimal Facts Approach dishonoring to God's Word? Isn't it sacrilege to subject the inspired text to the same historical scrutinizing that we subject secular texts to? Aren't we expressing that we doubt God's word when we need some criterion of authenticity to tell us whether an event mentioned in it is true?

It's important to realize that The Minimal Facts Approach is trying to reach people who don't believe The Bible is the inspired word of God, and maybe believers who are doubting. It's not meant to reach people who already believe its claims. The Minimal Facts Approach reaches unbelievers where they are epistemologically. It's not that **I personally** doubt or am skeptical of what The Bible says, but the people I'm trying to reach are. This approach is entirely biblical. The Apostle Paul was a skilled apologist. Acts 17 records two occasions on which Paul argued with people, trying to convince them of Christianity's truth. The first occasion was with Jews in a synagogue and the second occasion was with the Greeks on the hill in Athens. In the first occasion, Paul appealed to Old Testament prophecies to convince his fellow Jews that Jesus truly is the Messiah, but when speaking to the Greeks, he didn't use the Old Testament. He appealed to general revelation (i.e the natural world), he quoted their Greek poets, and he used philosophical arguments to reach his gentile hearers. He knew that the Athenians didn't care about The Old

Testament or what it had to say, so he changed his tactics. His message didn't change, but his **method** did.

To help you get in their shoes, imagine if a Muslim tried to convince you of Islam by citing from the Quran. You wouldn't be persuaded, would you? Why? Obviously, because you don't think the Quran is inspired! You think it's a fabrication by Muhammad. Well, atheists, agnostics, Muslims, and other non-Christians see The Bible the same way. If a Muslim were to convince me of Islam, he would have to take an approach to proving his religion that didn't presuppose the inspiration of his holy book.

The Minimal Facts Approach does this. When we Christian Apologists argue for the 5 minimal facts undergirding the inference to the resurrection, we don't quote from The New Testament as inspired scripture. We do use The New Testament, but not as scripture. We use it as we would any other ancient document that claims to tell of historical events. Extra-Biblical sources (like Josephus and Tacitus), and archeological evidence (like The Nazareth Decree) can also weigh in.

Question 5: Why Did The Women Go Down To The Tomb To Anoint The Body Of Jesus If They Knew That It Was Sealed? Do Their Actions Really Make Sense?

This is a question Lee Strobel posed to William Lane Craig in their interview in the book *The Case For Christ*. Craig responded to Strobel with the following: *"Lee, I strongly feel that scholars who have not known the love and devotion that these women felt for Jesus have no right to pronounce cool judgments upon the feasibility of what they wanted to do. "For people who are grieving, who have lost someone they desperately loved and followed, to want to go to the tomb in a forlorn hope of anointing the body— I just don't think some later critic can treat them like robots and say, 'They shouldn't have gone.' ... Maybe they thought there would be men around who could move the stone. If there were guards, maybe they thought they would. I don't know. Certainly, the notion of visiting a tomb to pour oils over a body is a historical Jewish practice; the only question is the feasibility of who would move the stone for them."* [9]

I find Craig's response to Strobel to be intellectually satisfying. Also, notice that even if this question went unanswered, it wouldn't have altered our case. It wouldn't have undermined any of the arguments for the 5 minimal facts nor would it have given us a non-supernatural way to account for them. This question, like the others in this chapter, have answers to them, but the majority of them wouldn't affect the case for the resurrection even if they went unanswered.

Question 6: You Said In Chapter 3 That Jesus' Death By Crucifixion Was Multiply Attested in 9 Independent Sources, But Why Aren't There More Sources?

For one thing, very few documents from ancient history have survived up to the present time. As Ryan Turner, author for CARM (Christian Apologetics and Research Ministry) wrote in an article on Carm.org: *"There are a number of ancient writings that have been lost, including 50% of the Roman historian Tacitus' works, all of the writings of Thallus and Asclepiades of Mendes. In fact, Herod the Great's secretary named Nicolas of Damascus wrote a Universal History of Roman history which comprised nearly 144 books and none of them have survived. Based on the textual evidence, there is no reason to doubt the existence of Jesus of Nazareth."*[10]

The fact of the matter is that there may have been more sources that spoke about Jesus and his death by crucifixion for all we know, but they most likely decayed away or they simply haven't been discovered yet by archeologists. If documents aren't copied over and over again at a quick enough pace, they aren't likely to survive for 2,000 years.

Moreover, the evidence we do have for Jesus' death by crucifixion is still overwhelmingly strong. Four secular sources, one Jewish source, and four biblical sources attest to His death by crucifixion, which adds up to a total of nine. As I said in chapter 3, it is statistically impossible for 9 independent sources to all make up the same fiction and then proceed to treat it as a historical event. The principle of multiple attestations applies here. Secondly, Jesus' death is attested in three enemy sources (sources which are ridiculing Christianity in the very passage they mention Jesus' death by crucifixion), those sources would be Tacitus, Lucian and The Talmud. So this minimal fact is likely to be true on the basis of the principle of enemy attestation. Also, the principle of embarrassment verifies Jesus' death by crucifixion in 3 different ways; (1) Crucifixion was not only a painful death but a shameful one. If the gospels fabricated a tale of Jesus' death, they would have had him die in a more dignified way, such as death by stoning. (2) All of the disciples except John abandon Jesus, and only the women stand before the cross to be with Him in His final moments. Why would the author of John's gospel paint the disciples in such a bad light if that didn't actually happen? (3) Jesus said on the cross "My God! My God! Why have you forsaken me!" Although an explanation for this saying exists, it's still extremely awkward as it makes Jesus look like He's doubting the Father and forgot his mission. It's unlikely this saying of Jesus is made up, but this saying is in the context of Jesus dying by crucifixion.

You can ask "Why aren't there more sources?" but it's foolishness to say that the evidence we **do** have is insufficient.

Question 7: Aren't Jesus' Postmortem Appearances Like Elvis Sightings?

Several years ago, when I was debating the evidence for the resurrection with an atheist on Twitter (Twitlonger to be precise), the atheist compared the postmortem appearances of Jesus to alleged sightings of Elvis. People have claimed to have seen Elvis after he died, yet we don't give these claims any credibility. In fact, we have a tendency to dismiss them out of hand. Why don't we do the same with sightings of Jesus?

First of all, Jesus left an empty tomb behind, Elvis didn't. Anyone interested in disproving any resurrection of Elvis could go down to his tomb, exhume the corpse and prove that Elvis didn't re-enter the building. Had the opponents of Christianity done this back in the first century, they would have persuaded everyone that Jesus was still dead. Christianity would have died before it even began. Since it's still around, we can conclude that they didn't exhume Jesus' corpse, and they didn't exhume Jesus' corpse because there was no corpse in the tomb to be exhumed.

Secondly, Elvis sightings can be explained naturalistically. If only one person saw him at one time, that might have been a hallucination. Certainly, we know that Elvis impersonators are about, so maybe what these people are seeing are just these impersonators. Thirdly, it's possible that Elvis never died, but faked his death. While this is somewhat unlikely, it's still possible. But we saw in chapter 7 that multiple people on multiple different occasions (including 2 skeptics) saw the risen Jesus, and group hallucinations (especially ones that occur over and over) are impossible. We also know based on medical evidence, that Jesus was dead when they took him down from the cross. There's no way Jesus could have faked his death. So while there are plenty of plausible non-supernatural explanations for Elvis, none exist for Jesus.

Thirdly, Elvis never claimed to be divine or performed any miracles. Jesus did (see chapters 2 and 12). Jesus' resurrection occurred in what scholars call "A religio-historical context".

Question 8: Why Don't You Take The Gnostic Gospels Into Account?

Some readers may be wondering why I don't consider what the gnostic gospels have to say on this subject. The gnostic gospels were documents about Jesus that were excluded from the New Testament canon in about 300 A.D. The primary reason I don't consult them at all is simply a matter of good historical methodology. All scholars agree that the 4 gospels of The New Testament along with Paul's epistles were written in the first century. Conservative or Evangelical scholars place the dates of all the synoptics and the book of Acts between A.D 55 and 61, but more liberal scholars place the dates between 70-90. But both conservative and liberal scholars agree that the entire New Testament was completed before the close of the first century. By contrast, the Gnostic gospels are dated from the late 2nd to even the 4th centuries! These gospels are written so long after the life of Jesus, that I don't think they have anything really worthwhile to tell us about the historical Jesus. The fact that even the latest gospel dates 50 years minimum before the first Gnostic gospel shows up is an indication that the Gnostic gospels are less reliable.

Question 9: Doesn't Darwinian Evolution Disprove Christianity?

Evolution has been a sticking point for people ever since Charles Darwin first published his ideas. People (both non-Christians and Christians) think that the theory of evolution serves as a sort of God Substitute. If one can explain the origin of all life by naturalistic processes, then we need not appeal to God as an explanation. Famous atheist and biologist Richard Dawkins wrote that *"Natural selection is the blind watchmaker, blind because it does not see ahead, does not plan consequences, has no purpose in view. Yet the living results of natural selection overwhelmingly impress us with the appearance of design as if by a master watchmaker, impress us with the illusion of design and planning."*[11] and that therefore, *"Darwin made it possible to be an intellectually fulfilled atheist".*[12] Even Christian Apologist Lee Strobel sees evolution as refuting Christian theism. He wrote *"If the origin of life can be explained solely through natural processes, then God was out of a job!"*[13] and *""you don't need God if you've got The Origin of Species,"*[14]

Are Dawkins and Strobel correct? Does evolution make atheism intellectually fulfilling? Does it leave God out of a job? I do not endeavour to argue against the theory of Darwinian evolution in this chapter. For one thing, I find that the theory actually has a lot going for it. It's probably correct. I'm what you would call a "Theistic Evolutionist" although I prefer the term "Evolutionary Creationist". Rather than attack the science, I'm going to attack the metaphysical assumptions attached to the science. That is, I will argue that evolution doesn't prove atheism, there are many arguments for God's existence that do an end-run around the issue of biological evolution VS. special creation, that there's no reason to think that God couldn't have **used** evolution as his chosen method of creating the animal kingdom, and that the minimal facts for Jesus' resurrection still need to be explained.

1: The Minimal Facts Still Need To Be Explained

Was my great, great, great, great, great, great, X10,000,000 great grandfather an ape? What if he was? What would that mean for the case for Jesus' resurrection? We still have good historical evidence that Jesus died on a Roman cross, His tomb was found empty shortly thereafter, and Jesus' 12 disciples, a persecutor named Paul, and a skeptic named James all sincerely believed they saw Him shortly after His execution. Additionally, we've seen that no naturalistic explanation can account for these 5 facts. The only explanation that can account for them is that God miraculously raised Jesus from the dead. Since this is the only explanation that can adequately account for all of the data, this is the explanation we should go with. How exactly would proving that humans and apes evolved from a common ancestor refute the argument I've defended throughout this book? How would proving that natural selection and random mutations took a single celled organism and gradually turned it into the great animal kingdom show that Jesus' resurrection isn't the best explanation for the minimal facts? Appeal to evolution is a red herring that doesn't deal with the evidence for Jesus' resurrection. The Minimal Facts remain historical facts in need of explanation.

2: There Are Arguments For God's Existence That Can Be Sound Even If Darwinian Evolution Is A Fact

There are many arguments for the existence of God that can be sound even if macro evolution is true. I'll briefly survey these arguments in Chapter 11. These arguments include The Kalam Cosmological Argument, The Cosmic Fine-Tuning Argument, The Local Fine-Tuning Argument, The Moral Argument, The Ontological Argument, The Argument From Beauty, and many, many more.

God would still be the best explanation of the origin of the universe (Cosmological Argument), the best explanation for the very delicate balance of the laws of physics to allow life to exist (The Cosmic Fine-Tuning Argument), and He would still be the best explanation for the hundreds of characteristics needed for a galaxy, solar system, and Earth-Moon planetary system to support advanced life, even if Darwinian Evolution were true. If objective moral values and duties cannot exist if God does not, and yet we find that they do indeed exists, it follows logically that God exists. You can't have a moral law without a moral law Giver. You can't have legislation without a Legislator. Moreover, as we'll see in chapter 11, The Ontological Argument is totally immune to scientific refutation. This argument is

100% modal logic, so to refute it, one needs to appeal to modal logic. If it's possible that God exists, God exists in all possible worlds including the actual world.

If these arguments are logically valid and have true premises, then it follows that God exists. Christians can give atheists Darwinian evolution for free if they want to. Evolution doesn't excuse atheists from having to deal with these arguments.

3: There's No Reason To Think That God Couldn't Have Used Evolution To Create Life

I don't see any reason to say "If evolution, therefore, no Creator". Christians of all stripes are well aware that miracles aren't the only way that God does things. God often works through natural processes and divine providence. For example, someone may be going into the ER to undergo a serious and risky operation. The members of the patient's church pray that the surgery goes well. Lo and behold, the surgery goes well! They praise God for answering their prayers. Did God perform a miracle? Did He suspend or override the laws of nature to bring about the answer to their prayer? No, and everyone knows it. Everyone knows that the reason the surgery went well is that the surgeons were skilled and well trained, and they did their job very carefully. The surgeons caused the surgery to go well, not a divine miracle. If you pointed this out to one of the church members, they would probably respond with something like "Yes, the surgeons are the reason the surgery went well, but I believe that God guided the surgeons' minds and hands so that they wouldn't make any mistakes." For some reason, Christians acknowledge God's ordinary providence in things like this, but they don't think he can work through the natural processes of mutations and natural selection. They think if evolution did all the work, that means God did not. Yet they would never argue "If the surgeons made the surgery go well, then God did not."

In chapter 1 of their book *Origins: Christian Perspectives On Creation, Evolution, and Intelligent Design*, astrophysicist Deborah Haarsma and physicist Loren Haarsma give an example of the way weather operates. They point out that The Bible clearly teaches that God governs the weather and yet we also know of solid and proven natural explanations for how the weather operates. Dr. Haarsma points to several Bible passages proclaiming that God causes rain and drought (see Deuteronomy 11:14-17; 1 Kings 8:35-36; Job 5:10; Job 37:6; Jeremiah 14:22), and they note that the writers of Deuteronomy, the Psalms, and Jeremiah refer specifically to storehouses of rain and snow (Deuteronomy 28:12, 24; Psalms 135:7; Jeremiah 10:13). Deborah and Loren Haarsma go on to point out the natural explanations behind these. They write *"...water evaporates from the ground level, rises to where the air is cooler, and condenses into water droplets that form clouds. We learned how cold fronts and warm fronts and low pressure systems bring rain.*

When we watch meteorologists on television, we hear that scientists now use sophisticated computer models to help them understand and predict the weather a few days in advance. Their ability to understand meteorology is especially important for farmers, airline pilots, military personnel, and coastal residents. Every year scientists develop increasingly accurate computer models of the weather."[15]

Dr. Haarsma then invites us to imagine heated debates between whether The Bible is correct or whether the natural explanations of weather are correct, and to imagine lawsuits being filed against schools for teaching the natural explanations, and so on. Dr. Haarsma then writes *"The majority of Christians say that when it comes to the weather, both science and the Bible are correct. God governs the weather, usually through the scientifically understandable processes of evaporation and condensation. And the majority of atheists today would also agree that having a scientific explanation for the weather, by itself, neither proves nor disproves the existence of God."* [16] Her conclusion is that we would never conclude that natural explanations behind the weather would contradict scripture and leave God with no role to play in the process, so why do it with evolution?

I agree with them. The Bible is correct that God controls the weather, but he uses nature to do it. In the same way, God created all of life. Could He not have used evolution to do so?

But what about the whole idea of "random" mutations? Doesn't that make the idea of Evolutionary Creationism incoherent? How can God have purpose in a "random" system? Those who make this argument against the validity of Theistic Evolution/Evolutionary Creationism are committing the fallacy of equivocation. When biologists say that a mutation is "random", they don't mean that it occured without purpose. Evolutionists who are atheists may believe mutations are random in that sense of the word as well, but primarily, it just means that the mutations are unpredictable and spontaneous ((at least from our human point of view)). No one can predict when and where a mutation will occur in a given part of the genome of a given individual animal. They happen spontaneously, without warning. In biology, mutations are "random" in a similar way that dice rolls are "random".[17]

Atheists who try to prove that God does not exist by appeal to evolution are making metaphysical assumptions about the scientific evidence that cannot in fact be drawn from the scientific evidence itself. They are making philosophical interpretations of the scientific data. Now, **IF** atheism were true, then of course the evolutionary process would be purposeless and undirected. After all, if atheism is true, then there is no God to guide the evolutionary processes, and if there is no God to guide the evolutionary processes, then whatever happens in the biological history of the universe is a blind, purposeless, accident of chance and necessity. **But that's a conclusion about evolution one can only come to after one**

concludes that atheism is true! You can only conclude that evolutionary history had no purpose if you presuppose atheism. In that case, it's circular reasoning to argue **to** atheism **from** the theory of Darwinian Evolution.

Atheists like Richard Dawkins presuppose atheism in interpreting the scientific data, then say that the scientific data confirms atheism. Too many Christians have allowed the atheists to get away with this circular reasoning and have opposed Darwinian Evolution on account of it.

<u>4: As For Genesis 1-3, There Are A Few Plausible Interpretations That Would Allow For Evolution</u>

Again, this is going beyond the scope of this book, but I want to point out that as far as Genesis is concerned, there are several plausible interpretations that are compatible with an Evolutionary Creationist view. I think the one that has the most merit behind it is the "Cosmic Temple Inauguration" view that Professor John Walton defends in his book *The Lost World Of Genesis One: Ancient Cosmology and The Origins Debate* and *The Lost World Of Adam and Eve: Genesis 2-3 and The Human Origins Debate*. Deborah and Loren Haarsma do a survey of various different interpretations of Genesis in their book *Origins: Christian Perspectives On Creation, Evolution, and Intelligent Design*.

If you're interested, check out these books. In any case, whether the content of Genesis 1-3 is compatible with an old earth and evolution, we can conclude that evolution certainly doesn't prove atheism, it doesn't necessarily remove God's role as Creator and sustainer of the universe, and it does nothing to refute the minimal facts case for Jesus' resurrection.

Question 10: A Good Chunk Of Your Arguments Rely On The Use Of The New Testament Documents, But How Do We Know The New Testament We Have Today Wasn't The Result Of Centuries Of Corruption?

This objection is that we don't have the original New Testament manuscripts; the ones that the apostles' pens actually made physical contact with. All we have are copies of copies of copies. How do we know that the text was reliably transmitted through the 2,000 years since the original documents were written down? Was The New Testament reliably preserved for us? Do The New Testament books we read today say the same thing as the very first copies do? If they were distorted over the eons, and say something vastly different, how can we know anything about the historical Jesus?

This is perhaps the only area of New Testament reliability that would affect The Minimal Facts approach. We needn't concern ourselves with who authored the 4 gospels or how early the 4 gospels were written, or whether Paul wrote the pastoral epistles, or whether the New Testament got 2 or 3 historical details wrong. However, we **do** need to know whether the gospels and epistles say the same thing as was initially penned.

Fortunately, we can demonstrate evidentially that The Bible we have today says the same thing as The Bible that was originally written down. The New Testament has 24,000 partial and complete manuscripts. Over 5,000 Greek manuscripts have been cataloged.[18] Compared to other generally accepted manuscripts, The New Testament fares surprisingly well. The New Testament, when compared with other works of antiquity, stand up remarkably well. As I said, The New Testament has over 5,000 Greek manuscripts alone, and the earliest complete New Testament dates to about 130 A.D. By contrast, the works of Tacitus survive in a total of 20 Greek manuscripts and the earliest copy between it is about 1000, given that Tacitus wrote in the early second century and the earliest surviving manuscript of his work dates to 1,100 A.D. Homer's Iliad was comprised in 900 B.C and it's earliest surviving copy dates to 400 B.C, about 500 years between the original and the earliest copy. The works of Plato were comprised between 427-347 B.C, and survive on a measly 7 manuscripts. The earliest surviving copy of it dates to 900 A.D! If anyone thinks we can't trust that The New Testament we have today says what the originals documents said, they would have throw out all of these other works as well, since the textual evidence for them is far less!.[19]

Now, you will hear it argued that there are thousands and thousands of variants in the manuscript copies so that therefore, we cannot trust anything these documents say. And at first, this does sound very damning! However, what the skeptics don't tell you is these thousands of variants are not found in each individual manuscript, but rather, they're spread out throughout multiple manuscripts. For example, if **one** misspelled word in **one** verse in **one** New Testament document is found in 20,000 manuscripts…that counts as 20,000 variants. In reality, it's only 1 error found in 20,000 manuscripts. But the way people word it, it makes it sound like there are 20,000 errors in a single copy, which is not true.

Let us imagine we have five written material copies of a first century document that isn't in existence any longer. All 5 copies are different in some way or another. The goal that we are aiming for is to compare the manuscript copies and find out what the original must have said. Here are the five copies:

Manuscript #1: Jes## Christ is the Savior of the w#### worl#.

Manuscript #2: Christ Jesus is the Savior of the wh###e world.

Manuscript #3: Jesus Christ ## the Savior of the whole world.

Manuscript #4: Jesus Christ is th# Savior of the wh#le world.

Manuscript #5: Jesus Christ is the Sav## of the whole w#rld.

Could you, by examination of these 5 documents, determine what is being said here? Yeah, you could! Most of the variants are resolved by the methodology I just illustrated. By comparing the various manuscripts, all of which contain very minor differences like in the above illustration, it becomes fairly clear what the original must have said. This is a simplistic illustration of how textual critics reconstruct the original message of an ancient text.

Moreover, even if all of the manuscripts of the New Testament documents were destroyed, we could still reconstruct most of what the originals said just from the quotations of it by the early church Fathers. As Ron Rhodes writes *"in addition to the many thousands of New Testament manuscripts, there are over 86,000 quotations of the New Testament in the early church fathers. There are also New Testament quotations in thousands of early church Lectionaries (worship books). There are enough quotations from the early church fathers that even if we did not have a single copy of the Bible, scholars could still reconstruct all but 11 verses of the entire New Testament from material written within 150 to 200 years from the time of Christ."*[20] According to New Testament Scholars, both Christians and Non-Christians, we know with 99% certainty what the original New Testament documents said. That 1% of uncertainty is affected by 50 of the variants, but these variants don't affect any major doctrine.[21]

Conclusion

We've seen that the lingering questions some of my readers may have had up until this point have good answers to them. Most of them wouldn't affect the case for the resurrection of Jesus even if they went unanswered. Only the last two questions addressed in this chapter would really affect the case if they went unanswered.

Now, some skeptics oppose Jesus' resurrection on the basis of what is called "antecedent probability". This objection will have an entire section dedicated to it. It is to this topic that we now turn.

Notes

1: This lecture can be purchased as an MP3 file at
http://www.catapes.com/viewresults.cfm?cid=363

2: See the previous blog post in this series.

3: I tackle this issue in chapter 9 of my book *A Hellacious Doctrine: A Defense Of The Doctrine Of Hell.* Losing a loved one who wasn't saved can be hard, but that's no reason why you should shake your fist at God and end up there yourself.

4: Thomas Nagel, *The Last Word*, Oxford, 1997

5: Nabeel Qureshi, "Seeking Allah, Finding Jesus: A Devout Muslim Encounters Christianity", February 11th 2014, Zondervan, page

6: J. Warner Wallace, from the article "How Can You Trust Christianity When There Are So Many Unanswered Questions?", March 26, 2014,
http://coldcasechristianity.com/2014/how-can-you-trust-christianity-is-true-when-there-are-so-many-unanswered-questions/

7: See Edwin Yamauchi, Jesus, Zoroaster, Buddha, Socrates, Mohammad, Revised Edition (Downers Grove, Ill.: InterVarsity, 1972), esp. 4– 7, 18, 38– 41.

8: This is because the early church fathers quote from The New Testament very frequently in their writings. These church fathers, like Polycarp, Irenaeus, Ignatius, Tertullian, etc. are writing in the second, third, and fourth centuries. Obviously, the books they're quoting from had to pre-exist their own writings. I can't quote from a book in a book of my own unless the former had already been written and published. This is why all scholars from all theological perspectives agree that the entirety of The New Testament had been completed before the end of the first century. Most scholars date Mark in the 60s, Matthew and Luke in the 70s, and John in the 80s, with Paul's epistles being completed between 50 and 60 A.D. More conservative scholars, like Craig Blomberg, have given very compelling arguments for gospel dates between 50 and 62. And I happen to agree with these arguments for more conservative dating.

9: Strobel, Lee; Strobel, Lee. Case for Christ Movie Edition: Solving the Biggest Mystery of All Time (Case for ... Series) (Kindle Locations 4436-4443). Zondervan. Kindle Edition.

10: Ryan Turner, "Did Jesus Ever Exist?", CARM - Christian Apologetics and Research Ministry, https://carm.org/jesus-exist

11: Richard Dawkins (2015). "The Blind Watchmaker: Why the Evidence of Evolution Reveals a Universe without Design", p.31, W. W. Norton & Company

12: ibid.

13: Strobel, Lee. The Case For a Creator: A journalist investigates scientific evidence that points toward God. Zondervan, 2004, 19.

14: ibid, 22.

15: Deborah and Loren Haarsma, *Origins: Christian Perspectives On Creation, Evolution, and Intelligent Design"*, Faith Alive Christian Resources, page 13.

16: ibid.

17: See, ibid, page 51

18: Norman Geisler & Peter Bocchino, Unshakeable Foundations, (Minneapolis, MN: Bethany House Publishers, 2001) p. 256.; "Christian Apologetics", by Norman Geisler, 1976, p. 307; the article "Archaeology and History attest to the Reliability of the Bible," by Richard M. Fales, Ph.D., in "The Evidence Bible", Compiled by Ray Comfort, Bridge-Logos Publishers, Gainesville, FL, 2001, p. 163; "A Ready Defense", by Josh Mcdowell, 1993, p. 45.

19: See the chart comparing the manuscript number and dating of The New Testament when contrasted with other ancient works of antiquity in Matt Slick's article "Manuscript Evidence For Superior New Testament Reliability" -- https://carm.org/manuscript-evidence

20: Ron Rhodes, "The Manuscript Evidence For The Bible", December 30th, 2011, http://www.thepoachedegg.net/the-poached-egg/2011/12/manuscript-evidence-for-the-bible.htm l

21: See Daniel Wallace's interview with Lee Strobel in "The Case For The Real Jesus", pages 85-87, Zondervan

PART 3

The Antecedent Probability Objection

Chapter 10
Is Jesus' Resurrection Too Improbable?

The objection that I will be devoting an entire section to in this book is known as "The Antecedent Probability Objection". If you wanted to sum up the argument in a single sentence, you would say "There is a huge mountain of probability against an event ever being an act of God."

Or to put it another way, to say that dead people remain dead far more often than they come back to life is a mega understatement. Of the people we know who died (friends and relatives) 10 out of 10 stayed in their graves. Of the friends of the friends we know of, 10 out of 10 of their loved ones stayed in their graves. In fact, if we interviewed 1,000 people, we'd probably get not one legitimate resurrection account. Therefore, argues the skeptic, even if one cannot explain what happened to Jesus after his crucifixion, the odds are against resurrection. The skeptic would argue "**Any** naturalistic theory is more likely than a miraculous resurrection."

This objection is sometimes expressed in terms of platitudes like "Extraordinary claims require extraordinary evidence". If the Antecedent Probability Objection succeeds, then it would seem we wouldn't be justified in concluding that Jesus rose from the dead.

I have basically a 3 legged stool of responses to this argument.

1: I'm Not Concerned With Probabilities, But With Explanatory Viability

I am not necessarily arguing here that a miraculous resurrection is the most **probable** explanation of the data, only that it is the **best** explanation. The resurrection is the best explanation of the facts no matter what number a person might ascribe to its probability. The resurrection is the best explanation because it explains all of the data, every single fact, while the naturalistic explanations we looked at in chapter 7 all fail miserably. The resurrection succeeds in explanatory power and scope. Even the best of the naturalistic explanations account for one minimal fact at most. However, most of them explain 0 of the facts. Every single possible naturalistic theory one could come up with fails, but the resurrection, the supernaturalistic explanation, succeeds. Therefore, we ought to conclude that this hypothesis is the true explanation. Detective Sherlock Holmes would agree with me. Sherlock Holmes once said, *"Once you eliminate the impossible, **whatever remains, no matter how improbable,** must be the truth."* (emphasis mine).[1] The Resurrection is the only explanation that remains, and it's the only one that adequately accounts for all five facts. Ergo, in Detective Holmes' reasoning, it must be the truth. If you can think of another explanation, be my guest, but until then, I'm sticking with "He is risen".

It passes all 6 of C.B Mccullagh's tests for a viable historical theory. Therefore, I believe we are epistemologically warranted in affirming that it occurred. It's the **only** hypothesis that works! I don't care about probability.

2: If Jesus Did Not Rise From The Dead, The Existence Of The Minimal Facts Is Improbable

I would argue that if Jesus didn't rise from the dead, then it's extremely improbable that the minimal facts should **be** facts. I would argue that in light of the hypothesis "Jesus did not rise from the dead", then His tomb should be occupied, His disciples should never have claimed and come to believe that they had seen him, and Paul and James should have remained skeptical for the rest of their lives.

Here's an analogy; let's say that a woman is brought before a jury on charges of murder. She's accused of having killed her young son. Now, at the start, you might think that it's extremely unlikely that she is guilty. After all, the vast majority of mothers who've ever lived do not harm their children. They love and care for them. In light of this background information, the claim that she is guilty is enormously improbable, and you'd be justified in thinking that the defendant was innocent if that background knowledge was all you had to go on. However, investigators found a bloody knife in the back seat of her car next to a mud-covered shovel. In her house, they found a pair of pants that also had been chemically spot cleaned. They also have several eyewitnesses who said that they heard a child screaming just before seeing the defendant carrying a black garbage bag and a shovel out her house in the middle of the night, the same night as the murder. When investigators found the dead child, he was in a black garbage bag. The defendant also had a history of mental illness and domestic violence. In light of these "minimal facts", the claim "She is not guilty" becomes improbable. The defendant's attorney threw out every alternative explanation he could think of, but the jury all saw the various holes in them and rejected them. They knew that the claim "This woman murdered her child" could explain **all** of the evidence. Even the best of the defense attorney's explanations could account for **one** piece of evidence at the crime scene at most, but the majority of his alternative explanations didn't even go that far. The only explanation that worked is "This woman murdered her child".

Now, it would be an invalid move on the part of the defense attorney to argue that the majority of mothers care for their children rather than killing them, and he's never witnessed a woman murder her child, and so the probability against any mother ever killing her child is so great that they should return with a "not guilty" verdict. Sure, the hypothesis "this woman killed her child" is improbable in light of the background information that mothers usually don't kill their sons and that we've personally never witnessed a mother kill her son, but the guilty verdict is still justified.

In fact, the existence of the evidence is improbable if she is not guilty. If she's not guilty, the detectives should not have found what they found. If she didn't do it, what are the odds that "the minimal facts" at the trial (the blood-covered knife in the back of the car, the muddy shovel in the trunk, the dead child being found in a black garbage bag, the eyewitness statements of her leaving the house with a black garbage bag and shovel, and the history of mental illness and domestic violence) should all exist? In the same way, the existence of the minimal facts (1) Jesus died by crucifixion, (2) Jesus' Empty Tomb, (3) Postmortem Appearances To The Disciples, (4) Postmortem Appearance To Paul, and (5) the postmortem appearance to James, should not exist if Jesus did not rise from the dead. It's enormously improbable that these five facts would be true if Jesus did not rise from the dead. Of all the dead people we know of, none of them left an empty grave behind and started showing up to us and everyone we knew. When my grandfather passed away in 2001, my parents and I didn't go down to the tomb the next day, find it empty, then come back home to find him standing in our living room saying "peace be with you". That didn't happen when my grandmother died in 2003 either. Her casket stayed occupied, and we didn't see her again after that. My cat Sunshine died in 2011. We buried him in a cardboard box in our front yard. To this day, his body remains in that box, and no one saw him meowing at the front door just a few days later. More recently, my dog Max died and my father and I buried him behind our shed. His grave also remains occupied, and none of us saw him sitting in the front yard wagging his tail 3 days later. Now, certainly there have been people who claimed to see the spirit of their loved one appear before them shortly after they die. You only need to watch one or two episodes of *Unsolved Mysteries* to know that. However, while Grandpa might show up to Grandma in their bedroom for a few moments before departing to the afterlife, Grandpa's not going to show up to Mom, Dad, his grandchildren, his siblings, an entire stadium of people, and his co-worker who hates his guts, and Grandma isn't likely to find to Grandpa's body missing from the cemetery. That kind of thing just doesn't happen with people who aren't resurrected. However, that happened following Jesus' death.

The skeptic can argue "Dead people usually stay dead", but I can retort "Dead people usually don't disappear from their graves and immediately proceed to appear in front of everyone they knew". It would be astonishing that the 5 minimal facts **are** facts if Jesus didn't actually rise from the dead.

To return to the analogy at the beginning of this subsection, if the woman didn't kill her child, there should at least be a viable alternative theory than "she is guilty". Likewise, there should at least be a viable explanation for the minimal facts than "He is risen". Alas, there is no other explanation. Hallucinations, Apparent Death, Stolen Body theories, all fail to account for the minimal facts.

3: There's More To Take Into Account Than The Ratio Of Dead People To Resurrections

The non-Christian who makes this type of objection is usually an atheist who adheres to a worldview called naturalism (i.e that matter, energy, space, and time are all that exist). You'll never hear an adherent to Judaism or Islam make this objection against the resurrection. Why? Because Jews, Christians, and Muslims all believe in the existence of an omnipotent God. If God exists, that upsets the whole probability structure. If we live in a theistic universe, that makes resurrections a lot more plausible. Additionally, if it can be demonstrated that Jesus had a 3 year ministry of miracle working and actually predicted his death and resurrection before hand, that gives us a strong religio-historical context in which a bodily resurrection would be right at home. If God exists, miracles are possible. That, by itself, upsets the whole probability structure. As even Anthony Flew put it; *"Certainly, given some beliefs about God, the occurrence of a resurrection does become enormously more likely."*[2] If Jesus had a ministry of miracles, that also increases the probability of a miraculous resurrection. If Jesus predicted His death and resurrection, that makes resurrection even more likely. Finally, the fact that **no naturalistic theory** whatsoever can account for the 5 minimal facts increases the probability that Jesus rose from the dead, since if He didn't rise from a viable naturalistic theory ought to be found by someone, somewhere.

Imagine a scale on which one side is placed (1) God's Existence, (2) Jesus' ministry of miracles, (3) Jesus' resurrection predictions, (4) The Minimal Facts, (5) The Fact that only "He Is Risen" can explain all 5 minimal facts, and (6) Most dead people don't appear to everyone they know. On the other side of the scale you have (7) Most people who die stay dead. The picture below illustrates this with metal balls.

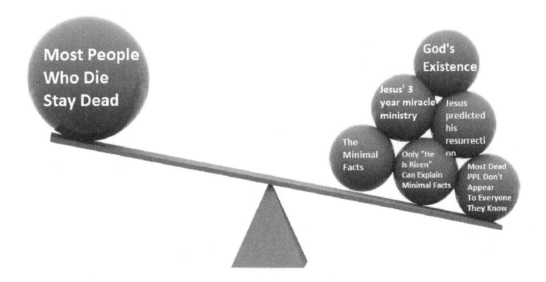

Does Jesus' resurrection or non-resurrection come out looking more probable? In light of the **full scope** of the evidence, in light of all the scale's metal balls, Jesus' resurrection becomes more probable than not. Now, it's true that I haven't demonstrated the factuality of all of the aforementioned metal balls, but I talk about the existence of God, Jesus' ministry as a miracle worker, and whether or not he predicted His resurrection in the upcoming chapters. I've obviously already demonstrated the factuality of three of the metal balls already. When you take all of the data into consideration, Jesus' resurrection comes out to be probable.

Notes

1: Arthur Conan Doyle, The Sign of the Four, ch. 6 (1890) Sherlock Holmes in The Sign of the Four (Doubleday p. 111)

2: Habermas and Flew, *Did Jesus Rise?* Page 142.

Chapter 11

The Existence Of God

If an omnipotent God exists, then Jesus' resurrection becomes enormously more likely. As I said in the previous chapter, The Antecedent Probability objection is only given by philosophical naturalists (a.k.a atheists). They believe that everything that exists is on the periodic table. Naturalism asserts that the natural world is all there is. If that worldview is true, then miracles are impossible. However, if there is a God, then miracles are at least possible. There is a being who is capable of causing the types of effects we call miracles.

Now, I for one think that Jesus' resurrection can be an argument for God's existence in and of itself. I would argue **to** God **from** the resurrection using the following syllogism

1: If Jesus rose from the dead, then a miracle has occurred.
2: If a miracle has occurred, then there must exist a miracle working God in order to perform the miracle.
3: Jesus rose from the dead.
4: Therefore, a miracle has occurred.
5: Therefore, a miracle working God exists.

This is a logically valid syllogism. The conclusion follows from the premises by the rules of logic. If the premises are true, then so is the conclusion. Now, I would think premises 1 and 2 would be indisputable. Clearly if a corpse is re-animated, that has to be a miracle. Natural processes just aren't going to revive a dead person. Moreover, if a miracle has occurred, there clearly has to be a being powerful enough to make it happen. The only debatable premise here would be the third one; that Jesus rose from the dead, and that's the premise I've been defending throughout this entire book.

Now, while I think The Minimal Facts Case For Jesus' Resurrection can serve as an argument on its own, there are arguments for God's existence independent of the case for the resurrection. What are those arguments? They are (1) The Kalam Cosmological Argument, (2) The Cosmic Fine-Tuning Argument, (3) The Local Fine-Tuning Argument, (4) The Moral Argument, and (5) The Ontological Argument.

There are many more arguments for the existence of God than these, but space does not permit an indepth look at all of them, and even with these 5, I'll only be doing a brief overview of them. Interested readers will be pointed to material at the end of this chapter that go into more depth.

Argument 1: The Kalam Cosmological Argument

I think a good place to start this overview would be at the beginning. By the beginning, I mean the beginning of the universe. The Kalam Cosmological Argument was formulated in its most sophisticated form by the 12th century Muslim philosopher Al Ghazali, and has been popularized by contemporary Christian philosopher William Lane Craig.

The argument goes like this

1: Whatever begins to exist has a cause.
2: The universe began to exist.
3: Therefore, the universe has a cause.

For an argument to be sound it must meet three criteria (1) the logic must be valid, (2) the premises must be true, and (3) we must have good reasons to believe the premises are true. This argument follows valid logic since it takes the form Modus Ponens. The only debate is whether the premises are true and can be verified. Are they true and can they be verified? Let's examine these premises.

1: Whatever Begins To Exist Has A Cause

*Nothingness has no properties and therefore no causal ability.
To deny premise 1 of this argument is to assert that things can pop into being from nothing. This is impossible because nothingness has no properties. Nothingness is not a thing, but the complete absence of being. Given that nothingness has no properties whatsoever, it follows that it has no causal properties either. If it has no causal properties, then it follows that it cannot bring anything into existence.

*If something could come into being from nothing, we'd expect to see it more often.

No one has ever seen things come into being from nothing before. If it could happen, we ought to be seeing it happen all the time. For example, we should hear news reports of things like a woman who was jogging in a park being mauled to death because a tiger popped into being out of nothing and mauled her. Why don't we see things popping into being more often? Maybe we don't see it happening more often because it never happens. Maybe it never happens because it cannot happen.

*Common experience and scientific evidence constantly confirms this premise and never falsifies it.

Not only do we not have any examples of things coming into being without a cause, we have an ocean of examples of things coming into being via a cause. Whenever we see something coming into existence, be it a sandwich, a house, a skyscraper, a baby, a car, a computer, or whatever, we see always see causes at work. No one's ever seen a sandwich, house, car, etc. simply poof into existence.

2: The Universe Began To Exist

*Scientific Confirmation 1: The Big Bang Theory

In 1915, the German scientist Albert Einstein formulated his theory of general relativity. This theory predicted that the universe should be in a state of either constant expansion or contraction, rather than being static. Einstein didn't like that implication of his theory, so he added a "fudge factor" to keep the universe walking a tightrope between expansion and contraction. Later, George Lemaitre and Alexander Friedman independently formulated math models that predicted the universe's expansion. The expansion of the universe was empirically verified by the American astronomer Edwin Hubble in 1929 when he noticed the red shift of the light coming from distant galaxies. Hubble concluded that the red shift is best explained by the light from the distant galaxies being stretched as they move away from us. This meant that the universe is expanding. The expansion entails the beginning of the universe because if the universe is getting bigger and bigger as it gets older and older, then if you rewind the clock, the universe gets smaller and smaller until the universe becomes smaller than the period at the end of this sentence. Rewind it farther still, and the universe shrinks down to nothing. The universe began to exist in a rapid explosion-like expansion. This explosion has been dubbed by Fred Hoyle "The Big Bang."

*Scientific Confirmation 2: The Second Law Of Thermodynamics

The second law of thermodynamics is the law of physics which is responsible for the transfer of heat from hot bodies to cold bodies, and it's also responsible for things decaying over time. The second law of thermodynamics is the reason my bedroom stays warm in the winter. When I turn the ceramic heater on in my bedroom, the heat doesn't stay confined to a small corner. The heat spreads all throughout the room. This is because the second law causes the heat to move from the hot body (i.e the ceramic heater) to the colder body (my bedroom). The second law is responsible for why your food cools a certain amount of time after you get it out of the oven. The heat travels from the hot body (i.e the food) to the cooler body (the room). This is why I sometimes smile when people say things like "Close the door! You're letting the cold in!" I'm like "Dude, do you even science? The second law of thermodynamics causes heat to travel from hot bodies to cold bodies, not the other way around!" When you leave the door open in the winter, the heat escapes, the cold doesn't get in.

The second law entails that the universe had a beginning because the universe is continuously running out of usable energy as time goes on. The amount of usable energy is diminishing more and more as time goes on. If that's the case, then if the universe has existed from eternity past, then the universe should have run out of usable energy from eternity past. Given that we still have usable energy (the sun being the most obvious example), that entails that the universe has not existed forever. There was a time that the universe came into being with 100% of its energy being usable.

3: Therefore, The Universe Has A Cause

Given the truth of the two premises, the conclusion logically and necessarily follows. Now, so far, we've concluded that the universe had a cause which brought it into existence, but just why should we conclude that the cause is God? This is where the conceptual analysis part of the argument comes into play.

The cause must be

Spaceless – Because space came into being and did not exist until this cause brought it into existence, the cause cannot be a spatial being. It must be spaceless or non-spatial. You cannot be inside of something if you are that something's cause. You cannot be inside of something if that something did not exist until you brought it into existence.

Timeless – Since time did not exist until The Big Bang, the cause cannot be inside of time. It must be a timeless being.

Immaterial – The cause's non-spatiality entails immateriality. How so? Because material objects cannot exist unless space exists. Material objects have mass and ergo occupy spatial dimensions. If there is no space, matter cannot exist. This means that because the cause is non-spatial, it is therefore non-material.

Unimaginably Powerful – Anything able to create all matter, energy, space, and time out of absolutely nothing must be extremely powerful, if not omnipotent.

Supernatural – "Nature" and "The universe" are synonyms. Nature did not begin to exist until The Big Bang. Therefore, a natural cause (a cause coming, by definition, from nature) cannot be responsible for the origin of nature. To say otherwise would be to spout incoherence. You'd basically be saying "Nature caused nature to come into being."

Uncaused – Given that the cause of the universe is timeless, the cause cannot itself have a beginning. To have a beginning to one's existence entails a before and after relationship. There's a time before one existed and a time after one came into existence. But a before and after of anything is impossible without time. Since the cause existed sans time, the cause therefore cannot have a beginning. It's beginningless.

Personal– This is an entailment of the cause's immateriality. There are two types of things recognized by philosophers that are immaterial: abstract objects (such as numbers, sets, or other mathematical entities) or unembodied minds. Philosophers realize that abstract objects, if they exist, they exist as non-physical entities. However, abstract objects cannot produce any effects. That's part of what it means to be abstract. The number 3 isn't going to be producing any effects anytime soon. Given that abstract objects are causally impotent, it therefore follows that an unembodied mind is the cause of the universe' beginning.

Whatever begins to exist has a cause, given that the universe began to exist, if follows that the universe has a cause of its existence. The cause of the universe must be a spaceless, timeless, immaterial, powerful, supernatural, uncaused, personal Creator.

This being that is demonstrated to exist by this argument is consistent with The Christian God. The Bible describes God as spaceless (see 1 Kings 8:27, 2

Chronicles 2:6), timeless (1 Corinthians 2:7, 2 Timothy 1:9, Titus 1:2), immaterial (John 4:24, 1 Timothy 1:17, 1 Timothy 6:16), powerful (Psalm 62:11-12, Job 9:14, Matthew 19:26), uncaused (Psalm 90:2, Isaiah 57:15, 1 Timothy 1:17, Revelation 1:8), supernatural, and is a personal being (John 1:12, James 4:8). Moreover, The Bible credits him with being the Creator of all physical reality (Genesis 1:1, John 1:1-3).

Additionally, as I point out in my book *"Inference To The One True God: Why I Believe In Jesus Instead Of Other Gods"* a study of comparative religions demonstrates that only 4 religions are consistent with the Cosmological Argument's conclusion: Judaism, Christianity, Islam (that's why Ghazali defended it), and Deism. All other religions involve either an eternal cosmos that have God or gods bringing order out of the eternally existing matter, energy, space and time, or else their god is the universe itself (pantheism). Therefore, if you're picking a view about God based on the cosmological argument alone, your list of options consistent with the evidence is limited to just 4 options, Christianity being among them. Only the Abrahamic religions (and Deism) teach that a God like the one described above brought all physical reality into existence from nothing.

Argument 2: The Fine-Tuning Argument

Over the past 50 years, scientists have been stunned to discover that the laws of physics which govern our universe unexpectedly conspire in an extraordinary way to make the universe habitable for life. The four fundamental forces, the low level of entropy in the universe, and other parameters have to be exactly the way they are if **any** kind of life **anywhere** in the universe was going to have a chance to exist. This has become known as "The Fine-Tuning of the universe". Just as dials on a radio have to be tuned to a precise location in order for a particular radio station to come through the speakers, so the many different "dials" of the universe had to be precisely calibrated to allow life to develop. If they were off by a little bit….eternal static.

I want to first give you several examples of this fine-tuning. Then when I'm done giving you examples of fine tuning, I'll give a syllogism arguing for design as the best explanation of that fine-tuning.

Examples Of Fine Tuning

1: The Strong Nuclear Force – This is the force which binds together protons and neutrons inside the center of every atom. If this force were any weaker, then it would not be strong enough to bind together protons and neutrons in the atomic nucleus. In that case, hydrogen would be the only existing element in the universe.

Why? Because the hydrogen atom has one proton and no neutrons in its nucleus. It also has only one electron orbiting its nucleus. It is the simplest atom there is. If the strong nuclear force were any weaker, the entire universe would be filled with atoms consisting of only a single proton. On the other hand, if the strong nuclear force were any stronger, protons and neutrons would stick together so efficiently that not one proton would remain by itself. Protons would find themselves attached to many other protons and neutrons. In this case, no hydrogen could exist at all. The universe would consist of only heavy elements. Life chemistry is impossible without hydrogen. It is also impossible if hydrogen is the only element.

2: The Weak Nuclear Force – This force is responsible for the radioactive decay of subatomic particles and it plays an essential role in nuclear fission. If this force were any stronger, matter would convert into heavy elements at a pace too rapid for life. Any weaker and matter would remain in the form of just the lightest elements. Either way, the elements crucial for life chemistry (such as carbon, oxygen, nitrogen, and phosphorous) wouldn't exist.

3: The Force Of Gravity -- The strength of the force of gravity determines how hot the nuclear furnaces in the cores of stars will burn. If this force were slightly stronger, stars would burn too rapidly and too erratically for life. This is bad because a planet capable of sustaining life must orbit a star that is both stable and long burning. On the other hand, if gravity were slightly weaker, stars would never become hot enough to ignite nuclear fusion, and therefore, many of the elements required for life chemistry would never form. Since these elements are essentially "cooked" inside the cores of stars, it's necessary that the stars be able to reach a certain temperature in order to synthesize them. A universe in which gravity were slightly weaker would be a universe in which no elements heavier than hydrogen and helium exist.

4: The Electromagnetic Force -- Astrophysicist Hugh Ross writes *"If the electromagnetic force were significantly larger, Atoms would hang on to electrons so tightly no sharing of electrons with other atoms would be possible. But if the electromagnetic force were significantly weaker, atoms would not hang on to electrons at all, and again, the sharing of electrons among atoms, which makes molecules possible, would not take place. If more than just a few molecules are to exist, the electromagnetic force must be…. delicately balanced."*[1]

5: The Expansion Of The Universe – If the universe expanded too rapidly, all of the matter in the universe would fly apart too quickly for gravity to have a chance to condense them into galaxies, stars, and planets. In such a universe, life would never be possible. The universe would forever be nothing but disperse gas and dust. On the other hand, if the universe expanded too slowly, the universe would collapse in on itself. Why? Because in physics the gravitational pull of 2 massive bodies attract one another, and the larger those bodies are relative to one another and the closer they are together, the more powerfully they attract. And when the universe is young (and therefore small), all the pieces of matter in the universe will be tightly clustered together, and therefore gravity will cause the universe's expansion to slow down. But as the universe gets older and older (and hence bigger and bigger), all of the matter will gradually grow farther and farther apart. As a result of the matter gradually growing farther apart, gravity will grow progressively insufficient in its ability to slow down the cosmic expansion, while dark energy grows progressively more efficient in its ability to expand the universe. I will talk about dark energy in a moment.

Anyway, if the universe expanded too quickly, no galaxies, stars, or planets would form, but if the universe expanded too slowly, the universe would collapse before galaxies, stars, and planets could form.

In either scenario, the universe would never develop galaxies, stars, and planets. This is obviously incompatible with the existence of life for if there are no galaxies, stars, or planets, then there's no home for creatures to live on.

6: The Ratio Of Electrons To Protons – If there were either too many electrons or too many protons, electromagnetism would dominate gravity, preventing galaxy, star, and planet formation. Again, no galaxies, stars, and planets mean no possible home for creatures to live on. A universe devoid of galaxies, stars, and planets is a universe devoid of life.

7: The Entropy Level Of The Early Universe -- Hugh Ross explains that *"If the rate of decay were any lower, galactic systems would trap radiation in such a manner that stars could not form. Starless galaxies would fill the universe. On the other hand, if the decay rate were slightly higher, no galactic systems would form at all. In either case there would be no "terrestrial ball" to serve as a home for life."*[2]

8: Dark Energy - The expansion rate of the universe is governed by two forces: gravity and dark energy. Gravity and dark energy serve as the equivalent of a break and gas pedal in a car. If you've got your foot more prominently on one pedal than the other, your car will either be going really fast, or will be going really slow. As explained above, the expansion rate of the universe is crucial to getting galaxies, stars, and planets. If the break and gas pedals of the cosmos weren't finely tuned with respect to one another, either the universe would expand too quickly, and, therefore, all the matter in the universe would fly apart before gravity could make planets out of it, or the universe would expand so slowly that gravity would pull everything back, resulting in a "big crunch". Dark Energy is the gas pedal of the universe. It is the reason why space expands.

An Argument For Design

The Fine Tuning is in need of explanation. I strongly believe that Intelligent Design is the best explanation for why the physical constants and quantities fell within the extremely narrow life permitting range. To make my case, I'll employ a syllogism formulated by philosopher William Lane Craig that he uses in his books Reasonable Faith[3] and On Guard.[4]

1: The Fine-Tuning of the universe is due to either physical necessity, chance, or design.
2: It is not due to physical necessity, or chance.
3: Therefore, it is due to design.

This is a logically valid syllogism. The conclusion follows from the premises by the rules of logic. I know this because the argument form is disjunctive syllogism. In order for us to reach the conclusion, we'll have to confirm that both of the initial premises are true. So are these premises true or are they false? Well, let's look at them.

Premise 1: The Fine-Tuning Is Due To Either Physical Necessity, Chance, Or Design

The fine tuning is in need of explanation. Of the explanations debated today in the scientific community, the three options are physical necessity, chance, or design.

Physical Necessity = the constants and quantities mentioned above have to be the way that they are. There was no chance of a life-prohibiting universe coming into being.

Chance = The laws of physics took the values that they did by accident.

Design = An intelligent Creator willed that the laws of physics took the values that they did.

This premise is uncontroversial because it's simply a list of possible explanations. Of the two premises of this argument, this one shouldn't be debatable. It is simply a list of possible explanations to account for the universe's extraordinary fine-tuning. If the skeptic can conjure up a 4th alternative, he's more than welcome to add it to the list, and then we'll consider it when we come to premise 2. However, in the 50 years since the fine-tuning of physics was discovered, these 3 are the only ones ever advocated. Since this premise is simply a list of possible explanations, it shouldn't be controversial.

Premise 2: The Fine-Tuning Is Not Due To Physical Necessity Or Chance.

The Fine-Tuning is not plausibly explained by physical necessity. There's simply no good reason to think that the constants and quantities of physics couldn't be different than what they are. Why couldn't gravity be more attractive or less attractive? Why couldn't the universe have expanded faster or slower than it did? Couldn't there have been a different ratio of electrons to protons? Physical necessity is just conjecture.

The Fine Tuning is not plausibly explained by chance either. The odds of each individual constant and quantity coming together is extremely improbable on their own, but when you consider them all together, improbability is multiplied by improbability by improbability by improbability until the mind gets sent reeling from the ocean of unfathomable numbers.

For example, gravity is finely tuned to 1 part in 10^{36} (that's a 1 followed by 36 zeros). In the film The Case For A Creator based on the book of the same name, Lee Strobel demonstrates this improbability by saying to imagine a ruler stretching from one end of the universe to another, and the ruler is separated by one inch increments. The number of inches represents the range of possible values that gravity could have taken. The odds that gravity should take the just right value would be if it fell on one specific inch out of 14 billion light years worth of inches!

The odds of the expansion rate of the universe being just right is 1 part in 10^{60}. According to Strobel, this would be the same odds as flying hundreds of miles into space, turning around, throwing a dart at the Earth, and nailing a target a trillionth of a trillionth of an inch in diameter!

In his book The Creator and The Cosmos[5] Astrophysicist Hugh Ross said that the odds of the just right number of electrons to protons coming about was 1 in 10^{37}. Ross said that that would be the same odds as covering one million continents the size of North America in dimes, stacked up to the height of the moon, then painting one dime red, mixing it in with the one million North American continents worth of dimes, and having a blindfolded friend pick out one red dime.

The odds that your blindfolded friend would pick out the one red dime is 1 in 10^{37}.

Roger Penrose of Oxford University has calculated that the odds of the Big Bang's low entropy condition existing by chance are on the order of 1 out of 10 to the power of 10^{123}

Such an incredibly huge number is impossible to appreciate without the aid of an illustration.

If you set a laptop computer in front of a 2-year-old toddler with Microsoft Word open and you told him to put his finger on the 0 key until he had 10^{123} zeroes typed after the number 1, how long would it take that child to type in 10^{123} zeroes? He would die as an old man before he got finished typing all the zeroes! In fact, if you replaced the old man with another 2-year-old toddler and told him to type in zeroes in order to finish the work of his predecessor, he too would die as an old man before he got finished! In fact, you could go through 10 generations of men spending their entire lives typing in zeroes and they still wouldn't be able to type this number out in full!

This isn't even counting the number of members in a collection of items that the written number is supposed to describe. The number of members in a collection of items always outnumbers the 0s in the numeral that's describing the number of members in the collection. For example, the number 100 only has 2 zeros but there are far more members in a collection of 100 items than there are 0s in the numeral 100! If you had a stadium of 1,000 people, there would be far more people in the stadium than 0s in the numeral 1,000. There are only 2 zeros in the numeral 100. There are 3 zeros in the numeral 1,000, but in both cases, the number of members in the collection of items outnumbers the number of 0s in the numerals! So if there are 10^{123} zeroes in the number, what would a collection of 10 to the 10^{123} items look like?

It would be absolute madness to believe that the fine-tuning of the laws of physics came about by sheer chance. Rationality demands that we reject the chance hypothesis.

Conclusion: Therefore, It Is Due To Design

Given the truth of the two premises, the conclusion follows logically and necessarily by the laws of logic. In this case, the law of logic that The Fine Tuning Argument goes by is known as "Disjunctive Syllogism".

This option eliminates Deism from the list of possible religions because it demonstrates that the Creator of the universe wanted life of some kind to exist. Physicist John Kinson explains it like this: *"The amount of care lavished upon creating the parameters ('knobs') and then fine tuning them with painstaking care and precision (to values that are conducive to life, and to intelligent life in particular) points to a being who cares about intelligent life, rather than a being who is indifferent to intelligent life. In other words, this clue points to a Theist God (who cares about his Creation) rather than a Deist God (who does not care about his Creation). Given this degree of care, it is not unreasonable to think that this being might choose to reveal 'Himself' to humans."*[6]

Argument 3: The Local Fine-Tuning Argument

In addition to the laws of physics being finely tuned for the existence of life, there are also many parameters that need to come together in a particular region of the universe in order to make that particular region life permitting. This fine tuning differs from the fine tuning in the previous section because the fine tuning in the previous affects the entire universe while the fine tuning in this section affects only a particular region of the universe. This is why I use the distinction between universal fine tuning and local fine tuning.

Let's look at a few of the parameters needed in order for our galaxy, solar system, and Earth-Moon planetary system to be capable of harboring advanced life.

*If we had no moon, life couldn't exist. The moon stabilizes Earth's axial tilt, keeping it from wobbling too severely. It also slowed the Earth's rotation down from its initial 5 hours per day to 24 hours per day, and the collision event (i.e a collision between a Mars sized planet named Theia and Earth) that produced the moon also blasted the majority of Earth's primordial atmosphere into outer space. So much fine tuning went into this collision event.

1: Theia's Speed
If faster: Earth would have either been destroyed or ejected out of the solar system.
If slower: There wouldn't have been enough dust and rocky fragments ejected from Earth's surface, resulting in a moon too small for life.
2: Theia's Size
If larger: Earth would have either been destroyed, or would have become Theia's moon (depending on how much larger).
If smaller: Not enough material would have been ejected into Earth's orbit to make a

big enough moon.

3: Theia's Angle

If it hit Earth head on, it would have destroyed Earth.

If it barely grazed Earth, there wouldn't have been enough material ejected from the Earth's surface to make a moon of sufficient size.

4: Theia's Material Constituents

Needed to ensure that the just right material melted into Earth's core to produce a magnetic field strong enough to block solar radiation and radiation from other sources in the universe from reaching the surface.

All of these things were needed to produce a moon of the just right size and ergo an atmosphere of the just right density and a rotation rate of the just right speed.

5: Earth's Rotation Rate

If faster: Surface wind velocities would be too severe for life to handle.

If slower: It would be far too hot in the day and far too cold at night for advanced life to exist.

6: The Moon's Size

If larger: The Earth's rotation rate would have slowed down too much, resulting in day to night temperature extremes too severe for advanced life to handle.

If smaller: The Earth's rotation rate would not have slowed down enough, resulting in surface wind velocities too severe for advanced life to handle.

7: Earth's Atmospheric Density

If too thick: The Earth would have experienced a runaway greenhouse effect, resulting in temperatures of approx. 900 degrees just like Venus.

8: Jupiter Distance

If farther away: too many asteroid and comet collisions would occur on Earth.

If closer: Earth's orbit would become unstable: Jupiter's presence would too radically disturb or prevent the formation of Earth.

9: Jupiter Mass

If greater: Earth's orbit would become unstable: Jupiter's presence would too radically disturb or prevent the formation of Earth.

If lesser: Too many asteroid collisions would occur on Earth.

10: Saturn Distance

If farther away: too many asteroid and comet collisions would occur on Earth.

If closer: Earth's orbit would become unstable. Saturn's presence would too radically disturb or prevent the formation of Earth.

11: Saturn Mass

If greater: Earth's orbit would become unstable: Saturn's presence would disturb or prevent the formation of the Earth.

If lesser: Too many asteroid and comet collisions would occur on Earth.

12: Neptune Distance

If farther away: It would be insufficient in shielding Earth from asteroids.

If closer: Earth's orbit would be thrown out of whack.

13: Neptune Mass

If too small: Not enough Kuiper Belt Objects (i.e asteroids beyond Neptune) would be scattered out of the solar system. Moreover, too many asteroid and comet collisions would occur on Earth.

If too large: Chaotic resonances among the gas giant planets would occur.

14: Uranus Distance (Stop laughing!)

If farther away: Too many asteroid collisions would occur on Earth.

If closer: Earth's orbit would be thrown out of whack.

15: Uranus mass (I mean it! Stop laughing!)

If larger: Earth's orbit would be too unstable.

If smaller: Its gravity would be insufficient to attract incoming asteroids and pull them into itself. More asteroids would strike Earth.

16: Oxygen Level Of Earth's Atmosphere

If greater: Fires would erupt spontaneously across the planet. You could catch on fire from walking down the street due to the friction between your legs.

If lesser: People would not have enough oxygen to breathe.

17: Thickness Of Earth's Crust

If thicker: No tectonic processes could occur. Therefore, no land masses could ever form. Landmasses and tectonic processes are important for recycling nutrients back into the ocean.

If lesser: Tectonic processes would be so severe that building a civilization would be impossible. Severe Earthquakes would be happening everywhere all the time!

18: Earth's Distance From The Sun

If closer: Earth would become too hot for liquid water to exist on the surface (i.e it would boil away).

If farther away: Earth would become too cold for liquid water to exist on the surface (i.e it would all be frozen).

19: Just Right Star

If larger: Star would not burn long enough for advanced life to evolve.

If smaller: Earth would need to be closer to stay in the "Goldilocks Zone" and this would result in a tidally locked planet (i.e one side always facing toward, and one side always facing away from the sun). Remember, 24 hour rotation speed is required for advanced life.

20: Galaxy Cluster Type

If too rich: Galaxy collisions and mergers would disrupt solar orbit

If too sparse: insufficient infusion of gas to sustain star formation for a long enough time

21: Galaxy Size

If too large: infusion of gas and stars would disturb sun's orbit and ignite too many galactic eruptions.

If too small: Insufficient infusion of gas to sustain star formation for long enough time.

These are just 21 of over 400 different characteristics that need to be just right in order for advanced life to exist. Astrophysicist Hugh Ross has calculated that the odds that they could come together by chance is on the order of 1 chance in 10^{500}. The most reasonable explanation is that a Creator made these parameters the way that they are.

Isaac Newton, one of the most famous scientists of all time, wrote in his Principia; *"This most beautiful system of the sun, planets, and comets, could only proceed from the counsel and dominion of an intelligent and powerful Being..."*[7] Scientific advance since Newton's time have increasingly verified this statement as the centuries have gone on.

Argument 4: The Moral Argument

The Moral Argument argues that objective morality is evidence for the existence of God. Christian Philosopher William Lane Craig defends the argument in the form of the following syllogism:

1: If God does not exist, objective moral values and duties do not exist.
2: Objective moral values and duties do exist.
3: Therefore, God exists.

Before we continue, it would be good for us to define our terms.

Moral Values = good and bad.
Moral Duties = right and wrong.

The Difference between these two: Values have to do with something's' worth. Duties have to do with your obligations. Just because something is good doesn't mean you're obligated to do it. For example, it would be good for you to be a doctor, but you're not morally obligated to become a doctor.

Objective = it is what it is regardless of what anyone thinks. Objective is the opposite of subjective. Subjective means that something is dependent on someone's opinion. For example, it is objectively true that chocolate ice cream is brown. It is only subjectively true that it tastes better than vanilla.

Premise 1: If God Does Not Exist, Objective Moral Values And Duties Do Not Exist

Moral Values:
If atheism is true, then why would humans be objectively, intrinsically valuable? On atheism, man is just a biological organism. There are other biological organisms on the planet. Why would humans be of more worth than any other? How could the life of a man be more valuable than the life of a cockroach or a tree? Most people don't believe you're committing murder when you stomp on a cockroach or cut down a tree, but they do believe you're committing murder when you end the life of a person. What basis is there for this on atheism? What basis is there for thinking that it's okay to cut down a tree but evil to cut down a man?

On atheism, both man and the cockroach are made of the same material that sprang into being at The Big Bang. Both man and the cockroach evolved out of the same primordial slime billions of years ago. According to Darwinism, all life came out of the same primordial slime and is related to one another, so what makes humans more valuable than they?

Could it be that humans are more advanced? More complex? More intelligent? If you say this, then that only raises another question: why is complexity a criterion for an organism's worth? Who or what decided that? Why is it not the simpler organisms that are of more value? I fail to see how on atheism, man's life isn't ontologically equal with the lowest life form. On the atheist's worldview, man is just a bag of chemicals on bones thrust into existence through a blind, purposeless process on a tiny speck of a planet in a universe that cares not whether he lives or dies. Why is this bag of chemicals on bones worth loving, worth saving, worth taking care of, worth praising? Objective moral values are totally unintelligible on an atheistic worldview.

Moral Duties
If moral values cannot exist in the absence of God, then moral duties are thrown out the window as well. The denial of moral values entails the denial of moral duties. If man's life is as worthless as a flea's, then you have as much of a moral obligation towards a man as you do a flea. In this case, the holocaust cannot be said to be truly, objectively wrong. There was no **moral** difference between killing 6 million

Jews and terminating a hill of ants. The only difference is **biological**; one was the mass extermination of insects and the other was the mass extermination of bi-pedal primates. As ghastly as it is to say such a thing, this is the logical entailment of atheism.

As Dostoevsky put it: *"If God does not exist, then all things are permitted."*[8]

Premise 2: Objective Moral Values And Duties Do Exist

Although good and evil and right and wrong cannot exist on the atheist's worldview, deep down, we all know that they do exist.

We can sense that some things are truly good, and that others are truly evil. We have moral intuitions that tell us that taking care of a baby is morally right and torturing a baby is morally wrong. Just as our sensory experience tells us that a world of physical objects is real, so our moral sense tells us that good and evil are real.

Moreover, just as no one can get outside of their 5 senses to see for sure whether or not they are giving them reliable information, so we cannot get outside of our moral sense to test whether it's giving us reliable information, but that should not give us reason to doubt whether physical objects or objective morality is real.

In my experience, atheists who try to cast doubt on our moral intuitions (and therefore, the ability to confirm this premise) typically make arguments that, if applied to our physical senses, would remove our ability to know things about the external world. For example, some of them argue that "People disagree on whether X is right or wrong, so our moral intuitions are unreliable in determining whether right and wrong exist." But imagine this logic being applied to our physical sense of sight. You would not be able to know whether color is an objective part of the physical world. After all, some people are color blind and others aren't! Some people can perceive color, but disagree on a particular shade of color. Don't forget that an entire internet sensation known as "The Dress" was founded on a disagreement as to whether the dress was gold and white or black and blue! The reductio ad absurdum shows that this is not a valid response.

Conclusion: Therefore, God Exists.

Given the truth of the two premises, the conclusion follows by the rule of modus tollens.

1: If P, then Q.
2: Not Q.

3: Therefore, Not P.

God is the best explanation for why objective morality exists. His moral character is the standard of good and evil, and His commandments are a reflection of His character, and these determine right and wrong.

Moreover, as I argue in chapter 4 of my book *"Inference To The One True God",* I think only the Christian conception of God is compatible with this argument's conclusion. This argument requires that a necessary, morally perfect, personal Being be the measuring stick of good and evil. He must be necessary because many moral truths appear to be necessarily true, and necessary truths can't be grounded in a contingent being. He must be morally perfect because an evil being can't be the standard of morality. Why? Because if that were the case, Hitler would be closer to meeting the standard of The Good than Mother Teresa. The moral perfection of this Being entails that He must be all loving and perfectly loving. He must be a Trinity in order to be a being of perfect love. If This being is not a triune being, then he cannot be a being of perfect love because love requires 3 things; (1) a lover, (2) someone to love, and (3) a relationship going on between the lover and the loved one. If God is only one person rather than three, then before He created any other persons (angels, humans), He had no one to love. Since He had no one to love, he, therefore, could not be perfectly loving. And if he wasn't perfectly loving, he was morally deficient since it seems to me at least that love is a moral virtue. Only a God who is multi-personal could be perfectly loving from eternity past. Christianity is the only religion in the world that has a multipersonal God. Therefore, only Christianity is consistent with this argument's conclusion.

Argument 5: The Ontological Argument

This argument, originally formulated by a Benedictine monk named St. Anselm and has gone through several revisions over the centuries. Anselm's version was, to be frank, a little silly. However, he laid the groundwork for future philosophers to make it into a robust argument for God's existence. The version I'll defend is called the "Modal" version. Its most famous contemporary defenders are Alvin Plantinga and William Lane Craig.

Now, before I go on to list and defend the premises of the argument, let me first explain some of the unique terminologies that will come into play for those without a background in philosophy. The Ontological Argument employs terms like "Possible Worlds" and "Maximally Great Being".

Possible Worlds = A maximal description of the way the world could be. It is simply a complete list of logically possible states of affairs that could be true of reality. At least one of these lists of logically possible states of affairs will be true of reality. If you still find the term "Possible Worlds" confusing, just substitute it for the term "Possible Lists" instead. Imagine you have multiple sheets of notebook paper, and each list has a sentence describing a logically coherent state of affairs which could be true of reality, such as "Evan Minton is writing a book on Jesus' Resurrection", "Evan Minton is currently writing a chapter overviewing 5 arguments for the existence of God", "Evan is wearing a t-shirt with Pokemon on it while he types", "Evan is using Google Docs to write this book", "Evan's room needs cleaning up", and so on. These statements listed one after another on your notebook paper are all states of affairs that could exist, and so, form a possible list. I'll confess, all of the prior statements are not only true of a possible world/list, they're true of the actual world/list. Now, if you change some statements on your sheet of paper, you arrive at a different list. This is really all a possible world is: an exhaustive list of statements that could be true of reality.

Maximally Great Being = This is a being that has all properties or attributes that go to make a person great (e.g power, knowledge, presence, moral goodness) and it has these properties to the greatest extent possible (i.e omnipotent, omniscient, omnipresent, morally perfect). If an attribute would make a person great if he had it, a Maximally Great Being will have that attribute, and moreover, will have it to the greatest extent possible.

Now that we've defined our terms, let's look at the premises of this argument.

1: It is possible that a Maximally Great Being exists.

2: If it is possible that a Maximally Great Being exists, then a Maximally Great Being exists in some possible world.

3: If a Maximally Great Being exists in some possible world, then it exists in every possible world.

4: If a Maximally Great Being exists in every possible world, then it exists in the actual world.

5: If a Maximally Great Being exists in the actual world, then a Maximally Great Being exists.

6: Therefore, a Maximally Great Being exists.

This is a logically valid argument. The conclusion follows from the premises by the rule of inference known as Hypothetical Syllogism.

Premise 1: It is possible that a Maximally Great Being Exists

By possible, I mean that something like a Maximally Great Being (MGB) could exist in reality. I don't mean it like a weak agnostic that says "Well, it's possible that a Maximally Great Being exists and it's possible that He doesn't." I mean that an MGB is metaphysically or logically possible. It does seem to me that this premise is true. I don't see any reason to think that it isn't possible that an omnipotent, omniscient, omnipresent, morally perfect, necessarily existent being exists. Such an entity seems intuitively possible.

Premise 2: If It Is Possible That A Maximally Great Being Exists, Then A Maximally Great Being Exists In Some Possible World

This premise follows from the first. If the existence of anything is logically possible, then it exists in some possible world. The only way it would exist in no possible world would be if the thing in question were logically impossible, such as a square circle, one ended stick, a married unmarried man, or a physical object with no shape. Such things are contradictions. A shape is either a square or a circle, but not both. A man is either married or unmarried, but he can't be both! A stick always has two ends. These things violate the laws of logic and therefore exist in no possible world. By contrast, things like a little green alien or a unicorn, while these don't exist in the actual world, they do exist in some possible worlds because their existence is possible. If God's existence is possible (see premise 1), then He at least exists in some possible worlds.

Premise 3: If A Maximally Great Being exists in some possible world, then He exists in every possible world.

This premise is true because of how one defines an MGB. A Maximally Great Being is, by virtue of being maximally great, necessarily existent. A Being who is necessarily existent is intuitively greater than one who is contingently existent. When something necessarily exists, this means that it could not possibly fail to exist. Its non-existence is impossible. Many mathematicians think that numbers, sets, and other mathematical entities exist in this way. If they exist, they have to exist and could not possibly fail to exist.

Now, if a necessary being exists in some possible world, it is impossible for it to not exist in all other possible worlds. 2+2=4 is a logically necessary truth. If it's necessarily true in some possible world, it will be true in all of them. 2+2=4 is a logically necessary truth. If it's necessarily true in some possible world, it will be true in all of them. 2+2 will not equal 4 in some possible worlds, but 5 in others. Necessary truths and necessarily existent being either exist in all possible worlds or none at all.

Premise 4: If A Maximally Great Being Exists in every possible world, then it exists in the actual world.

This premise follows from the previous one. If a Maximally Great Being exists in every possible world, then, of course, it will exist in the actual world. The actual world is a possible world. We know this precisely because it is actual. If it were an impossible world (like a world with a square circle) then it would not and could not exist. Given that it does exist, we know that it certainly is logically possible.

Premise 5: If A Maximally Great Being Exists In The Actual World, then a Maximally Great Being Exists.

Obviously, if something exists in the actual world, it actually exists.

Conclusion: Therefore, A Maximally Great Being Exists.

An omnipotent, omniscient, omnipresent, morally perfect, necessarily existent being exists in the actual world.

All of the premises of this argument are true, so it follows that a necessarily existent, morally perfect, omnipotent, omniscient, omnipresent, personal being exists.

Now, like the Moral Argument, I think only the Christian God is compatible with this conclusion. Various reasons have been given in chapter 5 of my book *"Inference To The One True God"*, but for the sake of length, I'll only go into one of them. In order to be a morally perfect being, this being would have to exist as more than one person. If God is not a trinity then God is not love. This is because love requires three things: someone to love, someone to do the loving, and a relationship going on between the lover and the Beloved. If these three things are not present then love is not present. But before any human beings were created, God was all by himself. So if God was all by himself, who was there to love? God had no one to love! Given that God had no one to love, God couldn't be love or loving until he created the first human beings or Angels or any persons other than himself. But in that case, God could not be maximally great, for in order to be maximally great, God would have to be morally perfect, which he could not be if God were only a single person. But the Ontological Argument established the existence of a being who is indeed morally perfect and ergo maximally great. So how does one resolve this dilemma? The doctrine of the Trinity provides the answer. If God is a trinity, then God can be an intrinsically loving being, because if God is a trinity then all of the necessary requirements for love are present. You have a lover, you have a beloved, and you have a relationship between them. The Father loves the Son and the Son loves the Father. The Holy Spirit is the spirit of love. Again, only Christianity has a God who is a Trinity. Therefore the Moral and Ontological Arguments demonstrate the truth of Christianity.

Conclusion

These 5 arguments powerfully demonstrate the existence of God. Now, unfortunately, I was only able to make brief positive cases for the soundness of these arguments. Some readers probably have objections to these arguments, objections I haven't addressed in this chapter. For example, one might respond to The Kalam Cosmological Argument with "Well, if God made the universe, who made God" or respond to the Fine-Tuning argument with the multiverse objection (i.e an infinite number of universes exist and life is bound to exist in one of them). It is unfortunate that I can't respond to all of the objections atheists raise against these arguments in this book. However, I have addressed these and a plethora of other objections in my book *Inference To The One True God: Why I Believe In Jesus Instead Of Other Gods*. In this book, I dedicate 20-30 page chapters to each of the 5 arguments overviewed above. I not only provide a positive case for the aforementioned arguments, but I respond to a plethora of atheistic objections to them as well. If you have objections to these arguments, please read *Inference To The One True God: Why I Believe In Jesus Instead Of Other Gods*. Authored by yours truly and available on Amazon.com.

I think these arguments are sound. I've been debating these arguments with skeptics for a long time, and I have never been able to find a knock down refutation of any of them. In fact, I've really stopped running into **new** objections to these arguments. Now, I just keep running into the same ones over and over. Seeing how these arguments have been able to stand up under the scrutiny of skeptics only increases my confidence in their soundness. And given that they are sound, the backdrop of atheistic naturalism collapses. One cannot claim that Jesus' resurrection can never be affirmed because "miracles are impossible". According to The Kalam Cosmological Argument, we know that one of the greatest miracles in history is backed up by scientific evidence, namely the creation of all physical reality out of nothing. If there's a God who can create whole universes by the sheer force of His will, raising a man from the dead is child's play! Additionally, The Ontological Argument shows us that a God exists who has the attribute of Omnipotence. If He's omnipotent, that means that He can do anything logically possible, and resurrecting a man from the dead certainly doesn't violate any of the laws of logic.[9] Therefore, we know that (A) Miracles are possible, and (B) at least one miracle (the creation of the universe) actually occurred. This makes the resurrection of Jesus far more probable, especially when combined with the fact that no explanation **but** a miraculous resurrection can account for all 5 minimal facts.

Notes

1: Hugh Ross, "The Creator and The Cosmos: How The Latest Scientific Discoveries Reveal God", Page 146, NAVPRESS

2: Hugh Ross, from the online article "Why A Decaying Universe?" /September 2008/ Reasons To Believe/ -- http://www.reasons.org/articles/why-a-decaying-universe

3: "Reasonable Faith: Christian Truth and Apologetics, Third Edition", by William Lane Craig, Crossway / 2008 /. Chapter 4 "The Existence Of God (2)", page 161.

4: "On Guard: Defending Your Faith With Reason and Precision" by William Lane Craig, David C. Cook / 2010 / chapter 5 "Why is the universe finely tuned?", page 111

5: Hugh Ross, "The Creator and The Cosmos: How The Latest Scientific Discoveries Reveal God", Chapter 14, Page 115, NAVPRESS

6: John M. Kinson, "Does Mathematics Point To God? Vignettes By An Ex-Atheist Scientist", Amazon Digital Services LLC, August 1st, 2016, page 189

7: Newton said this in his book Principia.

8: Fyodor Dostoyevsky, "A Hymn and a Secret", Part 4, Book 11, Chapter 4

9: Sometimes when I make this point, people get confused. When philosophers say that something is "logically possible", they mean that the concept doesn't violate any of the laws of logic, such as the law of non-contradiction (i.e it is impossible for both A and Not-A to both be true at the same time and in the same sense), excluded middle (it is either A or not-A), and identity (A = A).

Chapter 12

Was Jesus A Miracle Worker?

Just as God's existence and the lack of any non-miraculous explanation for the minimal facts increases the likelihood that Jesus rose from the dead, so also would the probability of Jesus' resurrection be bolstered if it could be historically demonstrated that, prior to His death, Jesus performed what appeared to be miracles. If this can be demonstrated, this gives us a religio-historical context (in addition to Jesus' claims to divinity) in which to situate a miraculous resurrection.

As with Jesus' claims to divinity and the minimal facts themselves, I will be appealing to the gospels to make my case, but I want to emphasize that I won't be treating them as divinely inspired scripture. I won't argue that because The Bible says Jesus did a certain miracle, that therefore, he must have done it. No, just as with Jesus' self-understanding and the 5 minimal facts, I will be treating the New Testament just as historians would treat any ancient document that purports to be recording historical events. I'll apply the criteria of authenticity that historians apply to any non-biblical source, such as the criterion of multiple attestation, the criterion of embarrassment, the criterion of enemy attestation, and so on.

What can these criteria tell us about Jesus' ministry? Which historical principles can be applied to which miracle narratives to affirm whether they are historical. Furthermore, is it possible that these actions Jesus did could be explained naturalistically, invalidating them from being true miracles? These are the questions this chapter seeks to answer. If it can be confirmed that Jesus performed miracles, then the supposed antecedent probability against Jesus' resurrection shrinks even more.

Miracle 1: Jesus, Water You Doing Out There?

Matthew 14:22-33 says *"Immediately Jesus made the disciples get into the boat and go on ahead of him to the other side, while he dismissed the crowd. After he had dismissed them, he went up on a mountainside by himself to pray. Later that night, he was there alone, and the boat was already a considerable distance from land, buffeted by the waves because the wind was against it. Shortly before dawn Jesus went out to them, walking on the lake. When the disciples saw him walking on the lake, they were terrified. 'It's a ghost,' they said, and cried out in fear. But Jesus immediately said to them: 'Take courage! It is I. Don't be afraid.' 'Lord, if it's you,' Peter replied, 'tell me to come to you on the water.' 'Come,' he said. Then Peter got down out of the boat, walked on the water and came toward Jesus. But when he saw the wind, he was afraid and, beginning to sink, cried out, 'Lord, save me!' Immediately Jesus reached out his hand and caught him. 'You of little faith,' he said, 'why did you doubt?' And when they climbed into the boat, the wind died down. Then those who were in the boat worshiped him, saying, 'Truly you are the Son of God.'"*

Right away, you should be able to anticipate one of the criterion I'm about to employ; the criterion of embarrassment. Again, whether you think the former tax collector and disciple Matthew wrote the gospel of Matthew or whether you think it was just someone in the early church (Polycarp? Tertullian? Bob the Jerusalem Church Janitor?), there can be no doubt that the writers had respect for the apostle Peter. Yet in this passage, when Jesus calls him to come out and walk on the water with him, Peter sinks because he doesn't have enough faith! Jesus helps him and then gently rebukes him for doubting. Why would the writer make this up? Why add this embarrassing detail about Peter if it didn't really happen? The writer could have emphasized the miraculous power of Jesus without making his chief apostle faithless and waterlogged. By the principle of embarrassment, I dub this miracle historically verified.

I also think this miracle is multiply attested, for it is not only recorded in Matthew's gospel, but Mark's as well. And this is one of those instances where I think Matthew probably didn't use Mark as a source because the details they include in this passage are different. Compare Matthew's telling with Mark's *"Immediately he made his disciples get into the boat and go before him to the other side, to Bethsaida, while he dismissed the crowd. And after he had taken leave of them, he went up on the mountain to pray. And when evening came, the boat was out on the sea, and he was alone on the land. And he saw that they were making headway painfully, for the wind was against them. And about the fourth watch of the night he came to them, walking on the sea. He meant to pass by them, but when they saw him walking on the sea they thought it was a ghost, and cried out, for they all saw him and were terrified. But immediately he spoke to them and said, 'Take heart; it is I. Do not be afraid.'And he got into the boat with them, and the wind ceased. And they were utterly astounded, for they did not understand about the loaves, but their hearts were hardened."* (6:45-52)

Notice that while Matthew includes Peter walking on water, doubting, and then sinking, Mark omits Peter's folly entirely. If Matthew were using Mark as a source for this particular instance, we would expect Matthew and Mark to both include Peter's doubt. Moreover, Mark says that the disciples were utterly astounded and didn't understand about loaves because their hearts were hardened. Matthew doesn't say anything about loaves in his account. Therefore, I have good reason to believe that Matthew and Mark recorded Jesus' walking on water independently of one another. They didn't use each other as a source in this particular instance. The gospel of John records this miracle as well in John 6:16-24. **No one** thinks John relied on **any** of the synoptic gospels. We therefore have 3 independent sources to Jesus' walking on water. Therefore, by the principle of multiple attestation, I dub this miracle historically verified.

Miracle 2: Color Me Wine.

The next miracle I want to put under historical examination is Jesus' turning water into wine at the Wedding At Cana, recorded in John 2:1-11: *"On the third day a wedding took place at Cana in Galilee. Jesus' mother was there, and Jesus and his disciples had also been invited to the wedding. When the wine was gone, Jesus' mother said to him, 'They have no more wine.' 'Woman, why do you involve me?' Jesus replied. 'My hour has not yet come.' His mother said to the servants, 'Do whatever he tells you.' Nearby stood six stone water jars, the kind used by the Jews for ceremonial washing, each holding from twenty to thirty gallons. Jesus said to the servants, "Fill the jars with water"; so they filled them to the brim. Then he told them, 'Now draw some out and take it to the master of the banquet.' They did so, and the master of the banquet tasted the water that had been turned into wine. He did not realize where it had come from, though the servants who had drawn the water knew. Then he called the bridegroom aside and said, 'Everyone brings out the choice wine first and then the cheaper wine after the guests have had too much to drink; but you have saved the best till now.' What Jesus did here in Cana of Galilee was the first of the signs through which he revealed his glory; and his disciples believed in him."*

Two historical principles can be applied to this text: embarrassment and historical fit. The former, because Jesus creating this much wine would seem to encourage drunkenness, which is condemned in The New Testament epistles. As Professor Craig Blomberg wrote *"Given the early Christian tendencies toward asceticism, it is unlikely that a story of Jesus deliberately producing large amounts of wine, with which at least some of the guests could have become quite drunk, would have been fabricated without a strong historical basis."*[1]

As for historical fit, again, Blomberg writes *"Archaeology has confirmed the use of the stone water jars described in verse 6 (Reich 1995). Verses 7-9 are striking in what they omit - no description of the miracle itself, precisely what later free invention would probably have created."*[2] Moreover, we have extra-biblical sources which give us some cultural background to this episode. Running out of wine at a wedding wasn't just a social embarrassment to the host. As Rachael M. McGill of Western Michigan University wrote: *"Wine was absolutely crucial to weddings. If a bridegroom ran out of wine at his wedding, there would be social and possibly even legal consequences. He could be shamed for years to come and could even be considered a disgrace to the family."*[3]

Miracle 3: Something's Fishy About This Miracle.

I often joke that Jesus would be a fantastic buddy to bring with you on a picnic. You can pack light and end up with a feast after you arrive at your picnic location. Jesus' feeding of the 5,000 is recorded in Matthew 14 and John 6. After Jesus had given a long sermon, his disciples urged Jesus to tell the people to go into town to get themselves something to eat. Jesus said "You get them something to eat." and the disciples were like "Bruh, you serious? We can't buy enough food to feed all these people!" Then a boy with 2 pieces of bread and some fish came up, and Jesus took the bread and fish, and multiplied them to feed all of the people who were there.

First of all, this miracle is multiply attested, being recorded in both Matthew's gospel and John's gospel. Again, I know of no scholar who thinks John used any of the synoptics as a source. Therefore, this miracle is multiply attested.

Secondly, I think the principle of embarrassment might be applicable here. The disciples should have recalled the many miracles they had seen Jesus do. Yet they seemed to think Jesus was unable to provide for their needs.[4] Andrew calculated the amount of manpower it would take to feed all those people and concluded that it couldn't be done.

Miracle 4: You Interrupted My Nap For This?

"Then he got into the boat and his disciples followed him. Suddenly a furious storm came up on the lake, so that the waves swept over the boat. But Jesus was sleeping. The disciples went and woke him, saying, 'Lord, save us! We're going to

191

drown!' He replied, 'You of little faith, why are you so afraid?' Then he got up and rebuked the winds and the waves, and it was completely calm. The men were amazed and asked, 'What kind of man is this? Even the winds and the waves obey him!'" - Matthew 8:23-27

I don't think that multiple attestation applies here. Although Mark and Luke also record this miracle, the amount of similarity between Matthew's account, Mark's account, and Luke's account all strongly suggest that Matthew and Luke were using Mark as a source. Therefore, we really only have one source, not three.

That said, the principle of embarrassment definitely applies here. Jesus is snoozing in the boat and the disciples are panicking because they think they are going to die. They wake Jesus up and he rebukes them for not having any faith before rebuking the storm and calming everything down. Again, why would the disciples or the early church depict the disciples in a bad light? In fact, this is just one of many occasions where the disciples are depicted as either dull or faithless. This does not look made up. By the principle of embarrassment, I dub this account historical.

Miracle 5: I'm All Ears.

Matthew 26:51-56 tells of Jesus' arrest. Peter whips out his sword and slices off Malchus' ear in an attempt to prevent his master's capture. Jesus rebukes Peter and heals Malchus' ear. It just grows back.

Two principles of authenticity can be applied to this event. Embarrassment and multiple attestation. The former, because Jesus rebukes Peter for trying to interfere with Old Testament prophecies being fulfilled. The latter, because not only is it recorded in Matthew's gospel, but John's gospel as well (John 18:3-11).

Miracle 6: Jesus The Exorcist

Do the passages about Jesus' exorcisms meet any of the tests of historical authenticity? They do. For example, in Matthew 12, a man was brought to Jesus and Jesus healed the man by casting out a devil. After he cast out the devil, the man's sight and ability to speak returned (verse 22). The people who were around Him watching the event were astonished and asked if Jesus could be the son of David (verse 23). But the Pharisees, who did not believe that Jesus was from God, came along and accused Jesus of casting out demons by the power of Beelzebub (verse 24). Then Jesus gave a very logical refutation to their claims. He said ""Every kingdom divided against itself will be ruined, and every city or household divided against itself will not stand. If Satan drives out Satan, he is divided against himself. How then can his kingdom stand? And if I drive out demons by Beelzebul, by whom do your people drive them out? So then, they will be your judges. But if it is by the

Spirit of God that I drive out demons, then the kingdom of God has come upon you."
- Matthew 12:25-28

We have more certainty that this historical event is true than false because of the principle of dissimilarity. In Matthew 12:32, Jesus says *"Anyone who speaks a word against the Son of Man will be forgiven, but anyone who speaks against the Holy Spirit will not be forgiven, either in this age or in the age to come."* In this verse of the passage, Jesus refers to Himself as the "Son Of Man".

Mark 9:14-29 says *"When they came to the other disciples, they saw a large crowd around them and the teachers of the law arguing with them. As soon as all the people saw Jesus, they were overwhelmed with wonder and ran to greet him. 'What are you arguing with them about?' he asked. A man in the crowd answered, 'Teacher, I brought you my son, who is possessed by a spirit that has robbed him of speech. Whenever it seizes him, it throws him to the ground. He foams at the mouth, gnashes his teeth and becomes rigid. I asked your disciples to drive out the spirit, but they could not.' You unbelieving generation,' Jesus replied, 'how long shall I stay with you? How long shall I put up with you? Bring the boy to me.' So they brought him. When the spirit saw Jesus, it immediately threw the boy into a convulsion. He fell to the ground and rolled around, foaming at the mouth. Jesus asked the boy's father, 'How long has he been like this?'*

'From childhood,' he answered. 'It has often thrown him into fire or water to kill him. But if you can do anything, take pity on us and help us.' 'If you can'?" said Jesus. 'Everything is possible for one who believes.' Immediately the boy's father exclaimed, 'I do believe; help me overcome my unbelief!' When Jesus saw that a crowd was running to the scene, he rebuked the impure spirit. 'You deaf and mute spirit,' he said, 'I command you, come out of him and never enter him again.' The spirit shrieked, convulsed him violently and came out. The boy looked so much like a corpse that many said, 'He's dead.' But Jesus took him by the hand and lifted him to his feet, and he stood up. After Jesus had gone indoors, his disciples asked him privately, 'Why couldn't we drive it out?' He replied, 'This kind can come out only by prayer.'"

Once again, the disciples show themselves to be faithless. Jesus had to cast out the demon because the disciples couldn't. Why couldn't they? Because they didn't have enough faith in God. Once again, the principle of embarrassment is applicable.

The Talmud

Recall from chapter 3 that the Jewish Talmud, the material of which dates from 70-200 AD. reports not only that Jesus was hanged but that prior to his hanging/crucifixion, some of the Jewish people were calling for his execution because they said that Jesus was leading Israel astray by acts of sorcery. If Jesus performed miracles as the gospels say he did, then it wouldn't be surprising that those didn't want to believe in Jesus would try to explain these away as acts of sorcery rather than acts of God. However, if Jesus never performed acts that appeared miraculous, then we would expect the Talmudic authors to say something like "Yeshu's followers claimed that he performed miracles, but we're here to tell you that he didn't." or something like that. However, they said no such thing. Instead, rather than denying Jesus did what appeared to be miracles, they chocked it up to sorcery. Therefore, we have enemy attestation to the fact that Jesus was a miracle worker.

This Is Only The Tip Of The Iceberg

Graham Twelftree did a 400 page historical study on this topic alone, and he concluded that a total of 29 different miraculous accounts talked about in the gospel narratives are historical. Twelftree determines that in 22 of these cases, the evidence is good enough to have *"high confidence,"* that the events described in these texts actually happened. Twelftree was careful to let his readers know that this doesn't mean the remaining reports didn't happen, just that they can't be verified with the same degree of historical certainty as the others.[5]

But, Are These Really Miracles?

Naturalists may be skeptical that the above mentioned events are actually supernatural, but according to the historical criteria of authenticity, they have no grounds on which to deny them altogether. They can try to explain these above instances naturalistically if they want to, but they shouldn't try to argue that the gospel authors simply made them up.

Of course, if the skeptic wants to deny that these actions of Jesus really are supernatural, what explanations would he put in their place? Let's examine each of these in the order I've presented them above.

Walking On Water

How would one explain naturally Jesus' walking on water towards the disciples?

Was Jesus Skipping Along Stones?

I'm reminded of a Red Bull commercial in which Jesus walks on water towards the disciples. The disciples are amazed and ask Jesus how he could be standing on top of the water, and Jesus says "You just have to know where the stones are". Jesus wasn't really walking on water. He was just standing on big rocks that were close to the surface, which gave Jesus the mere appearance of standing on water. Although the Red Bull commercial was probably intended merely as a joke and not a theory of serious scholarship, I still would like to examine it simply to cover all possible explanations.

First of all, this theory implies that Jesus was intentionally deceiving the disciples, which doesn't fit with the fact that Jesus truly believed His claims about Himself as we saw earlier. Jesus was martyred for His claims to be the Son of God and the messiah. If any of Jesus' miracles were simply tricks, Jesus would know that his "powers" weren't of God, and therefore not signs that He is who He claims to be. If this were not a miracle, we would expect Jesus to set the record straight, saying something like "Guys, I know I performed a lot of miracles, but this isn't one of them. I'm just skipping along rocks beneath the surface. Peter, come here, but watch your footing." Based on the historical evidence and logic, He was a liar.

Secondly, Jesus skipping along underwater stones would have given off a much different appearance than walking on water. Jesus would have been making carefully timed jumps from one rock to the other. That's not walking. Walking is putting one foot in front of the other. The disciples would have described Jesus not as "walking" on water, but "hopping" on water.

Were The Disciples Hallucinating?

One might posit that Jesus wasn't actually there at all, but rather the disciples were hallucinating. They **thought** they saw Jesus, but in reality, this was just a product of their imaginations. Hallucinations won't work for this account of Jesus walking on water anymore than it would account for Jesus' post-crucifixion appearances. As we saw in chapter 7 of this book, group hallucinations are statistically impossible. Hallucinations are products of an individual's brain. Hallucinations are like dreams. They don't spread like the common cold. All 12 disciples were on the boat when Jesus approached them, and they all saw him. If a hallucination occurred, one disciple would have seen Jesus, but the others wouldn't have.

Turning Water Into Wine

What about the account of Jesus turning water into wine? Can this be explained naturalistically?

Jesus The Hypnotist?

British author Ian Wilson has raised the question of whether Jesus was a master hypnotist and that this is how Jesus convinced the wedding guests at Cana that he had transformed jars of water into wine.[6]

In Lee Strobel's interview with psychologist Gary Collins in *The Case For Christ*, Collins said this about the suggestion that Jesus might have hypnotized the wedding guests into thinking they were drinking wine. *"....Look at the miracle of turning water into wine. Jesus never addressed the wedding guests. He didn't even suggest to the servants that the water had been turned into wine—he merely told them to take some water to the master of the banquet. He's the one who tasted it and said it was wine, with no prior prompting."*[7]

As Collins said in Strobel's interview cited above, hypnotists need to prompt the people they're trying to hypnotize in order for the hypnosis to work. They need to speak in a soothing tone of voice and coach them into a trance-like state, sometimes using a pendulum or some other visual focal point in addition. However, in the case of the wedding at Cana, Jesus did none of that. He didn't even say He was going to turn the water into wine and serve it to the guests. He didn't coach the servants nor the guests, so how exactly was Jesus supposed to have hypnotized them?

The Feeding Of The 5,000

How would one account for a few pieces of bread being multiplied in order to feed 5,000 individuals? Ian Wilson suggested hypnosis to explain this account. However, as psychologist Gary Collins explained in his interview with Lee Strobel, this explanation is untenable. Not everyone is equally susceptible to hypnosis. People who are really skeptical of hypnosis can't be put under quite as easily. How are we to honestly believe that Jesus successfully hypnotized a whopping 5,000 individuals? Surely some of them would have been unaffected by the hypnosis and called out Jesus' alleged miracle as a fraud.

The Calming Of The Storm

How would one explain naturalistically Jesus' calming of the storm? One possibility is the hypnosis explanation again. Jesus hypnotized the disciples to think it was storming and then his words to the storm was the vocal cue that snapped the disciples out of it. The problem though, is that Jesus was napping during this whole episode. Though I suppose the skeptic could respond that Jesus prompted the disciples prior to even leaving the shore. The skeptic might even argue that this explains why Jesus could sleep during the whole squall; namely because the squall only existed in the disciples' minds. Could hypnosis on Jesus' part explain why the disciples' believed he calmed the storm?

This is the only miracle of Jesus that I think the hypnosis explanation could actually be plausible. However, this is only if this miracle occurrence is taken in isolation from the rest of Jesus' ministry. If all of Jesus' other miracles actually are true miracles, that would make hypnosis in this particular instance less likely. Moreover, in every instance where hypnosis is appealed to, it is assumed that Jesus is intentionally trying to pull the wool over people's' eyes, but if Jesus knew he was a fraud, why would He go to His death claiming to be the Son of Man, The Son Of God, and the Messiah?

Jesus' Healing Of Malchus' Ear

Can this miracle be explained as a natural occurrence? Hypnosis won't help you here. Peter couldn't have been hypnotized into thinking he sliced off Malchus' ear when he really didn't. Malchus and the soldiers who would arrest Jesus would have been unsusceptible to being hypnotized by Jesus, given that they were opposed to Jesus' ministry. But, apart from a supernatural healing, what other explanation is there?

Jesus The Exorcist

Jesus' exorcisms are probably going to be the toughest to defend as actual casting out of demons. Even today, naturalists view the "demon possessed" as merely people who are mentally ill. Of course, I think that in many cases, mental illness is indeed probably the cause for their behavior. We Christians realize that while we live in a world inhabited by supernatural beings, we also recognize that lots of things can be explained by causes and effects within nature. Sometimes it's difficult to distinguish whether something is natural or supernatural, since you would get the same symptoms if either were the case. Behavior people exhibit from neurological malfunctions can often closely mirror actual demonic possessions. This is why psychiatrist Richard Gallagher is consistently hired by Catholic Priests to examine cases of people exhibiting bizarre behavior in order to determine which is which.[8] Has this person simply gone off their rocker? Then medical treatment needs to be applied. Is this person truly possessed by a demon? Then exorcism needs to be done. If a person is suffering mental illness, then exorcisms won't do them any good. If a person is possessed, then medicine won't do any good. Richard Gallagher is hired by priests because the priests realize they need to get a correct diagnosis before they can know whether performing an exorcism is appropriate.

But what about the specific cases of Jesus casting out demons? Did he actually cast out evil spirits? Well, in the specific passage I examined, Jesus' disciples tried to perform an exorcism and failed. When Jesus came along, He succeeded. The boy immediately got better. If this were a case of mental illness, one would expect Jesus to have failed just as badly as his disciples. Is it just a coincidence that the boy got better when Jesus commanded the "demon" to leave?

Where Do Scholars Stand On Jesus' Miracles?

It might surprise you to find that many scholars today affirm that Jesus performed works that appeared to the people around him to be miracles.

New Testament scholar Craig Blomberg said *"To begin with, they are deeply embedded in every layer, source and finished Gospel in the early Christian tradition. Jewish sources likewise attest to Jesus' miracles. Faced with the opportunity to deny the Christian claims that Jesus performed such amazing feats, Josephus and the Talmud instead corroborate them, even though they don't believe he was heaven-sent. The rabbis often made the charge that Jesus was a sorcerer who led Israel astray, much like certain Jewish leaders in the Gospel accounts (Mark 3:20-30) accused Christ of being empowered by the devil."*[9] New Testament historian Eric Eve wrote *"This leaves Jesus as unique in surviving Jewish literature of his time in being portrayed as performing a large number of healings and exorcisms".*[10] World leading Jesus scholar and New Testament scholar Craig Evans said *"It is no longer seriously contested that miracles played a role in Jesus' ministry."*[11] Craig Keener notes that *""Most historical Jesus scholars today, regardless of their personal theological orientation, do accept that Jesus drew crowds who believed that he performed cures and exorcisms."*[12] Non-Christian New Testament scholar and Jesus Seminar member Marcus Borg, wrote *"As a historian, however, I do think Jesus was a healer and an exorcist. To illustrate my reasoning, I use two factors. The evidence that Jesus performed healings and cast out what he and his disciples called evil spirits is widespread throughout in earliest Christian writing. There are stories and sayings, and both his followers and opponents accepted that he performed these acts… the second factor is evidence that paranormal healings happen. The evidence is ancient and modern, anecdotal and statistical. Since I am persuaded that paranormal healings do happen, then there is no reason to deny them to Jesus."*[13] Even Bart Ehrman admits that Jesus did what his followers perceived to be miracles, saying *""Whatever you think about the philosophical possibility of miracles of healing, it's clear that Jesus was widely reputed to have done them."*[14]

Conclusion

We have seen in this chapter that we are on good historical grounds for affirming that Jesus' ministry consisted of miracles and exorcisms. We also saw that attempts to explain these miracles naturalistically failed. The best explanation is that Jesus actually performed supernatural works in front of his followers and the crowds. If this is the case, then the antecedent improbability against Jesus' resurrection shrinks. If Jesus performed miracles before his death, that opens the door to a possible resurrection.

Notes

1: Craig Blomberg, "The Historical Reliability Of John's Gospel", IVP Academic, page 86.

2: ibid.

3: See Rachael M. McGill's paper: "God's Getting Married: The Wedding at Cana as a Dramatization of Covenantal Fulfillment", Western Michigan University. → https://scholarworks.wmich.edu/cgi/viewcontent.cgi?referer=&httpsredir=1&article=1152&context=hilltopreview

4: It just occurred to me that this would be a great point to make in a sermon about relying on God to provide for your needs.

5: Graham H. Twelftree, Jesus the Miracle Worker: A Historical and Theological Study (Downers Grove, IL: InterVarsity), see particularly pages 328-330, especially the summarized results; cf. even the skeptical inclination on page 427, note 21.

6: Wilson, "Jesus, The Evidence", 141

7: Strobel, Lee. Case for Christ Movie Edition: Solving the Biggest Mystery of All Time (Case for ... Series) (Kindle Locations 3129-3132). Zondervan. Kindle Edition.

8: See "Psychiatrist Admits Mental Illness Is Caused By Demonic Possession" -- https://yournewswire.com/psychiatrist-admits-mental-illness-is-caused-by-demonic-possession/

9: Craig Blomberg, from "The Credibility of Jesus' Miracles.",

10: As cited in "58 Scholar Quotes On Jesus' Miracles" by James Bishop. https://jamesbishopblog.com/2015/04/23/what-do-scholars-make-of-jesus-miracles-58-quotes-by-scholars/

11: Craig Evans, "Life-of-Jesus Research and the Eclipse of Mythology.",

12: Craig Keener, "'The Gospels as Sources for Historical Information about Jesus.",

13: Marcus Borg, from "Jesus, A New Vision: Spirit, Culture, and The Life of Discipleship.", May 10th 1991, HarperOne

14: Bart Ehrman, "The New Testament: A Historical Introduction to the Early Christian Writings.",

Chapter 13

Wrapping Up Response To The Antecedent Probability Objection

We're coming to see that Jesus' resurrection isn't as improbable as naturalists would have us believe. Yes, relative to the background information that every instance of dead people we know of, not a single resurrection occurred. However, in every single instance of dead people we know of, they didn't leave an empty grave behind and start appearing to everyone they knew, including people who hated them and thought they were crazy.

The Minimal Facts, The fact that no naturalistic explanation whatsoever can adequately explain the minimal facts, that God exists and is powerful enough to perform miracles, and that Jesus claimed to be God and had a 3 year ministry of miraculous deeds prior to His execution, all serve to upset the probability structure and cause the odds to lean heavily in favor of the "He Is Risen" hypothesis. Furthermore, if Jesus predicted His death and resurrection, that would lead further credence to the resurrection.

Did Jesus Predict His Resurrection?

There are at least four reasons for affirming that He did.

First of all, scholars usually deny Jesus' resurrection predictions because they also deny the resurrection itself as a historical event. However, if the resurrection happened (and we've seen good evidence in chapters 3-8 that it did), then scholar dudes aren't warranted in rejecting the prediction accounts.

Secondly, in many of the instances in which Jesus predicted his resurrection from the dead, the disciples are depicted as confused and not knowing what the heck Jesus is talking about (see Mark 8:31–33; 9:31–32; 14:27– 31; Luke 24:13–24). On the basis of the principle of embarrassment, we can conclude that these instances are historical. The gospel authors wouldn't depict the disciples as dim-witted. If Mark really wrote Mark and got his gospel from Peter (as church tradition says), then it would be especially unreasonable to believe Mark 8:31-33, Mark 9:31-32, and Mark 14:27-31 are made up. Can you imagine Peter telling Mark "Hey, write this down! Even though Jesus explained his death and resurrection to us over and over, we just didn't get it." if it weren't true? However, even if one wants to attribute these to some early church fathers or something, the principle of embarrassment can still be applied, as the early church had a high respect for the disciples.

Thirdly, Jesus' use of the title "Son of Man" in reference to his resurrection predictions (Mark 8:31; 9:31; 10:33–34) weighs in favor of authenticity. As I pointed out in chapter 2, this saying of Jesus is multiply attested. And moreover, the principle of dissimilarity applies since Jesus was never called "Son Of Man" anywhere else in The New Testament, and the early church fathers rarely referred to Jesus by this title. If this saying were made up by the early church and retroactively inserted into the mouth of Jesus, we would expect the early church fathers and NT epistles to use this title of Jesus more frequently.

Finally, the principle of multiple attestations applies to Jesus predicting that He would get out of his grave (see Matthew 12:38–40; 16:1–4,21; 17:23; 20:19; Mark 8:31–32; 9:31; 10:33; Luke 9:22; John 2:18–21. Cf. Mark 14:58; Luke 11:29–30).

For readers who want to go into more depth, I recommend reading Dr. Michael Licona's paper "Did Jesus Predict His Death and Vindication/Resurrection?" in the *Journal For The Study Of The Historical Jesus*, (2010), now available online to read for free. -->

http://booksandjournals.brillonline.com/docserver/14768690/v8n1_splitsection3.pdf?expires=1529252033&id=id&accname=guest&checksum=299BD2ECE796D7B2C759C4D7F82A4403

Jesus' Resurrection: Probable Or Improbable?

Let's return to the scale illustration. On one side of the scale is placed (1) God's Existence, (2) Jesus' ministry of miracles, (3) Jesus' resurrection predictions, and (4) The Minimal Facts, (5) The Fact that only "He Is Risen" can explain all 5 minimal facts, and (6) Most dead people don't appear to everyone they know. On the other side of the scale you have (7) Most people who die stay dead. The picture below illustrates this with metal balls.

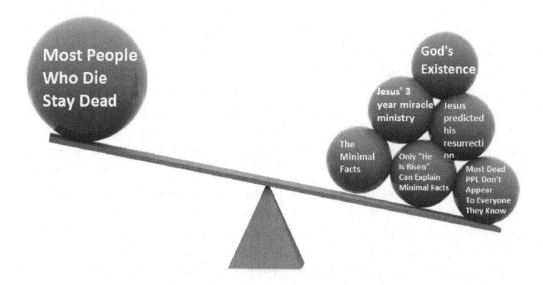

Does Jesus' resurrection or non-resurrection come out looking more probable? In light of the full scope of the evidence, in light of all the scale's metal balls, Jesus' resurrection becomes more probable than not. Now, I think many other things could be added to this scale to make Jesus' resurrection come out as more probable than not. For example, if it can be demonstrated that actual miracles are still occurring in our time, that lessens any antecedent improbability against the resurrection. If some Near Death Experiences can be evidentially verified, this proves that there is an afterlife, and if there's an afterlife, then you have to be open to a bodily resurrection, because that's a particular category of afterlife. My friend at Truth Ministries, Dave Glander, has given some talks on The Shroud Of Turin and makes a strong case for its authenticity. If The Shroud Of Turin is accurate as it seems to be, that would change everything.

I think the "metal balls" I **have** demonstrated in this book is enough to refute The Antecedent Probability objection. It is beyond the scope of this book to talk about modern day miracles or evidenced Near Death Experiences. If you want to investigate the former, I recommend reading Craig Keener's 2 volume work "Miracles" in which he documents thousands of well evidenced miracle claims. As for NDEs, Gary Habermas has some good material on that on his website www.garyhabermas.com. And please do check out Dave Glander's talks on the Shroud Of Turin. His talks can be found on YouTube. If you're unable to find Glander's lectures for whatever reason, Gary Habermas gives a defense of the Shroud in chapter 8 of his book *The Historical Jesus: Ancient Evidence For The Life Of Christ*. The Shroud Of Turin is talked about on pages 177-186.

In conclusion, I think The Antecedent Probability Objection is junk.

He Is Risen! What Follows?

In Chapter 2, I sought to evidentially establish that Jesus had a radical understanding of who He was and what His mission was. In chapters 3-8, I sought to evidentially demonstrate that Jesus died on the cross and rose from the dead. I think I succeeded in demonstrating those two things. I hope that by now, you, dear reader, concur. The reason it's important to establish Jesus' divine self-understanding and Jesus' resurrection from the dead is that if they are true, then Christianity is true. If Jesus claimed to be God and then died and rose from the dead, then the entire Christian worldview is true and any religion, philosophy, or worldview that contradicts Christianity must be false.

The significance of establishing those two facts (1) that Jesus claimed to be God and (2) rose from the dead is this; if Jesus said that he was God but he wasn't, then he was either a lying heretic or else he was crazy. If that were the case, there's no way God The Father would resurrect Jesus from the dead knowing that that would vindicate his blasphemous claims and lead many people astray. God would never raise a heretic and a blasphemer. But given the fact that God did raise Jesus from the dead, then God implicitly put his stamp of approval on everything Jesus said and did. Since Jesus rose from the dead, then that means God The Father agreed with Jesus' claims for which his enemies killed him as a blasphemer. Given that we've proven that God The Father raised Jesus from the dead then that means He agrees with Jesus' claims to be divine.

In that case, then whatever Jesus teaches carries a lot of weight.

Well, what did Jesus teach? He taught (1) that the Old Testament was the divinely inspired Word of God. He believed and taught that every word in The Old Testament was true. (2) He also seemed to believe that Adam and Eve were historical individuals, that (3) the flood story in Genesis 6-9 actually happened, that (4) angels and demons do really exist, and (5) that if you place your faith in him, you will have eternal life but that if you don't place your faith in Him, you'll end up in Hell (John 3:16-18, John 8:24).

So since Jesus rose from the dead after allegedly blaspheming the One who raised him, we can believe all of these things as well simply because Jesus believed them.

But how do we know Jesus believed the 5 things I mentioned above? We know them because of the standard principles of authenticity which historians use when examining documents.

(1) Jesus Believed That Old Testament was the divinely inspired Word of God.
Jesus believed The Old Testament was true. That's why he quoted it during his

temptations in the wilderness (Matthew 4, Luke 4:1-13). He believed that the Old Testament had power over the devils of Hell. In one of Jesus' temptations, he quoted from Deuteronomy 8:3 which says *"Man does not live by bread alone, but by every word that comes from the mouth of God."*(see Matthew 4:4). Jesus believed that the Old Testament proceeded from the mouth of God (c.f 1 Timothy 3:16). When the Sadducees questioned him about a man who had 7 wives who all died and asked whose wife will belong to the man at the resurrection (see Matthew 22;23-28), Jesus responded *"You are in error because you do not know the scriptures…"* (Matthew 22:29). According to Jesus, the Sadducees were in error because they were ignorant of what The Old Testament taught concerning the afterlife.

But how do we know that this instance of Jesus being tempted in the wilderness really happened? Can we establish it through any of the standard criteria of authenticity? Yes. Jesus' temptations in Matthew 4 and Luke 4 are most likely historical on the basis of the principle of multiple attestation. For not only do Matthew and Luke record it, but the writer of Hebrews also says that Jesus was tempted. Hebrews 4:15 says *"For we do not have a high priest who is unable to sympathize with our weaknesses, but we have one who has been tempted in every way, just as we are – yet was without sin."* So we have 2 independent sources which attest that Jesus was tempted by Satan. We have 3 if Matthew and Luke are independent sources, but the vast majority of scholars believe Luke used Matthew as a source. But since it's mentioned in **at least** 2 independent sources, it is therefore multiply attested and therefore likely to be true. It's unlikely that both Matthew and the writer of Hebrews would both independently make up the same thing.

In Matthew 21:12-17, we read of Jesus going into the Jerusalem temple, turning over the tables and chasing people with whips. Jesus then quotes Isaiah 56:7 which says "My house shall be called a house of prayer" but then says that the people there made it "into a den of thieves". Later in the passage, he quotes Psalm 8:2. This instance is likely to be true for two reasons. **Number 1;** it's multiply attested. It's not only recorded in the gospel of Matthew but also in the gospel of John. Matthew and John are independent sources, and therefore, it's multiply attested. It's unlikely both Matthew and John would make this up independent of one another. **Number 2;** it's not very flattering towards Jesus because it makes him appear to have anger issues. And he's not just angry, but he goes so far as to turn over tables, and chase after people with whips! Why would the gospel authors depict Jesus in such a bad light?

This is significant because in Matthew 21:12-17, Jesus appeals to two Old Testament documents, indicating that he believes that they have authority.

So by the historical principles of authenticity, we've established that Jesus believed the Old Testament was true.

(2) He also seemed to believe that Adam and Eve were historical individuals, and that (3) the flood story in Genesis 6-9 actually happened.

Jesus seemed to imply that Adam and Eve were real people when he taught about marriage and his second coming.

"When Jesus had finished saying these things, he left Galilee and went into the region of Judea to the other side of the Jordan. Large crowds followed him, and he healed them there. Some Pharisees came to him to test him. They asked, 'Is it lawful for a man to divorce his wife for any and every reason?' "Haven't you read," he replied, "that at the beginning the Creator 'made them male and female,' and said, 'For this reason a man will leave his father and mother and be united to his wife, and the two will become one flesh'? So they are no longer two, but one flesh. Therefore what God has joined together, let no one separate.' 'Why then," they asked, 'did Moses command that a man give his wife a certificate of divorce and send her away?' Jesus replied, 'Moses permitted you to divorce your wives because your hearts were hard. But it was not this way from the beginning. I tell you that anyone who divorces his wife, except for sexual immorality, and marries another woman commits adultery.'" – Matthew 19:1-9

"As it was in the days of Noah, so it will be at the coming of the Son of Man. For in the days before the flood, people were eating and drinking, marrying and giving in marriage, up to the day Noah entered the ark; and they knew nothing about what would happen until the flood came and took them all away. That is how it will be at the coming of the Son of Man."– Matthew 24:37-39

While its true that Jesus **could** use a fictional story to make his point, why would Jesus say *"As it was in the days of Noah…"* if the Genesis flood story were mythological or merely an allegory? What would you think if I said "As it was in the days of Santa Claus, so will it be when I get a job delivering mail"? People don't usually preface a fictional story with "As it was in the days of…". If the story of Noah's Ark were an allegory (as many theistic evolutionists propose) then we would expect Jesus to say something like *"As it was in the **story** of Noah…"* or something like that. "In the days of…" seems to imply these things happened in history.

Since Jesus is God, then certainly He would be in a position to know whether or not Genesis chapters 1 through 11 really happened or not.

But how do we know that the historical Jesus really said what I cited above (apart from presupposing biblical inspiration)? The passage quoted from Matthew 24 is very likely a historical saying of Jesus. This is based on the principle of dissimilarity. Jesus claimed to be the Son Of Man 88 times in the gospels, but Jesus is hardly ever called the Son Of Man outside the gospels. The Church Fathers refer to Jesus frequently as "God", "Son Of God", "Jesus", "Christ", and "Jesus Christ", but never "Son Of Man". Even in the New Testament epistles, Jesus is rarely called Son Of Man. If Jesus' claim to be the son of man were an invention of the early church retroactively inserted into the mouth of Jesus, we'd expect the early church to refer to Jesus by that title far more often than we do. Therefore, it's likely the self ascribed title "Son Of Man" really was used by the historical Jesus. **This also means that any instance in which he uses the title is also historical** (like the instance cited above).

(4) Angels and demons do really exist.

Jesus definitely believed in the existence of angels and demons. In fact, he spent a lot of time casting them out of people. When Jesus was being tempted in the wilderness, after having endured a few temptations, he said *"Get away from me Satan…"* (Matthew 4:10) He believed that he was being tempted to sin by a fallen angel, and he commanded that fallen angel to get away from Him.
Even non-Christian historians are now beginning to admit that being an exorcist was part of the historical Jesus' ministry (as we saw in the previous chapter)". In the previous chapter I showed how the criteria of authenticity show that the specific instance of Jesus being accused of casting out demons by Beelzebub's power by the pharisees really was a historical instance. So I won't rehash that here.

(5) That if you place your faith in him, you will have eternal life but that if you don't place your faith in Him, you'll end up in Hell

*"Therefore everyone who confesses Me before men, I will also confess him before My Father who is in heaven. But **whoever denies Me before men, I will also deny him before My Father who is in heaven."** - Matthew 10:32-33*

*"For God so loved the world that he gave his only begotten son so that whosoever believes in him will not perish but have everlasting life. For God did not send his son into the world to condemn the world but that the world might be saved through him. Everyone who believes in him will not perish **but whoever does not believe in him***

is condemned already because he has not believed in God's only son." – John 3:16-18

We know Jesus taught this because it's multiply attested. While the specific saying of Jesus in both of these instances are not multiply attested, nevertheless two different sayings where Jesus expresses the same principle certainly is. Matthew and John are independent sources and therefore it's multiply attested. Both of these gospels contain statements of Jesus expressing that only belief in Him will grant you eternal life and that unbelief in him will result in condemnation.

Jesus' resurrection is very significant. Since Jesus claimed to be God, and then he died and rose from the dead, then that means that He was telling the truth (i.e He really is God). God The Father would never raise a heretic and a blasphemer, knowing that by raising him he would be vindicating Jesus' claims to be divine, and thus would lead many people astray. So since Jesus rose from the dead, then anything Jesus teaches carries a lot of weight, doesn't it? Jesus taught that The Old Testament was the word of God, that it had authority. Jesus taught that Adam and Eve were real people, that the story of Noah's Ark is actual history, that angels and demons do exist, and that only by believing in Him, will you go to Heaven.

We don't have very much direct evidence for these things. There's not a lot of evidence for the Genesis flood, or angels and demons, or of the existence of Heaven and Hell, but I believe in them anyway. Why? Because Jesus believed in them, and He rose from the dead! I feel intellectually justified in believing these things because Jesus' ministry was vindicated by his resurrection.

I don't believe in Jesus because I believe The Bible. I believe The Bible because I believe in Jesus!

Conclusion

I have given the best defense of Christianity that I could. Hopefully, some of my non-Christian readers have found my case compelling and have concluded that Christianity is true. In that case, you may be ready to make a decision for Christ. If you want to commit your life to Jesus Christ, turn to the next and final chapter.

Conclusion

If you've taken the time to read through this book, I commend you. The resurrection of Jesus is the most important event in human history. If it occurred, the Christian worldview is true. If it did not occur, then we need to search for worldview truth elsewhere. However, we saw throughout this book that the historical evidence for Jesus' resurrection is shockingly strong.

There have been times when I gave refuting the resurrection a shot myself, but I could never think of a naturalistic theory other than the ones I refuted in chapter 7. And according to Dr. Habermas, scholars are the same way. The fact that non-Christian historians admit the 5 minimal facts, and have basically just given up trying to explain them only bolsters my confidence in the resurrection's historicity.

A Message To The Non-Christian Reader

If you were a non-Christian who became convinced by these arguments in this book that Jesus has risen, I want you to know that you can't just stop here. It isn't enough to acknowledge that Christianity is true, you have to place your trust in Christ for salvation. This is the difference between "Belief That" and "Belief In". Those aren't my terms, I got those from Frank Turek and J. Warner Wallace. "Belief That" is an acknowledgment that God exists, that God is a Trinity, that Jesus died and rose from the dead, etc. While "Belief That" is certainly a necessary condition for obtaining salvation (see Hebrews 11:6), it is not a sufficient condition. After all, James 2:19 says that even the devil believes that God exists yet Revelation 20:10 says he's going to Hell! Acknowledging that Christianity is true isn't enough to get you into Heaven. You need belief that **and** belief in. What is "Belief In"? Belief In is when you act on what you know. It's when you place your trust (the actual definition of faith) in Christ for your salvation. It's when you receive Christ as your personal Lord and Savior and devote your life to serving Him.

Lee Strobel explains this in mathematical terms. Believe + Receive = Become. Become what? A child of God (see John 1:12 - *"To all who received him, he gave the right to be called children of God."*). "Belief That" is the first part of the equation.

"Belief In" is the second part. For years, I had only the first part of the equation until God wore me down and brought me to my knees.

You're a sinner according to Romans 3:23; *"All have sinned and fallen short of the glory of God."* The *"wages of sin is death"* (Romans 6:23a) because God is holy and just (Psalm 9:7-8, Psalm 9:16, Psalm 10, Psalm 11:16, Psalm 103:6). But God isn't only just, He is also loving. In fact, 1 John 4:8 says that love is a vital part of who God is. *"God is love".* Because God's very nature is love, He *"so loved the world that he gave his one and only son, so that whoever believes in him will not perish, but have everlasting life."* (John 3:16). God loves "the world". Are you a part of the world? If you are, then this verse applies to you. God loves you and gave his son Jesus to die on the cross to atone for your sins (cf. 1 Peter 3:18). Jesus was crucified in order to experience the wrath of God. He experienced God's wrath so that you wouldn't have to. God's word promises that if you place your faith in Christ, He will be registered as your substitute. His blood will cover you, and God will look at you as though you had never sinned. He will see you the same way he sees Jesus; as a son who is without sin. This is the gift that God offers you. It's a free gift. You don't have to work for it. *"The gift of God is eternal life in Christ Jesus our Lord."* (Romans 6:23b). Ephesians 2:8-9 says *"For by grace you have been saved, through faith, and this is not of yourselves. It is a gift from God. Not by works lest anyone should boast."*

Will you receive this gift? Will you receive the free gift of salvation that God offers you? If so, call upon God and ask Him to save you. You don't need a special "Sinner's Prayer". God knows your heart. Just call out to him. *"For all who call upon the name of The Lord will be saved"* (Romans 10:13). Your prayer doesn't have to be eloquent or scripted. It can be as simple as "God, I now know that this Christianity stuff is true. Now that I'm convinced, I want you to save me. Please give me salvation in Jesus' name. Amen."

If you have received Christ as your personal Lord and Savior, I'd love to hear from you. Send me an email at CerebralFaith@Gmail.com to tell me about your decision. I'd love to know that this book made an impact on someone's eternity.

A Message To The Christian Reader

For readers who are already Christians, I hope you study this book and master these arguments so that you will *"always be ready to give a defense to anyone who asks you to give a reason for the hope that you have."* (1 Peter 3:15). One of my goals as an apologist is to equip my fellow believers like you to be able to give people the reasons to believe that Christianity is true. Not every unbeliever will take the time to read an apologetics book or even a single article. Either because they just don't like to read, or maybe they just don't know that good answers to their questions are available. However, they may be more than happy to engage in a conversation with you about God. You may be the only apologist they ever hear or you may be the first one they ever hear.

You may be thinking "This is interesting and all, but I'm just not smart enough to be an apologist. Don't you have to get Ph.Ds and spend years in seminary?" Let me tell you a story: I can still remember my first exposure to Christian Apologetics. I was 18. The year was 2010. I had been wrestling with doubts that were planted by an atheist I had tried to share my faith with. I wrestled with these doubts for months, but I didn't tell anyone, not because I was ashamed of my doubts, but because I was worried that I would spread them around like the common cold. One night, while I was scrolling my timeline on Facebook, one of my Facebook friends had posted a link to a YouTube video. It was the documentary adaption of Lee Strobel's "The Case For A Creator". I was blown away at what I was seeing and hearing; several credentialed scientists were talking about scientific evidence for the existence of a transcendent Creator (from the origin of the universe, the cosmic and local fine-tuning, the information content in DNA etc.). My faith was restored. I bought Strobel's books and read them. And although the evidence from science and history were good, I wasn't able to articulate the arguments very well because I had only gotten the gist on my first read. I would try to share my faith with non-believers online, and they would pelter me with questions and objections that I couldn't answer. When I prayed for their souls, I prayed that God would send someone to them who could walk them through the evidence for His existence and for the reliability of The Bible.

One day, after I prayed for these atheists a few times, I prayed once more "Lord, please lead these people to salvation. Lead them to a saving relationship with yourself. If they need reasons to believe, please send someone who can articulate the reasons for them." And then I felt The Holy Spirit say to me "I want you to give them the reasons." I was confused. I was terrible at articulating the Cosmological Argument or the case for the resurrection. How could God want me to be the one? The very next day, I was scrolling my Facebook timeline, and I saw a captioned image that said; "God doesn't call the qualified. He qualifies the called." That's when I realized that although I wasn't currently equipped to deal with the challenges the non-believers I tried to witness to brought my way, I could, through rigorous study and training, **become** equipped. If God really wanted me to be a Christian Apologist, then he would help me learn the stuff I needed to skillfully contend for the faith (Jude verse 3).

I read Lee Strobel's books cover-to-cover several times, trying to remember what I read. My Mom helped me by getting me several books on Christian Apologetics as presents for my 19th birthday. Those books were *"On Guard:*

Defending Your Faith With Reason and Precision" by William Lane Craig, *"Who Is Agent X: Proving Science and Logic Show It's More Rational To Think God Exists"* by Neil Mammen, *"The Holman Quicksource Guide To Christian Apologetics"* by Doug Powell, *"I Don't Have Enough Faith To Be An Atheist"* by Frank Turek and Norman Geisler, *"Intelligent Design 101"* by multiple authors, *"The Apologetics Study Bible",* and *"The Case For Faith"* by Lee Strobel. I didn't just read these books, I studied them. I read them cover-to-cover multiple times. My copy of Turek's and Geisler's book is actually starting to fall apart due to overuse.

I joined a Facebook group called "The Christian Apologetics Alliance" and I would frequently ask questions that had either occurred to me or was posed to me by someone I was dialoguing with on the internet. I downloaded lectures and debates from Apologetics315.com to my MP3 Player and would listen to these lectures over and over while I did housework and yard work. Later in my 19th year, I attended The National Conference On Christian Apologetics so I could learn even more. I bought Hugh Ross' book *"The Creator and The Cosmos"* and Josh McDowell's *"The New Evidence That Demands A Verdict"* at that conference. Over the years, I've bought many different books by many different authors on theology and apologetics, and I have read many of them multiple times.

In 2012, I decided to start a blog to share what I was learning; Cerebral Faith (www.cerebralfaith.blogspot.com). Since then, I've written nearly 500 posts on a variety of different topics; arguments for God's existence, the historicity of Jesus' resurrection, the problem of evil, the Arminianism/Calvinism debate, the creation/evolution debate, and others.

As of this writing, I confess that I have never been to seminary (though I hope to be able to attend some day). All of my knowledge comes from the self-taught method, with the mindset that I was going to learn and master apologetics no matter what. I was hell-bent on improving my skills. Through hard work, discipline, and determination, you too can become a skillful defender of the faith. The knowledge isn't locked away in universities. You can gain it simply by studying the books. However, it won't be easy, and it won't come quickly. You will have to be dedicated to learning this material, but it's worth it. It is so satisfying to be able to go toe to toe with unbelievers.

J. Warner Wallace, in a talk called "Call Of Duty" given at 2017's National Conference On Christian Apologetics, said; *"We don't need another million dollar apologist. We need a million one dollar apologists."* [1] What is a million dollar apologist? What is a one dollar apologist? My friend Zachary Lawson gave this helpful analogy: A million dollar apologist is like Led Zepplin while a dollar apologist is like your friend who can play the guitar really well. A million dollar apologist is someone who has many letters after his name and probably belongs to a few philosophy clubs, and they are experts in their respective fields; people like Dr. William Lane Craig, Dr. Alvin Plantinga, Dr. Gary Habermas, Dr. Michael Licona, Dr. Craig Blomberg, N.T Wright, J.P Moreland, and Dr. Hugh Ross would fall under this category. One Dollar Apologists would be people like me; who do a lot of reading and then write about what they learned. Or they'd be people who didn't get a degree in a field relevant to apologetics (like philosophy, physics, ancient near eastern culture) but got a degree **in** apologetics itself.

I don't mind being called a "One Dollar Apologist". I don't find it degrading or insulting. I believe we need both the million dollar apologists like Craig and Plantinga, but we also need One Dollar Apologists.

This world is full of people who don't know Jesus. A lot of them don't believe simply because they don't want to. They are in rebellion against their Creator. However, there are those who are earnestly searching for the truth, who are open to following the evidence wherever it leads, and if asked "If you knew Christianity were true, would you become a Christian?" would answer with a resounding "Yes". We need to be equipped to reach these people. Don't be like I was. Don't pray "God, please send someone like Evan Minton who can answer all their objections." God wants **you** to be that person. Jesus said, *"Go, therefore, and make disciples of all nations"* (Matthew 28:19). We are **all** called to share our faith, and since in many cases, questions will arise, it logically entails that we are all called to defend our faith as well.

I've heard way too many stories of people either going to their pastor, their parents, or their Christian friends with tough questions about and even arguments against Christianity, and honestly wanted to know if they could be successfully answered. These people were either rebuked for questioning The Bible, told "You just need to pray and God will give you more faith", or were simply told that they didn't know how to respond. Their doubts grew until they finally ended up leaving Christianity entirely, often once they went to a university. You may at some point have someone like this attend your church. Your pastor may not be equipped to deal with the challenges he brings up. But if you take the time to study this book, and some of the other resources I've mentioned (e.g my own blog, and some of the books I've mentioned reading in the preceding paragraphs), then you will be equipped to deal with them. You will be the friendly neighborhood apologist, and people will start to take notice and will begin coming to you when they have questions. I have often joked that I'm "The Bible Answer Man" of my family. My friends and family come to me with questions all the time. Questions like "What happens to a person who commits suicide?", "Can people lose their salvation or not?", "Why did Jesus say He didn't know the time of His second coming if He's God and God is omniscient?" are a few examples.

No, you don't have to go to seminary to get the skills you need to defend your faith. You don't need to have an IQ of 130. You just need to study hard, and you should. This world can never have too many apologists. It will be well worth the time and effort you pour into it, I promise you.

C.S Lewis put it well: *"If all the world were Christian, it might not matter if all the world were uneducated. But, as it is, a cultural life will exist outside the Church whether it exists inside or not. To be ignorant and simple now — not to be able to meet the enemies on their own ground — would be to throw down our weapons, and to betray our uneducated brethren who have, under God, no defense but us against the intellectual attacks of the heathen. Good philosophy must exist, if for no other reason, because bad philosophy needs to be answered."*[2]

Let us be salt and light in this skeptical era.

Notes

1: This talk can be downloaded as an MP3 file at
http://www.catapes.com/viewresults.cfm?cid=363

2: C.S. Lewis, The Weight of Glory and Other Addresses

More From Evan Minton

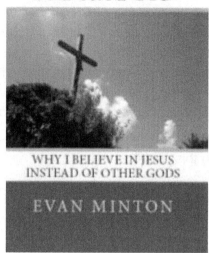

Inference To The One True God: Why I Believe In Jesus Instead Of Other Gods

There are so many religions in the world that it can be confusing for a spiritual seeker to figure out which, if any, are true. There are as many gods in mythology as there are people to believe in them. In fact, one of the common retorts from atheists when talking to Christians is "Why do you believe your God is real while thinking all these other gods are false?" In this book, Christian Apologist and blogger Evan Minton gives evidence for the existence of the God of The Bible, and shows why it's rational to believe the God of Christianity while disbelieving in all others. Mr. Minton argues for the biblical God, using arguments that draw from a wide range of disciplines such as science, philosophy, and history. This book is a must for any spiritual seeker.

Available Now In Paperback, Kindle, and Audiobook.

More From Evan Minton

A Hellacious Doctrine: A Defense Of The Biblical Doctrine Of Hell

Why would a good God send people to Hell? Isn't infinite punishment too severe for crimes of finite significance? Do babies go to Heaven when they die, or do they go to Hell? What happens to those who have never heard the gospel before they died? These questions and others are answered in Evan's newest book "A Hellacious Doctrine: A Defense Of The Biblical Doctrine Of Hell". Using The Bible and reason, Mr. Minton shows that the doctrine of Hell does not impugn God's goodness as skeptics of Christianity often say. The biblical doctrine of Hell is entirely compatible with a morally perfect God.

Available Now In Paperback and Kindle.

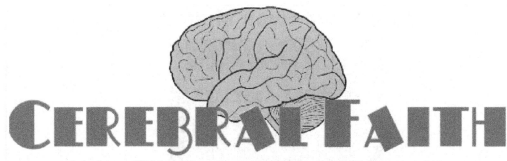

Using The Brains That God Gave Us

Cerebral Faith is an online blog ministry dedicated to Christian Apologetics and theology. It was founded and run by Evan Minton. Since its inception in August 2012, Minton has written over 400 articles on a variety of different subjects, such as the arguments for God's existence, the evidence for the resurrection of Jesus, responses to various things atheists say, the age of the earth, evolution, and soteriological issues (Arminianism, Calvinism). All of Minton's debates can be found on this site as well. Cerebral Faith gets it's name from the fact that Minton takes a very cerebral approach to faith and treats theological issues in a very analytical manner. To read Evan Minton's articles, visit www.cerebralfaith.blogspot.com

About The Author

Evan Minton is a Christian Apologist and is the author of the blog Cerebral Faith (www.cerebralfaith.blogspot.com). He has engaged in several debates which can be viewed on Cerebral Faith's "My Debates" section. Mr. Minton has been vigorously defending the faith against attacks from skeptics since 2011.

Made in the USA
Monee, IL
18 November 2019